A NATION UNDER GOD?
THE ACLU AND RELIGION IN AMERICAN POLITICS

D1304451

Thomas L. Krannawitter

Daniel C. Palm

THE CLAREMONT INSTITUTE
FOR THE STUDY OF STATESMANSHIP AND POLITICAL PHILOSOPHY
ROWMAN & LITTLEFIELD PUBLISHERS, INC.
Lanham • Boulder • New York • Oxford

ROWMAN & LITTLEFIELD PUBLISHERS, INC.

Published in the United States of America
by Rowman & Littlefield Publishers, Inc.
A wholly owned subsidary of The Rowman & Littlefield Publishing Group, Inc.
4501 Forbes Boulevard, Suite 200, Lanham, Maryland 20706
www.rowmanlittlefield.com

PO Box 317
Oxford
OX2 9RU, UK

British Library Cataloguing in Publication Information Available

Library of Congress Cataloging-in-Publication Data

Krannawitter, Thomas L., 1969-
 A nation under God? : the ACLU and religion in American politics /
Thomas L. Krannawitter, Daniel C. Palm.
   p. cm.
"The Claremont Institute for the Study of Statesmanship and Political
Philosophy."
Includes bibliographical references and index.
ISBN 0-7425-5087-7 (cloth : alk. paper) — ISBN 0-7425-5088-5 (pbk. : alk. paper)
1. American Civil Liberties Union. 2. Religion and politics—United States.
I. Palm, Daniel C., 1957- II. Claremont Institute. III. Title.
JC599.U5K735 2005
322'.1'0973—dc22   2005018979

Printed in the United States of America

⊗™ The paper used in this publication meets the minimum requirements of American National Standard for
Information Sciences—Permanence of Paper for Printed Library Materials, ANSI/NISO Z39.48-1992.

We are a religious people, whose
institutions presuppose a Supreme Being.
—*Justice William O. Douglas,* Zorach v. Clauson, *1952*

TABLE OF CONTENTS

ACKNOWLEDGEMENTS

The authors wish to thank the John Templeton Foundation, Paul and Gwyneth Hoff, and the Windway Foundation Inc. for the generous funding that made this work possible.

We wish also to thank Claremont Institute President Brian Kennedy for his unwavering commitment to developing scholarship in defense of the politics of freedom.

Our colleague Bob Gransden, who is tireless in his work, has been a source of constant encouragement and advice. We thank the staff at the Claremont Institute for their valuable assistance in the production of this book, especially David Skarka and Beth Gostlin, who provided many hours of assistance in collecting information on Supreme Court cases, and Matt Peterson, who helped edit the documents in the appendix. Professor Edward Erler and his delightful wife Fran have proven to be invaluable in editing and preparing the text for publication. Generously reading through the manuscript with critical eyes, their thoughtful suggestions have strengthened the book significantly.

Finally, both authors wish to acknowledge the great debt they owe to their teacher, Harry V. Jaffa, whose scholarship on the natural right principles of the American Founding remains unmatched as a source of timeless wisdom. The opinions expressed herein do not necessarily reflect the views of those who supported our work, and the authors alone are responsible for any mistakes that might appear in the pages that follow.

INTRODUCTION

[W]e here highly resolve that ... the nation shall,
under God, have a new birth of freedom.
—Abraham Lincoln, Gettysburg Address, 1863

In the summer of 2004, Los Angeles County officials found themselves under assault from the American Civil Liberties Union. The ACLU threatened a lawsuit unless the County removed a small cross from its seal. Stories of the ACLU attacking America's moral beliefs and religious institutions—from prayers in schools to local communities which display nativity scenes at Christmas—have become so common that many Americans merely shrug their shoulders instead of raising an eyebrow. But these battles deserve attention because they lay bare the radical "progressive" agenda driving the ACLU.

The Southern California ACLU chose to pick this particular fight after a recent victory in nearby Redlands, California, where they threatened to sue about a cross and a church depicted on that city's seal. City officials were aware of ACLU successes in similar cases in Illinois and New Mexico. Facing a budget deficit of $1.2 million, the city capitulated, replacing the cross and church with a tree and a house, instead of risking a lengthy and costly court battle which they likely would have lost.

ACLU supporters then called attention to the Los Angeles County seal, which includes a symbol of the Hollywood Bowl, a cross, and two stars. These representations on the seal reflect the Christian roots of the county named after "the queen of the angels," as well as the Hollywood Cross, which has stood near the Hollywood Bowl for more than eighty years and is one of Los Angeles County's most familiar icons.

What is it that drives the ACLU to attack public symbols of religious faith and morality with such vengeance?

From its inception, a powerful faction within the ACLU has been determined to remake America along "progressive" (if not communist) lines. ACLU founder, Roger Nash Baldwin, had close ties with communist movements in the United States. Two of the ACLU's first board members, William Z. Foster and Elizabeth Gurley Flynn, would go on to become prominent members of the Communist Party USA.[1] In the 1920s, Baldwin developed a deep admiration for the recently founded Union of Soviet Socialist Republics. Indeed, his biographer, Robert C. Cottrell, writes that Baldwin, "like many other Western intellectuals, seemed to view the Soviet leaders as superprogressives of a sort."[2]

Baldwin and his ACLU colleagues understood that making America into a "progressive" or proto-Soviet state would require two fundamental changes: First, constitutional limitations on government power had to be removed; and second, moral, free, self-sufficient citizens needed to be transformed into needy, subservient citizens dependent on government. Removing God from the American mind advances both goals.

The distinction between a government of limited powers, versus one of unlimited powers, rests on the source of rights. If men are endowed with rights from God, then the power of government ought to be commensurate with its purpose, which is limited to the protection of those God-given rights. If rights come from government, on the other hand, then any limitation on government power is a limitation on rights. It is no coincidence that the worst modern tyrannies have been rigidly atheistic, amassing power by claiming the more power government has, the better off the people under it will be.

People who are fiercely independent, however, people who take care of themselves, their families, and their businesses, don't like government bossing them around or trying to act as their "nanny." A culture of dependency and victim-hood must be created if big, "progressive" government is to be successful. The best way to create that culture is to sap the moral will of the people.

In the American political tradition, religion and morality have been mutually reinforcing. Religion offers strong support for the moral character of Americans, teaching them to exercise self-restraint while being charitable to their friends, neighbors, and fellow citizens. Indeed, America has witnessed more philanthropic acts of good will, individuals using the fruits of their labor to advance the common good, than any nation in history. At the same time, moral, God-fearing, law abiding citizens tend to be deeply religious. America has always been and remains among the most religious nations in the world.

Anyone seeking to corrupt the morals of America, therefore, would want to drive religion out of the public square. No organization has been more persistent than the ACLU in the relentless assaults on religion and the natural law, family-based morality that has been the unifying force in the American political tradition. It is important to note that the ACLU is not opposed to all morality; indeed, it supports a certain kind of liberal or progressive morality, which will be discussed further below. It is the traditional morality of the family, the moral law that has been taught from most American pulpits and is confirmed by reason, which the ACLU opposes. Based on its record and continuing efforts, it appears the ACLU will not rest until every remnant of this older moral faith in America has been jettisoned from the public square, erased from the public mind, and replaced with the new morality approved by the ACLU.

The fight in Los Angeles County and the scores of similar challenges to public religious expression occurring around the country represent much more than the display of religious symbols. These challenges by the ACLU present to us the question of how we understand ourselves. Will we look up to the "laws of nature and of nature's God," as stated in our Declaration of Independence, for the source of our freedom, our rights, and all that is good? Or will we look to government? The position of the ACLU is clear. For the sake of discharging our duty to God as we understand it, and for the sake of preserving free society and the constitutional government that has served us so well, let us pray, in private and public places, that their view does not prevail.

✛✛✛✛

Previous Claremont Institute publications have addressed questions and problems posed by the ACLU and like-minded advocacy groups.[3] Here we focus on the ACLU's reading of the First Amendment's Religion Clause— "Congress shall make no law respecting an establishment of religion, or prohibiting the free exercise thereof"—that has resulted in a radical effort to stamp out all public expressions of faith in the name of preserving religious liberty.

We begin our study with a survey of contemporary American politics and the role assumed by the ACLU in transforming the way American citizens and law view public expression of religion. In chapter two, we describe the American Founders' policies toward religion by examining the historical development of religion and politics, focusing on the role of Christianity in Western Civilization. In chapter three, we highlight the political and moral conditions necessary for free society, as understood by early American statesmen and thinkers, and the important role assigned to religion.

In chapter four we turn to the widespread critique of the principles of the American Founding that occurred during the Progressive era and gave rise to modern liberalism, the philosophic inspiration for the ACLU. Throughout the book, we use the terms "progressivism" and "modern liberalism" as synonymous. The new liberal view of politics and morality emerged during the Progressive era, stretching roughly from 1880 through World War I. Prominent political thinkers of this period such as Woodrow Wilson referred to themselves and their new historicist political philosophy as "progressive." Later political reformers, such as John Dewey and Franklin Delano Roosevelt, incorporated the principles of "progressivism" in their work. Roosevelt simply called his policies "liberal," while John Dewey was more precise, making a distinction between the old liberalism of the Founding and what he called "new liberalism" or "modern liberalism." Whether labeled "progressivism" or "modern liberalism," this new political theory and its adherents share in their rejection of the natural right principles of the American Founding in favor of a standard of political and moral right rooted in history or evolution.

In chapters five and six we discuss the birth of the organization itself, and its close connection to modern liberalism as it developed through the last eighty-five years. We also trace the ACLU's concerted effort in the courts to transform the nation's understanding of the Establishment Clause in order to construct a "wall of separation" between government and religion. The seventh chapter considers the ACLU's rigorous but select defense of religious free exercise, and explains why that position is in keeping with its other attempts to remove religion from the public square.

We conclude by laying what we hope is the groundwork for a reformation in American politics respecting questions of church and state. Like all reformations, we hold that our current troubled politics has gone astray from its foundations, and that we would do well now to look again to our political roots, re-examining as a nation the principles of the Founding respecting the important questions of religion and religious liberty. In order to provide citizens with a guide to the political principles and policies of the American Founding, we have included in an appendix a number of documents from the Founding period that bear directly on the current controversies over religion. It is our hope that our readers will find these documents helpful in developing a public philosophy, and a public rhetoric to support it, built on the firm principles set forth in the American Founding.

Endnotes

1. Samuel Walker, *In Defense of American Liberties: A History of the ACLU* (Carbondale, Illinois: Southern Illinois University Press, 1990), 52, 132-133.

2. Robert C. Cottrell, *Roger Nash Baldwin and the American Civil Liberties Union* (New York: Columbia University Press, 2000), 176.

3. See William H. Donahue, *On the Frontline of the Culture War:*

Recent Attacks on the Boy Scouts of America (Claremont: The Claremont Institute, 1993); Harry V. Jaffa, *Emancipating School Prayer: How to Use the State Constitutions to Beat the ACLU and the Supreme Court* (Claremont: The Claremont Institute, 1996); Douglas A. Jeffrey, *The American Civil Liberties v. The Constitution* (Claremont: The Claremont Institute, 1998); John C. Eastman and Philip J. Griego, *One Nation Under God: The Pledge of Allegiance Under Attack* (Claremont: The Claremont Institute, 2002).

CHAPTER ONE

THE ACLU AND RELIGION IN AMERICAN POLITICS TODAY

*Of all the dispositions and habits which lead to political prosperity,
Religion and morality are indispensable supports. In vain would that
man claim the tribute of patriotism who should labor to subvert these
great Pillars of human happiness, these firmest props of the duties of
Men and citizens.*
—*George Washington,* Farewell Address, *1796*

Designed in 1957, the great Seal of the County of Los Angeles was intended to reflect the county's history, including the Christian missionaries
who first brought men and women of
European decent to California. The
Seal, therefore, featured a small cross
among other symbols. On September
14, 2004, three of the five Los Angeles County Supervisors voted to
remove the cross from the county seal,
explaining that the cross represents an
unconstitutional establishment of religion.[1] Their decision was made

1

under threat of litigation by the Southern California chapter of the American Civil Liberties Union.

On July 14, 2003, the National Park Service at Grand Canyon National Monument removed a bronze plaque which reproduced Psalms 104:24: "O Lord, how manifold are thy works! In wisdom hast thou made them all: the earth is full of thy riches." This plaque and two others quoting Psalms 66:4 and 68:4 were removed from the popular lookout points at Hermits Rest, Lookout Studio, and Desert View Tower where they had stood for thirty-three years since the Evangelical Sisterhood of Mary donated them. Reuters reported that "[o]fficials said they had no choice but to remove the plaques from three popular spots at the majestic canyon's busy South Rim after an inquiry was made by the state chapter of the American Civil Liberties Union. 'They are religious plaques on federal buildings and that's not allowed based on the law,' said Maureen Oltrogge, a Grand Canyon National Park spokeswoman."[2]

In March of the same year, National Park Service employees placed a tarp over the Mojave Cross, an eight-foot monument located in the desert eighty-five miles northeast of Barstow, California. First erected in 1934 by the Veterans of Foreign Wars, the cross was intended to honor American doughboys killed in the First World War. The Park Service was not acting on its own, but in accord with a federal judge's order, the outcome of a March 2001 lawsuit by the American Civil Liberties Union, which claimed that because the cross is a "religious fixture" on federal land, it represented a clear violation of the First Amendment's Establishment Clause.

These are merely three recent examples of the hundreds advanced, often to court, by the ACLU. They are worthy of special note because they illustrate so well the extreme lengths the ACLU is willing to go in its efforts to purge religious references from the public square. The ACLU argues that in these cases it is simply defending the Bill of Rights. Indeed, the organization maintains that its actions are in defense of religion and religious liberty—that "religious liberty can flourish only if the government leaves religion alone," and that the only way to "ensure religious liberty" is rigorous enforcement of the First Amendment's religion clauses.

But are government employees covering up a cross in the desert as if it were an obscenity, or removing a plaque from a scenic overview, or removing a small cross from a county seal (at great expense to taxpayers) merely instances of government "leaving religion alone?" We know that America's Founders distinguished between an establishment of religion like the Church of England, on the one hand, and expressions of faith by Americans in public situations and on public property on the other. These views are manifest in their writings, some of which have been reproduced in this book's appendix and will be discussed at length in the chapters that follow. In sum, the Founders believed that an established church—where political rights depend on religious belief, and where membership in the political community depends on membership in a state-sanctioned church—is a dangerous threat not only to religious liberty but to all forms of liberty. This is why the First Amendment's Establishment Clause prohibits Congress from passing laws "respecting an establishment of religion." But the Founders also believed that public expressions of religious faith, sometimes emanating from government itself, are an important if not essential support for republican government.

How is it, then, that some Americans have come to regard a cross in the desert, or bronze plaques with a Biblical verse donated to the public by a convent of nuns, or a religious symbol on a county seal, as dangerous and illegal?

✦✦✦

As quoted in the epigraph above, George Washington argued that "religion and morality are indispensable supports" for free society and just government. He continued to emphasize the importance of religion and morality by sounding a warning to his fellow countrymen: "In vain would that man claim the tribute of Patriotism who should labor to subvert these great pillars of human happiness, these firmest props of the duties of Men and citizens."

Today the ground upon which those "great pillars" stand is under constant assault, as religion and morality are often interpreted to be anathema to a free society. Washington and the other Founders understood that religion and morality are necessary for the happiness of individuals and the nation. In their understanding, there exists an intrinsic harmony between the classical precept that happiness is living a virtuous and moral life, and the principles of modern republicanism. The political philosopher John Locke, whom the Founders read and borrowed from in their own political writings, also believed religion and morality to be indispensable for free society.[3] As Locke wrote in his *Essay Concerning Human Understanding*: "For God, having by an inseparable connection, joined Virtue and public Happiness together; and made the practice thereof necessary to the preservation of Society, and visibly beneficial to all."

In his First Inaugural Address, George Washington echoed Locke, reminding his fellow Americans:

> that there is no truth more thoroughly established than that there exists in the economy and course of nature an indissoluble union between virtue and happiness; between duty and advantage; between the genuine maxims of an honest and magnanimous policy and the solid rewards of public prosperity and felicity; since we ought to be no less persuaded that the propitious smiles of Heaven can never be expected on a nation that disregards the eternal rules of order and right which Heaven itself has ordained.

In Washington's words we find what is perhaps the most eloquent and succinct summary of the moral teaching of the Bible no less than classical moral philosophy.

From a political point of view, the American Founders supported religion because they understood that only a people capable of self-restraint and self-reliance would be able to live freely and prosper under a government of limited power, and religion promoted these moral qualities. The American Founders understood that political freedom requires a limited government—that is, government should leave people alone, for the most part, in their private associations such as family, religion, and business. But the Founders also understood that limited government presents certain risks as well: When people are left alone, they might use their freedom to violate the rights of others, or they might live irresponsibly, depending on others with money and resources to care for them. As political freedom requires limited government, so does limited government require certain kinds of civic virtue. James Madison observed in *Federalist* 55 that "republican government presupposes the existence of [moral virtue] in a higher degree than any other form." If a people do not possess the requisite virtue, he continued, then "nothing less than the chains of despotism can restrain them from destroying and devouring one another."

Today numerous organizations are at work to eliminate the influence of religion and morality from American public life. Foremost among these groups is the American Civil Liberties Union, which holds that the government—that is, the people acting in their public capacity—must avoid practicing, teaching, or supporting religious or moral views of any kind. Since the 1947 Supreme Court case *Everson v. Board of Education*—in which the Supreme Court, aided by ACLU attorneys, opined that any government aid to or support of religion violates the First Amendment's supposed "wall of separation" between church and state—the ACLU has been a driving force in the attempt to rid the public square of the last traces of religion and morality.

So what motivates the ACLU—an organization that claims to defend the civil liberties and rights of citizens—in its fierce and persistent war against religion and morality? The ACLU makes two arguments in defense of its anti-religious zeal: one is constitutional and the other is political. The organization and its backers believe public support of religion and morality is unconstitutional, and they believe that religion and the morality of the natural family are anathema to free society.

Religion and the Constitution: The ACLU's View

The ACLU claims to be fulfilling a constitutional mission. It insists that however some Americans might dislike the idea of driving religion and morality out of American public life, nothing less is required by the Constitution, in particular the Constitution's First Amendment. Here the ACLU is simply wrong. What the ACLU defends as the true meaning of the Constitution is nothing but the meaning the ACLU has fabricated. Indeed, their opinion is almost laughable, were it not held so firmly by so many in positions of power and influence, including former and current members of the United States Supreme Court.

First is the massive fact that the First Amendment was meant to place restrictions on the actions of Congress only, not state or local governments ("Congress shall make no law respecting an establishment of religion..."). On its face the First Amendment in no way precludes local governments from supporting religion, because local governments do not fall within the jurisdiction of the First Amendment. During the debates over the drafting and ratification of the First Amendment much was made of the importance of the police powers of the states, which include the power to regulate the health, safety, and morals of the various communities. A central object of the First Amendment was to protect these state police powers from interference from the national government, which is why the First Amendment does nothing but limit the power of Congress. As Robert Goldwin has written, the religion clause of the First Amendment "prohibits Congress from establishing a religion, [while] it simultaneously prohibits Congress from interfering with any existing state establishment of religion, and it leaves open the possibility of general, nondiscriminatory government encouragement of religion."[4]

The ACLU relies on the dubious doctrine of "incorporation"—the doctrine invented by the Supreme Court that the Fourteenth Amendment "incorporates" select (but not all) provisions of the Bill of Rights to apply directly to state and local governments—in order to advance its agenda through the national government. Thus the ACLU concludes that promotion of religion and morality by government at any level violates the Establishment Clause of the First Amendment.[5]

The First Amendment's Establishment Clause was meant to do one thing: prevent the establishment of an official national religion, so that sectarian differences could be taken out of the political realm, thus securing the possibility of free government that operates by majority rule and protects minority rights. In principle the Establishment Clause does nothing more than re-affirm the Article VI prohibition against religious tests for "any office of public trust under the United States." The Establishment Clause of the First Amendment was never intended to prohibit government from advancing religion and morality.

Morality and Freedom: The ACLU's View

Perhaps more pernicious, and more fundamental to the cause advanced by the ACLU, is the idea that religion and morality are somehow dangerous to free government. The ACLU clings to its strange interpretation of the First Amendment because of its devotion to a radical new theory about human beings, the theory of modern liberalism (discussed below in chapters four and five). According to this new view, human freedom means doing whatever one wants, whatever feels good, with little or no regard to the distinction between right and wrong or the social consequences of one's behavior. Right and wrong mean whatever we choose—which means that right and wrong cease to have any meaning.

The new liberal view of morality stands in direct opposition to the view widely accepted by the Founding generation of Americans. Consider, for example, a sermon preached by Samuel West in 1776.[6] Emphasizing the political nature of human beings, West argues that, "our wants and necessities being such as to render it impossible in most cases to enjoy life in any tolerable degree without entering into society, and there being innumerable cases wherein we need the assistance of others, which if not afforded we should very soon perish; hence the law of nature requires that we should endeavor to help one another to the utmost of our power in all cases where our assistance is necessary." What does it mean to "help one another?" West continues: "It is our duty to endeavor always to promote the general good; to do to all as we would be willing to be done by were we in their circumstances; to do justly, to love mercy, and to walk humbly before God." These, West argues, are not only the dictates of the Bible, but "some of the laws of nature which every man in the world is bound to observe, and which whoever violates exposes himself to the resentment of mankind, the lashes of his own conscience, and the judgment of Heaven." This "plainly shows," West concluded,

> that the highest state of liberty subjects us to the law of nature and the government of God. The most perfect freedom consists in obeying the dictates of right reason, and submitting to natural law. When a man goes beyond or contrary to the law of nature

and reason, he becomes the slave of base passions and vile lusts; he introduces confusion and disorder into society, and brings misery and destruction upon himself. This, therefore, cannot be called a state of freedom, but a state of the vilest slavery and the most dreadful bondage. The servants of sin and corruption are subjected to the worst kind of tyranny in the universe. Hence we conclude that where licentiousness begins, liberty ends.

For the Americans of 1776, right and wrong were not subjective and freedom did not mean doing whatever one pleases. Fixed in the unalterable "laws of nature and of nature's God," right and wrong provided a moral framework within which freedom was understood. As West wrote, the "most perfect freedom" was "obeying the dictates of right reason, and submitting to natural law." When human beings act contrary to the dictates of reason, when they ignore the distinction between right and wrong, they are no longer acting freely because they have become slaves to "base passions and vile lusts." Any living being can satisfy its appetites and desires, but it is the unique mark of the human being that he can distinguish what is right from what is pleasurable, knowing that some pleasures are morally wrong and to be avoided. In short, liberty is not license.

The moral relativism accepted and promulgated by the ACLU, however, denies any distinction between liberty and license. This denial, in turn, lends itself to radical individualism, the idea that the highest good for any individual is the unfettered expression of the autonomous individual will. The ACLU cloaks its moral relativism in the guise of civil liberties. Indeed, the ACLU identifies itself with the Bill of Rights. As former ACLU President Ira Glasser put it, anyone who disagrees with the ACLU's agenda is "attacking the Bill of Rights itself." And according to the current president of the ACLU, Nadine Strossen, "to say what we're doing is controversial is to say that the Bill of Rights is controversial."[7] But the ACLU uses the Bill of Rights as an instrument by which their view of civil liberties, a view strikingly different from those who framed and ratified the Bill of Rights, can be advanced. As Professor Harry V. Jaffa has pointed out, "civil liberties are, as their name implies, liberties of men in civil society. As such, they are to be correlated with the duties of men in civil society, and they are therefore subject to that interpretation which is consistent with the duty of men to preserve the polity which incorporates their rights."[8] Contrary to Jaffa and the American Founders, the ACLU holds a radical understanding of civil liberties. For the ACLU, civil liberties are ends in themselves, unconnected to any concerns about civic duty or responsibility, much less moral right and wrong. When the ACLU speaks of civil liberties, therefore, they equate civil liberty with license, thereby promoting moral relativism as constitutionally protected civil liberties.

From the ACLU's morally relativistic perspective, religion necessarily becomes a problem, because religion is intrinsically moral. All religion is premised upon the belief in a higher source of moral authority than man— that man looks up to discover right and wrong. According to modern liberalism, however, man does not *discover* right and wrong, he *creates* them. In this new liberal view, therefore, religion represents nothing but an antiquated restriction of freedom. This explains the ACLU's historically unsupportable position that "the Constitution commands that public schools may not take sides in matters of religion and may not endorse a particular religious perspective or any religion at all." According to ACLU founder Roger Baldwin, children should not even be allowed any time for personal meditation because "the implication is that you're meditating about the hereafter or God or something," which might suggest to their tender minds moral ideas of right and wrong.[9] Therefore, so long as the ACLU remains dedicated to modern liberalism it will continue in its zealous opposition to religion and morality in American public life, even if it requires inventing new and fantastic meanings for the Constitution.

If the principles of the American Founding are true—if freedom requires limited government, and limited government requires morality and religion—then the ACLU's constant assaults on religion and morality represent a serious threat not only to religion and morality, but to the American constitutional form of government that rests upon those principles. Indeed, Washington's warning against those who would "claim the tribute of patriotism," yet subvert religion and morality, is prescient with regard to the ACLU: No organization boasts of its patriotism while laboring as much as the ACLU does to subvert religion and morality, those "great pillars of human happiness."

Endnotes

1. Supervisors Gloria Molina, Yvonne Burke, and Zev Yaroslavsky voted to remove the seal, while Supervisors Don Knabe and Michael Antonovich voted against the seal's removal.

2. San Diego Union Tribune, "Biblical Verses on Plaques in Grand Canyon Taken Down," July 15, 2003, A4.

3. For a recent discussion of this point, see James Hutson, *Forgotten Features of the Founding: The Recovery of Religious Themes in the Early American Republic* (Lanham, Md.: Lexington Books, 2003).

4. Robert A. Goldwin, *From Parchment to Power: How James Madison Used the Bill of Rights to Save the Constitution* (Washington, D.C.: AEI Press, 1997), 164.

5. It is not insignificant that the ACLU proudly lists *Gitlow v. New York,* 268 U.S. 652 (1925), the Supreme Court decision that established the doctrine of incorporation, as its first victory. See "ACLU Greatest Hits," available at: http://www.aclu.org/ Files/OpenFile.cfm?id = 12590.

6. Relevant portions of the text of Samuel West's sermon, titled, "On the Right to Rebel Against Governors," is provided in the appendix.

7. Quoted in William A. Donahue, *Twilight of Liberty: The Legacy of the ACLU* (New Brunswick: Transaction Publishers, 2001), 307.

8. Harry V. Jaffa, "On the Nature of Civil and Religious Liberty," in *Keeping the Tablets: Modern American Conservative Thought*, William F. Buckley Jr. and Charles R. Kesler, eds. (New York: Harper and Row, 1988), 147.

9. Donahue, *Twilight of Liberty,* 102.

CHAPTER TWO

RELIGION AND POLITICS IN HISTORICAL PERSPECTIVE

*The unprecedented character of the American Founding is that it
provided for the coexistence of the claims of reason and of revelation in
all their forms, without requiring or permitting any political decisions
concerning them. It refused to make unassisted human reason the arbiter
of the claims of revelation, and it refused to make revelation the judge of
the claims of reason. It is the first regime in Western civilization to do
this, and for that reason it is, in its principles or speech ... the best regime.*
—*Harry V. Jaffa,* The American Founding as the Best Regime

In order to better understand the question of religion and politics, we
must first step back and take a brief historical tour of the development of
Western religion—Christianity in particular—and the special challenge it
posed for politics. With an historical understanding of religion, the American Founders' understanding of religion becomes clear.

Christianity ushered in a kind of politics utterly unknown to the ancient world, the world of the pagan Greeks and Romans. In particular, the
triumph of monotheistic Christianity in the Western world created a new
political problem—the problem of political obligation, or the "theological-
political" problem. In every ancient city, the laws were understood by

11

citizens to be of divine origin, and hence there was no question of political obligation. A citizen obeyed the laws because the laws came from the gods of the city. Disobedience of the law was disobedience to the gods and tantamount to inviting their wrath. In other words, there was a political logic to paganism: the many different cities of the ancient world had many different gods.[1] In this respect, the Israel of Moses was typical of any city; being a pious Jew and being a law-abiding Jew were inseparable from one another.[2] With the rise of Christianity and the demise of the Roman Empire, however, the connection between law and God was severed.

In 312 A.D. the Roman Emperor Constantine declared Christianity the official religion of the Roman Empire. Although on a scale far larger than ever before witnessed, Rome followed the political logic of the ancient city—that is, a universal empire was supported by a universal religion. Rome became the universal City of God. As Rome crumbled, however, and feudal states began to spring up throughout Europe in its wake, a new situation was created: There now existed many nations, but only one God in the minds of most Westerners, the Christian God. Divine sanction for the particular laws of particular states was impossible. As Professor Harry Jaffa has written:

> The decline and fall of the [Roman Empire] replaced centralized Roman administration with the most decentralized, and most lawless, of regimes: feudalism. The Christian God of the Holy Roman Empire was not the author of the laws of France, Germany, England, Spain or any other part of the Holy Roman Empire, in the sense in which He had been the author of the laws of Moses. He was the sanction for obedience to all rulers—and laws—that were to be obeyed. But these laws were regarded as laws for a variety of reasons, ancient custom or tradition being foremost. And the divine law—the characteristic form of all law in the ancient world—was no longer the law of the earthly but of the heavenly city.[3]

Put another way, if the Christian God is the God of all peoples, but different peoples possess different laws, then God cannot be a legislating God for any particular people. The most important challenge for modern political philosophy was to find some principle of obligation upon which the law could stand in the Christian world, a principle which would not offend the piety of those who lived under the law. Put differently, if piety in the modern Christian world concerns only the relationship of the individual to God, what moral claims of obligation can positive, man-made law have on the citizen? Why should any pious man obey man-made law, especially if that law is opposed to his understanding of Christian piety? Leo Strauss, a professor of political philosophy at the New School for Social Research and the University of Chicago, devoted himself to studying the theological-political problem, especially as that problem was formulated in the most important works of modern political philosophy. In closing his seminal work, *Natural Right and History*, Strauss commented: "The quarrel between the ancients and moderns concerns eventually, and perhaps even from the beginning, the status of 'individuality'."[4]

As Europe suffered centuries of bloody religious warfare, an attempt was made to re-connect the law and God with doctrines of the "divine right of kings," which claimed that political sovereigns were ordained by God and ruled through and with His grace. According to the divine right of kings theory, a monarch ruled as God's surrogate on earth, and as God's surrogate, he was entitled to rule without the consent of the governed. By the seventeenth century, political theorists such as John Locke refuted the divine right of kings as an incoherent theory and demonstrated the fraudulent claims of political power it was used to justify.[5] Locke, among others, suggested that true political sovereignty and legitimate government arise from the consent of the governed, itself a logical and political implication of the natural law teaching that all men are created equal and possess equal rights by nature.

While Locke solved the political problem of Christianity in theory, it remained unresolved in practice until the American Founding. It is the principles of the American Founding—principles built upon the ideas of human equality, individual natural rights, and government by compact, and understood in light of the morally obligatory "laws of nature and of nature's God"—that provide the only ground for a regime in which one can be a good citizen, and a good man of religious faith, simultaneously. While the ultimate claims of reason and revelation can never be reconciled at the level of pure theory, the principles of the American Founding nonetheless represent a solution to the theological-political problem at the political and moral level. Only on the basis of human equality and equal natural rights is a regime of majority rule and minority rights possible—a regime where those who live under laws participate in making the laws, and where no citizen is excluded because of his religious faith.

✛·✛·✛

The problem of political obligation forms the heart of the "theological-political" problem, ultimately pointing to the conflicting claims of reason and revelation: man-made, or positive law finds its ultimate authority in reason, whereas God-given law is discerned through divine revelation. In the modern, monotheist world, it becomes problematic when one particular nation claims the authority of God for its laws when the peoples of many nations worship the same God. On the other hand, laws grounded in human reason are problematic because reason does not command obedience; its authority arises not by threat of divine punishment but through persuasion; where men are not open to rational persuasion, even the most reasonable laws will not be viewed as obligatory. Thus James Madison writes in *Federalist* 49 in the course of defending the supreme reasonableness and wisdom of the Constitution of 1787, that even "the most rational government will not find it a superfluous advantage, to have the prejudices of the community on its side."[6]

The conflict between the political claims of reason and revelation can be traced to the insolubility of the problem of reason versus revelation: that as reason can never fully vindicate its own claims, as the conclusions of human reason are always accompanied by skepticism, reason can never fully refute revelation. Stated differently, reason cannot provide a complete account of all the causes of the universe, and without such a comprehensive account, reason must always be open to the possibility of a divine power as the ultimate and first cause. On the other hand, as revelation rests on a faith in miracles, revelation can never refute reason on reason's own ground. Any argument from revelation can never satisfy the claims of reason, it can never be wholly rational, lest it would no longer be an argument that rests on faith in divine revelation. The conflict between reason and revelation, therefore, remains a permanent problem. But for Strauss, it was the very conflict between reason and revelation, and the moderation of both reason and revelation caused by the inability of each to refute the other, that formed "the core, the nerve of Western intellectual history."[7] In addition, Strauss qualifies the conflict between Greek philosophy and Biblical revelation, pointing out that while they disagree on the highest questions—the ultimate end of human life and "the ultimate insufficiency" of morality—they agree in large measure about the ground or foundation of morality and politics:

> One can say, and it is not misleading to say so, that the Bible and Greek philosophy agree in regard to what we may call, and we do call in fact, morality. They agree, if I may say so, regarding the importance of morality, regarding the content of morality.[8]

Drawing from Aristotle, Strauss explained the relationship of the "good man" and "good citizen":

> Aristotle suggests two entirely different definitions of the good citizen. In his more popular *Constitution of Athens*, he suggests that the good citizen is a man who serves his country well, without any regard to the differences of regimes—who serves his country well in fundamental indifference to the change of regimes. The good citizen, in a word, is the patriotic citizen, the man whose loyalty belongs first and last to his fatherland. In his less popular *Politics*, Aristotle says that there is not *the* good citizen without qualification. For what it means to be a good citizen depends entirely on the regime. A good citizen in Hitler's Germany would be a bad citizen elsewhere. But whereas good citizen is relative to the regime, good man does not have such a relativity. The meaning of good man is always and everywhere the same. The good man is identical with the good citizen only in one case—in the best regime. For only in the best regime is the good of the regime and the good of the good man identical, that goal being virtue.[9]

In Book Ten of Aristotle's *Ethics*, the good man, the man who most achieves virtue in its complete understanding, is the philosopher. The American Founding did not aim to produce a nation of philosophers, thereby falling short of Aristotle's standard of the good man.[10] But the Founding did aim to foster the moral conditions of virtue, providing a ground common to Aristotle from which philosophy arises. As seen in the Massachusetts Constitution of 1780, "the fundamental principles of the Constitution" were identified with "those of piety, justice, moderation, temperance, industry, and frugality," all being "absolutely necessary to preserve the advantages of liberty, and to maintain a free government."[11] As we saw above, George Washington argued in his First Inaugural Address "that the foundation of [American] national policy will be laid in the pure and immutable principles of private morality," because "there is no truth more thoroughly established than that there exists in the economy and course of nature an indissoluble union between virtue and happiness."[12] By identifying happiness with virtue, Washington suggests something approximating Aristotle's teaching of the highest good for man, philosophy. At least on the level of morality, therefore, the virtues encouraged by the American regime and the virtues required by Aristotle's understanding of the good man, are nearly identical. A good American may or may not become a philosopher in the strict Aristotelian sense. But the principles of the American Founding do not preclude the development of philosophy; they form the foundation of it. In light of the principles of the Founding, one can become a good man, in the Aristotelian sense, while remaining a good citizen.

The morality that is common to reason and revelation formed the ground of citizenship in the American Founding. As Harry Jaffa has suggested, Jesus Christ assumed no more and no less than the Declaration's principle of human equality when issuing the injunction to do unto others as one would have others do unto him.[13] In other words, while the theological-political problem remains unsolvable at the level of ideas, the problem was solved in practice by political men—the American Founding Fathers. The rational ground of morality would form the basis of law and citizenship for men of reason no less than men of faith, so long as the moral dictates of the natural law are not violated. In addition, members of various religions, including Christian and Jewish denominations, could remain faithful to their religion and obedient to American law; there was no necessary conflict between the claims of religion and the claims of American positive law, so long as a religion did not reject the rational moral law which informed the positive law. It was precisely the rational moral law that made religious liberty possible in the American Founding.

Writing in the early 1830s, Alexis de Tocqueville noted that "there is no country in the world where the Christian religion retains a greater influence over the souls of men than in America." Yet, he continued,

> [t]he [religious] sects that exist in the United States are innumerable. They all differ in respect to the worship which is due to the Creator; but they all agree in respect to the duties which are due from man to man. Each sect adores the Deity in its own peculiar manner, but all sects preach the same moral law in the name of God....All the [religious] sects of the United States are comprised within the greater unity of Christianity, and Christian morality is everywhere the same [in the United States].[14]

Consider President George Washington's letter to the Newport Congregation of Hebrews—the first time a leader of a sovereign political nation welcomed Jews as equal and full citizens: "The citizens of the United States of America have a right to applaud themselves for having given to mankind examples of an enlarged and liberal policy—a policy worthy of imitation. All possess alike liberty of conscience and immunities of citizenship."[15] Not denying the gulf between Jews and Christians in terms of ultimate theological understanding, Washington nonetheless reminded them that the government of the United States "requires only that they who live under its protection should demean themselves as good citizens in giving it on all occasions their effectual support," because the rational moral ground of American citizenship and law was shared by most religious sects in America at the time of the Founding. As Tocqueville rightly observed, "religion in America takes no direct part in the government of society, but it must be regarded as the first of their political institutions; for if it does not impart a taste for freedom, it facilitates the use of it."[16]

Strauss caught a glimpse of the genius of the American Founding when, in the middle of his essay "On Classical Political Philosophy," he cites the republicanism of Thomas Jefferson as an example of what the ancients meant by the "best regime." But it was Strauss's student Harry Jaffa who articulated the supreme importance of the principles of the American Founding within the much larger context of the political crisis ushered in by monotheistic Christianity. This also explains the importance Jaffa places on the statesmanship of Abraham Lincoln: For it was Lincoln above all others who saved the only possible grounds of free government, at a critical moment when those principles were attacked and rejected.[17]

Strauss took his bearings from what he called the "crisis of the West," which he summarized as the West becoming uncertain of its purpose. This forgetfulness, or confusion, stems from the influence of modern doctrines asserting that right and wrong are arbitrary, and ultimately understanding human life as purposeless—doctrines that have come to inform modern liberalism in the United States. The proponents of these doctrines have convinced themselves that through reason, men come to understand that moral truth cannot be discerned by either reason or revelation. Thus Strauss sometimes referred to modern philosophy as the "self destruction of reason." In response to this crisis, Strauss wrote and spoke on many occasions of the need to return to the orientation of classical political philosophy. As Strauss wrote in the introduction to *The City and Man*: "We cannot reasonably expect that a fresh understanding of classical political philosophy will supply us with recipes for today's use."[18] This is because monotheistic Christianity and modern philosophy have ushered into the world a kind of politics unknown to the ancients. Nevertheless, "an adequate understanding of the principles as elaborated by the classics may be the indispensable starting point for an adequate analysis" of present-day society by "us."

But what is it about the principles of classical political philosophy that Strauss thought so indispensable for our current understanding of things, especially in light of the fact that Strauss himself said the precepts of classical thought cannot be applied today? In arguing for the return to the classical understanding, Strauss distinguished classical from modern political philosophy by "its direct relation to political life." Classical philosophy begins from the perspective of the citizen or statesman, albeit an "enlightened" citizen or statesman, which is a perspective guided by the distinctions of right and wrong, justice and injustice. In short, the things that are paramount for the citizen, and the things by which classical philosophy takes its bearings, are the claims of moral virtue. As Strauss wrote:

> Classical political philosophy is non-traditional, because it belongs to the fertile moment when all political traditions were shaken, and there was not yet in existence a tradition of political philosophy. In all later epochs, the philosophers' study of political things was mediated by a tradition of political philosophy which acted like a screen between the philosopher and political things, regardless of whether the individual philosopher cherished or rejected that tradition. From this it follows that the classical philosophers see the political things with a freshness and directness which have never been equaled. They look at political things in the perspective of the enlightened citizen or statesman ... they look further afield in the same direction as the citizens or statesmen. They do not look at political things from the outside, as spectators of political life.[19]

Thus, insofar as Strauss worked to rediscover the older, common sense understanding of politics and morality, the understanding of the "citizen or statesmen," the claims of moral virtue fundamentally animated and informed his philosophic writing.

The significance of the American Founding with regard to religion may be understood by contemplating the difference between religious toleration and religious liberty. Unlike the ancient city, where there was no distinction between church and state and where priests were the political leaders, modernity requires a distinction between the two. In post-Reformation Europe, the idea of religious toleration was gradually and sometimes reluctantly introduced, with a region's or a nation's established faith granting limited allowance to the practice of other faiths within its borders. But it was only with the American Founding and its Constitution that a regime emerged characterized by no government preference for any one faith—religious liberty in the true and full sense. That freedom receives its full expression in the Constitution's stricture against religious tests (Article VI). Alongside their having established a regime grounded upon equality of rights, the Founders may be said to have made a second great contribution to humankind, namely, resolving the political problem posed by religion.

One recent writer, commenting on the religious rhetoric of Abraham Lincoln, complains that Lincoln's "attempt to synthesize liberal democracy and Christianity" is "distant" from the rational, natural right principles of the American Founding. Indeed, on the eve of the Civil War, and in the most dire circumstances, Lincoln found no opposition between the principles of the Founding and Christianity. As he pleaded in his First Inaugural Address, only six weeks prior to the bombardment of Fort Sumter: "Intelligence, patriotism, Christianity, and a firm reliance on Him, who has never yet forsaken this favored land, are still competent to adjust, in the best way, all our present difficulty." But the "synthesis" of liberal democracy with Christianity attempted by Lincoln was no less the synthesis attempted by the American Founders. Further, by looking at the sermons from the Founding period, one can conclude that this attempted synthesis was successful in the minds of the Christian preachers. In these sermons it is clear that Christian preachers easily combined reason and revelation, at least to the extent necessary to support morality and the law, as the positive law in America would be based upon the "laws of nature and of nature's God." The proposition of natural human equality was identified by early American Christians as corollary to the Biblical account of God making "of one blood all nations." Consider, for example, the words of Rev. Samuel Cooper in 1780:

> We want not, indeed, a special revelation from heaven to teach us that men are born equal and free; that no man has a natural claim of dominion over his neighbors, nor one nation any such claim

upon another; and that as government is only the administration of the affairs of a number of men combined for their own security and happiness, such a society have a right freely to determine by whom and in what manner their own affairs shall be administered. These are the plain dictates of that reason and common sense with which the common parent of men has informed the human bosom. It is, however, a satisfaction to observe such everlasting maxims of equity confirmed, and impressed upon the consciences of men, by the instructions, precepts, and examples given us in the sacred oracles; one internal mark of their divine original, and that they come from him "who hath made of one blood all nations to dwell upon the face of the earth," whose authority sanctifies only those governments that instead of oppressing any part of his family, vindicate the oppressed, and restrain and punish the oppressor.[20]

The moral precepts derived from human equality are compatible, if not identical, with the Biblical injunctions about the individual's obligation to his neighbor. This idea received extensive discussion in colonial and revolutionary America, but was perhaps never expressed more succinctly and clearly than by Catharine E. Beecher, writing in 1841 as the debate about slavery began to intensify:

> The great maxim, which is the basis of all our civil and political institutions, is, that "all men are created equal," and that they are equally entitled to "life, liberty, and the pursuit of happiness."

> But it can readily be seen, that this is only another mode of expressing the fundamental principle which the Great Ruler of the Universe has established, as the law of His eternal government. "Thou shalt love thy neighbor as thyself;" and "Whatsoever ye would that men should do to you, do ye even so to them." These are the Scripture forms, by which the Supreme Lawgiver requires that each individual of our race shall regard the happiness of others, as of the same value as his own; and which forbids any institution, in private or civil life, which secures advantages to one class, by sacrificing the interests of another. The principles of democracy, then, are identical with the principles of Christianity.[21]

Beecher's last line is worth repeating: "The principles of democracy, then, are identical with the principles of Christianity." But the principles of democracy are the rational, self-evident moral truths announced in the Declaration of Independence. When those moral truths are denied or rejected—as the ACLU denies and rejects them—democratic self-government and religious liberty are left without support.

Endnotes

1. Intrinsic to the political logic of paganism was the precept that when a city was defeated on the battlefield, its gods were understood to be defeated as well by the gods of the victorious army. For the conquered people who were allowed to survive, their fate was to abandon the worship of their defeated gods and embrace the gods of the city that had conquered them.

2. On religion in ancient societies, see Fustel de Coulanges, *The Ancient City* (Garden City, New York: Doubleday and Co., 1956 [originally published 1874]).

3. Harry V. Jaffa, *The American Founding as the Best Regime: The Bonding of Civil and Religious Liberty* (Claremont: Claremont Institute, 1990), 22-23. The authors have also borrowed generously from the argument presented in chapter two of Professor Jaffa's *A New Birth of Freedom: Abraham Lincoln and the Coming of the Civil War* (Lanham, Md.: Rowman and Littlefield, 2000).

4. Leo Strauss, *Natural Right and History* (Chicago: University of Chicago Press, 1965), 323.

5. See for example, Robert Filmer's *Patriarcha, or the Natural Power of Kings* (1680) which was attacked and refuted at length in the first of John Locke's *Two Treatises of Civil Government* (1690).

6. Alexander Hamilton, James Madison, John Jay, *The Federalist Papers*, with Introduction and Notes by Charles R. Kesler, Clinton Rossiter, ed. (New York: Signet Classic, 2003), 312.

7. Leo Strauss, "Progress or Return?" in *An Introduction to Political Philosophy: Ten Essays by Leo Strauss,* Hilail Gildin, ed. (Detroit: Wayne State University Press, 1989), 289.

8. Leo Strauss, *An Introduction to Political Philosophy*, 274.

9. Ibid., 33.

10. Cf. *Federalist* 49.

11. Massachusetts State Constitution, accessed on May 5, 2005, at http://www.mass.gov/legis/const.htm.

12. George Washington, *Washington: Writings*, John Rhodehamel, ed. (New York: The Library of America, 1997), 732-733.

13. Harry V. Jaffa, *The American Founding as the Best Regime.*

14. Alexis de Tocqueville, *Democracy in America* (New York: Vintage Books, 1990), I: 303

15. George Washington, *Washington: Writings*, 767.

16. Alexis de Tocqueville, *Democracy in America*, 305.

17. See Harry Jaffa, *A New Birth of Freedom.*

18. Leo Strauss, *The City and Man* (Chicago: Rand McNally and Company, 1964), 11.

19. Leo Strauss, "What is Political Philosophy?" in *An Introduction to Political Philosophy*, 24-25.

20. An edited version of the sermon is in the appendix.

21. Catharine E. Beecher, *A Treatise on Domestic Economy* (Boston: March, Capen, Lyon, and Webb, 1842), 3.

CHAPTER THREE

RELIGION AND THE MORAL CONDITIONS OF FREEDOM IN THE AMERICAN FOUNDING

Before any man can be considered as a member of Civil Society,
he must be considered as a subject of the Governor of the Universe.
—James Madison, A Memorial and Remonstrance, *1785*

The religion supported and propagated during the Founding was a religion capable of providing the public law with a public defense of right. That is, the defense of public right was not limited to a particular group of religious believers. Rather, the religious arguments in defense of morality and free, republican politics while emanating from the pulpit, were often addressed to the public at large—and many times were part of official election ceremonies—because they were at their core not simply sectarian or religious, but rational as well.

Christianity in particular and revelation in general, were understood not simply as matters of faith, but as a body of objective moral and political truth as well, discoverable by reason no less than revelation. The Reverend John Witherspoon, Revolutionary preacher and signer of the Declaration of Independence, remarked that "[i]f Scripture is true, the discoveries of reason cannot be contrary to it, and therefore it has nothing

25

to fear from that quarter." For the Founders, and the preachers of the day, the moral and political teachings of Christianity are true, and are therefore the proper object of unassisted reason, whether exercised by believers or non-believers. By locating the defense of right and the republican cause in reason no less than revelation, the moral teaching of Christianity preached during the American Founding appealed to citizens of all faiths. It was the closest thing to the "political religion" called for by Abraham Lincoln in his 1838 Lyceum speech.

Because the Christianity of the Founding era held that right reason leads to the same moral and political conclusions as revelation, Christian preachers used the pulpit to defend free political institutions. As the Rev. John Tucker explained in a 1771 sermon:

> Civil Government ... is the dictate of nature: it is the voice of reason, which may be said to be the voice of God....All men are naturally in a state of freedom, and have an equal claim to liberty. No one, by nature nor by any special grant from the great Lord of all, has any authority over another. All right therefore in any to rule over others must originate from those they rule over, and be granted by them. Hence all government, consistent with that natural freedom, to which all have an equal claim, is founded in compact, or agreement between the parties, between Rulers and their Subjects, and can be none otherwise. Because Rulers, receiving their authority originally and solely from the people, can be rightfully possessed of no more than these have consented to, and conveyed to them.[1]

The American Founders and the preachers of the time understood, however, that while the basis of equal rights is something we can know by human reason—human equality and natural rights are rational, self-evident truths—questions of religious faith are not. There is no rational principle by which government can declare one religion to be the official or true religion and prohibit others. Reason cannot, for example, resolve the theological disputes over predestination, transubstantiation, or the theological status of Mary, Mother of Jesus Christ. As stated in the Virginia Declaration of Rights of 1776: "That religion, or the duty which we owe to our Creator, and the manner of discharging it, can be directed only by reason and conviction, not by force or violence; and, therefore, all men are equally entitled to the free exercise of religion, according to the dictates of conscience." In the Founders' view, government must guarantee religious liberty because citizens have a right and duty to give that which they "owe their Creator," but they cannot force citizens to engage in any particular religion. Rather it is through the free exercise of religion, according to the conscience of each citizen, that we are able to fulfill our duty to God as we understand it, and live peacefully as neighbors with those of other religious faiths.

The recognition of the liberty of conscience, however, is also a source of duty on the citizens' part. As Rev. Samuel Davies explained in a sermon to the militia of Hanover County, Virginia, on May 8, 1758:

> When our enemies would enslave the freeborn mind and compel us meanly to cringe to usurpation and arbitrary power ... what then is the will of God? Must peace be maintained? Maintained at the expense of property, liberty, life, and everything dear and valuable?...No. In such a time even the God of Peace proclaims by His Providence, "To arms!" Then the sword is, as it were, consecrated by God, and the art of war becomes part of our religion....Blessed is the brave soldier; blessed is the defender of his country and the destroyer of its enemies ... But, on the other hand, cursed is he who, when God, in the course of His Providence, calls him to arms, refuses to obey and consults his own ease and safety more than his duty to God and his country.[2]

The natural law doctrine of the Declaration of Independence, supported by early American Christians, but not dependent upon Christian piety *per se*, was an attempt to re-connect the foundations of law with the divine. In so doing, the natural law—resting on the idea of a Creator and the intelligible universe He created—was grounded in a natural theology compatible with Western Biblical religions. And because it was not the province of any one of those particular religions it proved to be the ground of religious liberty.

✢ ✢ ✢

At the conclusion of *Federalist* 55, James Madison wrote: "As there is a degree of depravity in mankind which requires a certain degree of circumspection and distrust, so there are other qualities in human nature which justify a certain portion of esteem and confidence. Republican government presupposes the existence of these qualities in a higher degree than any other form." In other words, in popular government the character of the people is essential. In a monarchy, the moral qualities of the people matter less because, so long as the king remains sober and sensible, the government will mirror his character. But in a self-governing regime, mindless and barbarous citizens will not respect each other's rights, they will elect bad rulers, and their liberty will soon be lost.

What's more, the American Founders understood that republican government requires not just one but four kinds of civic virtue: First, the people must know and be devoted to the principle of natural rights and be committed to republican government, the purpose of which is the protection of those rights. According to James Madison in *Federalist* 62: "A good government implies two things; first, fidelity to the object of government, which is the happiness of the people; secondly, a knowledge of the means by which that object can be best attained." The American Founders built into the Constitution a number of mechanisms that would curb the power of government, making it difficult for government to violate the liberties and rights of citizens.

As important as these improvements were over past governments, however, they were at best "auxiliary precautions." As Madison explained in *Federalist* 51, "a dependence on the people is … *the primary control* on the government." The principal responsibility for keeping American government within the confines of the Constitution, and therefore protecting the liberty of the American people, belongs to the American people themselves. Or, as Ben Franklin once quipped, the Americans have been blessed with a republican form of government, "if they can keep it!"

Citizens have a number of ways to maintain control over the government. The most obvious way is voting into office candidates who understand and will defend the Constitution. But citizens can also influence those officials already in office by writing letters or e-mails, or calling them on the telephone. Also, citizens can run for office themselves, and challenge in the next election those who currently hold office. With all these options, and so many ways of exercising each of them, how are citizens to know what they should do? How, for example, should they vote in an upcoming election, or what kind of letters should they write to their Representatives or Senators?

Citizens must understand what the Constitution says about how the government works, and what the government is supposed to do and what it is prohibited from doing. Americans must also understand their responsibilities as citizens, no less than their rights, and be able to recognize when government, or other citizens, infringe upon those rights. This civic knowledge should form the core of American public education. In his First Annual Address to Congress, President Washington explained the importance of civic knowledge in America:

> Knowledge is, in every country, the surest basis of public happiness. In one in which the measures of government receive their impression so immediately from the sense of the community as in ours, it is proportionally essential. To the security of a free constitution it contributes in various ways: by convincing those who are entrusted with the public administration, that every valuable end of government is best answered by the enlightened confidence of the people; and by teaching the people themselves to know and to value their own rights; to discern and provide against invasions of them; to distinguish between oppression and the necessary exercise of lawful authority; between burdens proceeding from a disregard to their convenience, and those resulting from the inevitable exigencies of society; to discriminate the spirit of liberty from that of licentiousness—cherishing the first, avoiding the last; and uniting a speedy but temperate vigilance against encroachments, with an inviolable respect to the laws.

In his Farewell Address, delivered at the end of his second term of office, President Washington said: "Promote then as an object of primary importance, institutions for the general diffusion of knowledge. In proportion as the structure of a government gives force to public opinion, it is essential that public opinion should be enlightened." Thomas Jefferson was even more direct: "If a nation expects to be ignorant and free in a state of civilization, it expects what never was and never will be." Washington, Jefferson, and the other Founders knew that without enlightened citizens keeping a close eye on their government, the American experiment in freedom would be short-lived.

Second, the people must possess self-restraint. They must be able to control their passions at least enough to respect the rights of others. They also need the capacity to postpone immediate gratification of their desires and appetites. "The law of nature," in the words of Samuel West, "gives men no right to do anything that is immoral, or contrary to the will of God, and injurious to their fellow creatures." Under a limited government—one based on the distinction between the public and private spheres and that preserves a large realm of personal freedom—the challenge for citizens is to possess self-restraint so that the "strong propensities of our animal nature" do not "overcome the sober dictates of reason and conscience and betray us into actions injurious to the public and destructive of the safety and happiness of society." As West summed up, "men of unbridled lusts" are especially dangerous to the public good and need to be "restrained from doing mischief." Citizens must respect those who deserve respect, pay their debts, obey the law, and perform their daily duties. In a word, they must be capable of living responsibly.

Third, the people must also be self-assertive. They must possess the spirit of the old Gadsden flag of the Revolution which read "Don't Tread on Me!" and later described by James Madison in *Federalist* 57 as that "vigilant and manly spirit ... a spirit which nourishes freedom, and in return is nourished by it." That citizens should be assertive in defending their rights springs from the sense of duty and obligation bound up in the principles of the Founding. Americans today are familiar and comfortable with discussions of their rights, but some have forgotten the duties that correspond to those rights. As the Declaration states, the end of government is the "safety and happiness" of the governed. And while "governments long established should not be changed for light and transient Causes," nonetheless it "is their right, it is their duty, to throw off such government and to provide new guards for their future security" when "a long train of abuses and usurpations ... evinces a design to reduce them under absolute despotism." Notice that what is a *right* in the Declaration is also a *duty*. In other words citizens not only have a right to resist tyranny and defend their liberty, they have a duty to do so. That, in short, is why the Founders were not pacifists.

The political theology of the Founding also conveyed a strong sense of duty. If our natural rights are gifts from God, then it is an affront to God to allow those rights to be violated; it communicates the message to God that we care little about His gift to us. According to the political and theological principles of the Founding, Americans have a duty to themselves, their fellow citizens, and to God to be self-assertive in the defense of their liberty. "If magistrates are ministers of God only because the law of God and reason points out the necessity of such an institution for the good of mankind," Samuel West argued,

> it follows that whenever they pursue measures directly destructive of the public good they cease being God's ministers, they forfeit their right to obedience from the subject, they become the pests of society, and the community is under the strongest obligation of duty, both to God and to its own members, to resist and oppose them, which will be so far from resisting the ordinance of God that it will be strictly obeying his commands.[3]

"Whenever magistrates abuse their power and authority to subverting the public happiness," West concluded, "their authority immediately ceases, and it not only becomes lawful, but an indispensable duty to oppose them; that the principle of self-preservation, the affection and duty that we owe to our country, and the obedience we owe the Deity, do all require us to oppose tyranny."

Self-assertive Americans, mindful of their duty and honor, will be ready to stand against those at home or abroad, in or out of government, who wish to trammel their rights, so that in hard times they will stand and fight, and not slink away slavishly to avoid trouble and danger. Fortunately, Americans have possessed a model of self-assertiveness from the beginning, George Washington, who embodied the "vigilant and manly spirit" that Madison and the other Founders thought indispensable for freedom. Consider, as just one example, Washington's address to the Continental Army of July 2, 1776, only two days before the Declaration of Independence was formally adopted by the Continental Congress:

> The time is now near at hand which must probably determine, whether Americans are to be freemen or slaves; whether they are to have any property they can call their own; whether their houses and farms are to be pillaged and destroyed, and they consigned to a state of wretchedness from which no human efforts will probably deliver them. The fate of unborn millions will now depend, under God, on the courage and conduct of this army. Our cruel and unrelenting enemy leaves us no choice but a brave resistance, or the most abject submission; this is all we can expect. We have therefore to resolve to conquer or die: Our own country's honor, all call upon us for a vigorous and manly exertion, and if we now shamefully fail, we shall become infamous to the whole world. Let us therefore rely upon the goodness of the cause, and the aid of the Supreme Being, in whose hands Victory is, to animate and encourage us to great and noble actions. The eyes of all our countrymen are now upon us, and we shall have their blessings, and praises, if happily we are the instruments of saving them from the tyranny meditated against them. Let us therefore animate and encourage each other, and show the whole world, that a free man contending for liberty on his own ground is superior to any slavish mercenary on earth.

Finally, citizens must be self-reliant. In order to be truly free, citizens should provide the basic necessities of life for themselves. This will ordinarily require hard work, but so long as citizens can keep most of what they earn they will have a powerful incentive for work, and work makes the character of citizens sturdier. Indeed, the economic well-being of the American people is left primarily to them. This presents unlimited opportunities for exercising industry and creativity, which is the single greatest cause of the rise of American economic prosperity and power. But it is also risky. The freedom to succeed is inseparable from the freedom to fail.

Where then do people turn for support and help when they fail? The Founders expected them to turn first to their families.

The Founders understood that strong families and hard work go hand-in-hand with limited government. In 1790, James Wilson emphasized the importance of family this way: "The family is that seminary on which the commonwealth, for its manners as well as for its numbers, must ultimately depend, as its establishment is the source, so its happiness is the end, of every institution of government that is wise and good."[4]

Citizens who could not provide for themselves, and who did not have strong families, were expected to turn for help to their churches or synagogues or to local charities. If these were not adequate to their needs they might turn to government for assistance. While some amount of government assistance or welfare might be available, usually at the local or state level, the Founders recognized a danger intrinsic to government welfare or assistance. The danger is that as people become increasingly dependent on government for their basic needs, they are no longer in a position to act as independent citizens and demand that government stay limited within the confines of the Constitution. As Jefferson remarked in his *Notes on the State of Virginia*: "Dependence begets subservience and venality, suffocates the germ of virtue, and prepares fit tools for the designs of ambition" by those in government.

Self-reliant citizens are free citizens in the sense that they are not dependent on others for their basic needs. They do not need a large provider-government, which has the potential to become an intrusive or oppressive government, to meet those needs. In a letter to a recent immigrant, George Washington wrote of the benefits available in America to self-reliant, virtuous citizens: "This country certainly promises greater advantages, than almost any other, to persons of moderate property, who are determined to be sober, industrious, and virtuous members of society."[5] Only an industrious, self-reliant citizenry is able to enjoy fully the blessings of liberty.

The Founders were concerned with virtue not merely in a utilitarian way, as a necessary condition for republican government. They also believed that the pursuit of virtue was itself the pursuit of happiness, and said so frequently. Thus to be truly happy a people must be virtuous, and if a people are virtuous they will be happy. This is not to say that it will be in every circumstance easy for all to agree on what is or is not virtuous behavior—indeed, so long as human beings remain fallible there will always be such disagreement. But it is at least to admit that virtue and virtuous behavior exist, and that for every moral or political question—hard though it may sometimes be to know—we can know that a right answer exists.

The Founders employed or endorsed several means to promote moral education, including political means (constitutions, laws, and the examples of statesmen), educational means (private and public schools), and private institutions such as families and churches. In each, they saw reason and revelation offering mutual support for free political institutions.[6]

Political Means

The connection between religious faith and politics in the United States is enshrined throughout its political documents. One cannot but help note that the Declaration of Independence—which stands to this day the first of the nation's organic laws in the U.S. Code—includes no fewer than four explicit references to God. The document refers at the outset to the "Laws of Nature and Nature's God," and to the "Creator," concluding with a reference to the "Supreme Judge," and an appeal to "Divine Providence." Moreover, the Declaration carries in all its language the unmistakable message that politics must be understood within a moral order. The colonists' profession that they are acting out of a "decent respect to the opinions of mankind," their discussion of government's "just powers," and the idea of "sacred Honor" each convey a clear sense of right, just as the document's mention of "evils," "cruelty and perfidy," with the adjectives "barbarous," and "merciless," all directed against the Crown, convey a clear sense of wrongdoing.

The Constitution of 1787 begins by carrying over this same clear sense of morality in its Preamble, referring to the "blessings of liberty." "Alone among the ends of the Constitution," writes Harry V. Jaffa, "to secure liberty is called a securing of 'blessings.' What is a blessing is what is good in the eyes of God. It is a good whose possession—by the common understanding of mankind—belongs properly only to those who deserve it."[7] Thus a legal document that lays down the foundation for the day-to-day governance in the new nation begins with subtle recognition that there exists something higher than human law, and that liberty is to be used to good ends.

Throughout the remainder of the Constitution of 1787, the framers created a document remarkable for having solved the question of religion's connection to politics. There are three instances where the document requires that oaths be made—for Senators sitting for impeachment trials, for presidential inaugurations, and for all elected or appointed officers of the United States. The Constitution allows as well for "affirmation" to accommodate those (Quakers and Jews, for example) whose religious convictions barred the swearing of oaths. Most famously, Article VI includes the provision that "no religious test" can be made a prerequisite for holding office, thereby settling at once the question of religious establishment. James Madison's *Notes on the Debates in the Federal Convention of 1787* record that Roger Sherman "thought it unnecessary, the prevailing liberality being a sufficient security against such tests."[8] But the members of the convention had also received and considered correspondence from Jonas Phillips, a Jew from Philadelphia, making note of the Pennsylvania Constitution's provision requiring officeholders to "acknowledge the scriptures of the Old and New Testament to be given by divine inspiration," and that such a provision would deprive Jews from "holding any public office or place of Government."[9] The "no religious test" provision was then approved.

Despite having already drawn a clear line between politics and a particular religious faith in this simple—albeit unprecedented—provision, the Founders do not hesitate to conclude the Constitution by noting that the document has been agreed to "in the Year of our Lord one thousand seven hundred and Eighty seven, and of the Independence of the United States of America the Twelfth." It is not only to their fellow Americans ("in witness whereof") that the framers are answering as they sign their names. We have in an apparently merely functional conclusion a subtle reminder that human government is not to be understood only in human terms, but must be understood with reference to the Divine.

The same understanding of religion holds true in the *Federalist*, that great exposition of the Constitution. While the authors famously describe religion as one of the most durable sources of faction in *Federalist* 10 and elsewhere expound upon the importance of the "no religious test" provision, in other passages they refer to "the Almighty" and to "the transcendent law of nature and of nature's God." In *Federalist* 45, the Old World doctrine "that the people were made for kings, not kings for the people"—an idea directly contrary to the equality of men laid down in the Declaration—is described as "impious." This is to say nothing of Publius' frequent use of the words "virtue" and "honor." Clearly, discussion of free government for Publius does not mean that any reflection upon or discussion of morality and religion alongside is prohibited.

Beyond the founding documents, political freedom itself fosters citizen virtue. We have already cited Tocqueville's *Democracy in America* to the effect that: "Local institutions ... put [liberty] within the people's reach; they teach people to appreciate its peaceful enjoyment and accustom them to make use of it." Specific constitutional provisions are also helpful for purposes of education. Bills of Rights are an example. Of these, Madison wrote in a 1788 letter to Jefferson that "[t]he political truths declared in that solemn manner acquire by degrees the character of fundamental maxims of free government, and, as they become incorporated within the national sentiment, counteract the impulses of interest and passion."

John Adams credited state militia laws—requiring most adult males to be armed and ready to fight—and the habits of local self-government with being a source of "that prudence in council and that military valor and ability, which have produced the American Revolution." Other examples were laws on public decency and providing support to family life.

Of increasing importance after the American Revolution were laws to protect property. The emphasis was placed not on existing property—though they protected it as well—but on the right of all to acquire and use property. Thus these laws too had a moral purpose: to make it possible for families to be independent by producing enough wealth to do away with degrading dependence on others, and to foster such self-reliant virtues as sobriety and industry.

Beginning at the first Congress in 1789, to the present day, Congress has authorized and paid for chaplains, to serve both in its two houses, to say nothing of the hundreds of chaplains who have served the nation's military forces.

The tone of American life was also affected by the speeches and actions of statesmen, who are looked up to by the people as models. In our early history, this was most evident in the respect accorded George Washington. As Washington said in his First Inaugural Address, the foundation of American national policies "will be laid in the pure and immutable principles of private morality." When Washington died, President Adams said in an address to Congress: "His example is now complete, and it will teach wisdom and virtue to magistrates, citizens, and men, not only in the present age, but in future generations." We can also add to these examples the manifold and continuous references to the importance of religious faith by American presidents, legislators, and judges throughout American history.

It is this firm sense at the American Founding that led later statesmen, as their states were admitted to the union, to include in their own constitutions references to moral virtue, understood to stem from religious faith. Forty-five of the fifty state constitutions include preambles that invoke God.[10] California's is typical: "We, the people of California, grateful to Almighty God for our freedom, in order to secure and perpetuate its blessings, do establish this Constitution." Other states refer to God with different language: the Colorado Constitution appeals to "the Supreme Ruler of the Universe." Iowa's Constitution refers to "the Supreme Being." And the preamble to Maine's Constitution invokes the "goodness of the Sovereign Ruler of the Universe." Only two state constitutions, Oregon and Tennessee, do not make explicit reference to God in their respective preambles, although both refer to "Almighty God" later in the text (Article I, Section 2 in the Oregon Constitution; Article I, Section 3 in the Tennessee

Constitution). The remaining three state constitutions—New Hampshire, Vermont, and Virginia—do not have preambles, beginning instead with bills of rights. But even these three state constitutions invoke God: In Part I, Article 5 of the New Hampshire Constitution there are two references to "God;" Article III of the Vermont Constitution invokes both "Almighty God" and "God;" and Article I, Section 16 of the Virginia Constitution acknowledges the "duty which we owe to our Creator." All fifty state constitutions include provisions equivalent to the "no establishment" and "free exercise" clauses of the United States Constitution's Bill of Rights, clearly finding no inconsistency in their references to God and limitations on its political influence.[11]

Acknowledgements of God also appear in several state mottos, including Colorado's *Nil Sine Numine* ("Nothing without Providence"), Arizona's *Ditat Deus* ("God Enriches"), South Dakota's "Under God, the People Rule," and Ohio's "With God, All Things Are Possible."

If the Founders' understanding of moral education receives expression in grand speeches and statements, it as well was embedded in our national symbols. Professor Thomas G. West has observed that the Founders had no qualms about reminding their countrymen of the importance of Providence to the American Revolution. This extends from the numerous sermons from the Founding era to the details of the Great Seal of the United States, adopted by Congress in 1782 as the revolution neared its end. That seal, readily found on American paper currency, includes an eye. Any doubt about whose eye it represents is dispelled by reference to Charles Thomson, the Great Seal's co-designer, who noted that "[t]he eye over it and the motto allude to the many signal interventions of Providence in favor of the American cause."[12]

Likewise, the inscription on the Liberty Bell, now enshrined on National Park Service property at Independence National Historic Park in Philadelphia, reads as follows: "Proclaim liberty throughout all the land unto all the inhabitants thereof - Lev. XXV, v. x. By order of the Assembly of the Province of Pennsylvania for the State House in Philada." The order for that inscription came from Speaker of the Pennsylvania State Assembly Isaac Norris in 1751 upon ordering the bell for the Pennsylvania State

House (Independence Hall). In a state founded by William Penn in 1682 with the principle of religious liberty as its hallmark, the inclusion of this particular Biblical quotation was hardly understood as an establishment.

Congress on April 22, 1864, resolved that "In God We Trust" should appear on American currency, with the same motto appearing in many federal, state and local court buildings across the land. The Congress received its inspiration for this act from the fourth verse to the national anthem, which includes the words: "Let this be our motto, In God is our Trust."

Inscribed upon and within U.S. government buildings in Washington, D.C., quotations from the Bible abound. In the Library of Congress' Thomas Jefferson Building, above the figure of Science, appears Psalm 19:1, "The Heavens declare the glory of God; and the firmament shewith his handiwork." In the same series, above the figure representing religion, appears Micah 6:8, "What doth the Lord require of thee, but to do justly, and to love mercy, and to walk humbly with thy God?" In the same building bronze statues of Moses and St. Paul appear alongside likenesses of Sir Isaac Newton and Herodotus, while in the paintings of the library dome appear, in Hebrew, Leviticus 19:18, "Thou shalt love thy neighbor as thyself." In the Members of Congress Reading Room are ceiling panels painted by Carl Gutherz in the 1890s, representing aspects of civilization, including a depiction of God speaking the words of Genesis, 1:3, "Let there be light." Another panel, representing the light of truth, includes cherubs wielding the level, the plumb, the square, and the Bible.[13] Gutherz and his government patrons found no violation of the Establishment Clause in these Biblical references appearing alongside quotations from Homer, Shakespeare, Virgil, and Confucius. A more recent government structure, the offices of the Central Intelligence Agency in Langley, Virginia, completed in 1959, includes a quotation from the Gospel of John: "You shall know the truth, and the truth shall make you free." (8:32).[14] Further, representations of the Ten Commandments grace the rotunda of the Library of Congress, the exterior rear façade of the U.S. Supreme Court as well as inside the Supreme Court's courtroom, the exterior of the Ronald Reagan Building, and the floor of the National Archives building.[15]

Educational Means

Vigorous public school systems, known as "common schools," and state-supported universities could be found in the North, and occasionally in the South, well before the Civil War. Of the leading Founders, Jefferson devoted the most thought and effort to this cause. The main purpose of pre-university education, he wrote, was to "instruct the mass of our citizens in ... their rights, interests, and duties as men and citizens." This included reading, writing, arithmetic, the information they might need for their own business, and, perhaps most importantly, a basic understanding of the rights and duties of citizenship and the general constitutional structure of government.

Jefferson, whose letter to the Danbury Baptists is the source for the phrase, "a wall of separation between church and state," and editor of a Bible with the stories of miracles removed, is typically portrayed as the Founding era's great opponent of religion. But in 1803 Jefferson signed into law a bill providing for a treaty with the Kaskaskia Indians including an appropriation of $100 annually for seven years to support the work of a Catholic priest ministering to and teaching the Kaskaskia Indians in the Ohio River valley. The legislation included "the sum of three hundred dollars to assist the said tribe in the erection of a church." Similar treaties with the Wyandotte Indians in 1806, and with the Cherokees in 1807, were enacted by Jefferson's administration.[16] Also during his presidency, Jefferson granted no fewer than three extensions for a previously passed "act regulating the grants of land appropriated for Military Services, and for the Society of the United Brethren for propagating the Gospel among the Heathen."

As for university education, Jefferson said it was "to form the statesmen, legislators and judges on whom public prosperity and individual happiness are so much to depend." The university is to "develop their reasoning faculties" and "enlarge their minds, cultivate their morals, and instill into them the precepts of virtue and order." All of this is in order "to form them to habits of reflection and correct actions, rendering them examples of virtue to others, and of happiness within themselves."[17]

Constitutionally, the federal government had no role in public educa-tion, although the first six presidents tried to persuade Congress to establish a national university in Washington. But in the territories that had not yet become states, the federal government had to act in the absence of state governments. In the Northwest Ordinance of 1787, organizing the lands north of the Ohio River and west of Pennsylvania, Congress therefore called for public schools in which moral and religious instruction would take place: "Religion, morality, and knowledge, being necessary to good govern-ment and the happiness of mankind, schools and the means of education shall forever be encouraged." The document's authors saw no inconsistency in appealing for instruction in religion on the one hand, and guaranteeing religious liberty in Article I.[18]

It goes without saying that the education of the young emphasizing self-restraint as opposed to self-indulgence is itself necessary to the con-tinued health of a republic. In practical terms, this means that teachers must convey the message "what can I do today that is right and good" rather than "what can I get away with today?"

Private Institutions

The Founders did not expect education to be conducted only by public authorities. In those days, as today, the main educational institution was the family. The precepts, discipline, religion, and example of parents were foremost in the moral and intellectual development of children. As John Adams recorded in his diary:

> The foundation of national morality must be laid in the private families … How is it possible that children can have any just sense of the sacred obligations of morality or religion if, from their earliest infancy, they learn their mothers live in habitual infidelity to their fathers, and their fathers in as constant infidel-ity to their mothers?[19]

Of course, America's Founders supported the separation of church and state. They enshrined that separation in the First Amendment, no less than the prohibition against religious tests for public office found in Article VI of the Constitution. There would be no sect or faith designated as the official religion of the nation which citizens would be penalized for failing to accept.

But government *approval* and *support* of religion was thought to be not only compatible with liberty, but indispensable for it. For instance, Jefferson and Madison supported a Virginia bill prescribing penalties for anyone doing business on the Sabbath. They did so in the very same year that Madison successfully persuaded the Virginia legislature to pass Jefferson's Bill for Establishing Religious Freedom, an outstanding expression of freedom of conscience.

In his Farewell Address, President Washington expressed the consensus of the Founders on the need for government support of religion:

> [L]et us with caution indulge the supposition that morality can be maintained without religion. Whatever may be conceded to the influence of refined education on minds of peculiar structure, reason and experience both forbid us to expect that national morality can prevail in exclusion of religious principle.

The second to the last clause of the Virginia Bill of Rights says: "no free government, or the blessings of liberty, can be preserved to any people, but by a firm adherence to justice, moderation, temperance, frugality, and virtue, and by frequent recurrence to fundamental principles." The cultivation of virtue through laws and through various means of upholding property rights, local self-government, schools, religion, and strong families was considered one of the government's chief duties.

Endnotes

1. John Tucker, "An Election Sermon," in *American Political Writing During the Founding Era, 1760-1805,* Charles Hyneman and Donald Lutz, eds. (Indianapolis: Liberty Press, 1983), I: 161-162.

2. Samuel Davies, "The Curse of Cowardice," reprinted in *On Faith and Free Government,* Daniel C. Palm, ed. (Lanham, Md.: Rowman and Littlefield, 1997), 93-94.

3. An edited version of the sermon is in the appendix.

4. James Wilson, "Lectures on Law," 1790, available at http://teaching americanhistory.org/library/index.asp?document = 831.

5. George Washington, letter to Reverend Francis Adrian Vanderkemp, May 28, 1788.

6. We have relied extensively on the fine analysis provided by Thomas G. West and Douglas A. Jeffrey in *The Rise and Fall of Constitutional Government* (Claremont: The Claremont Institute, 2004).

7. Harry V. Jaffa, *The American Founding as the Best Regime: The Bonding of Civil and Religious Liberty* (Claremont: The Claremont Institute, 1990), 1.

8. James Madison, *Notes of the Debates in the Federal Convention of 1787* (Athens, Ohio: Ohio University Press, 1966), 561.

9. Max Farrand, ed., *The Records of the Federal Convention of 1787* (New Haven: Yale University Press, 1937), III: 78.

10. The relevant passages from the 50 state constitutions have been reproduced in the appendix.

11. Harry V. Jaffa, *Emancipating School Prayer* (Claremont: The Claremont Institute, 1996).

12. As cited in Thomas G. West, "The Theology of the United States," *Crisis* (December 1996), 40-41.

13. *On These Walls: Inscriptions and Quotations in the Buildings of the Library of Congress*, available at http://www.loc.gov/loc/walls/jeff1.html#swpav.

14. See "The CIA Headquarters Buildings," available at http://www.cia.gov/cia/publications/facttell/building.htm.

15. Carrie Devorah, "God in the Temples of Government" posted on *Human Events Online*, Nov. 24, 2003.

16. John Eidsmoe, *Christianity and the Constitution*, (Grand Rapids, Mich.: Baker Book House, 1987), 243.

17. Thomas Jefferson, et al., *Report of the Commissioners for the University of Virginia*, August 4, 1818, reprinted in *The Portable Thomas Jefferson*, Merrill D. Peterson, ed. (New York: Viking Press, 1975), 334-5.

18. Thomas G. West, "Religious Liberty: The View from the Founding" in *On Faith and Free Government*, 18.

19. Quoted in *The Founders' Almanac*, Matthew Spaulding, ed. (Washington D.C.: Heritage Foundation, 2001), 160.

CHAPTER FOUR

THE PROGRESSIVE REJECTION OF THE PRINCIPLES OF THE AMERICAN FOUNDING

The business of every true Jeffersonian is to translate the terms of those abstract portions of the Declaration of Independence into the language and the problems of his own day. If you want to understand the real Declaration of Independence, do not repeat the preface.
—Woodrow Wilson,
An Address to the Jefferson Club of Los Angeles, *1911*

In the late nineteenth century, a new and radical movement began in the United States that sought nothing less than the transformation of American constitutional government into an administrative-welfare state. This movement has both informed and been advanced by the ACLU. Originally it was an intellectual movement, made up of American academic scholars enamored with the doctrines of historical or evolutionary "progress" produced by European thinkers such as G. W. F. Hegel, Karl Marx, Charles Darwin, and Max Weber. The principal goal of this new movement was the rejection of the natural right principles of the American Founding. The intellectual leaders of this fledgling group, some of whose works we will examine shortly, insisted that American politics should be guided by the new understanding of evolutionary right and historical "progress," and thus they described themselves and their new political philosophy as "Progressivism." By the time of Franklin Roosevelt's election in 1932, the "Progressive" intellectual movement had become a powerful political movement. Roosevelt and other political progressives began adopting the more marketable term "liberal" to describe their policies and they abandoned their previous willingness to make direct attacks on the principles of the Founding, although they never waivered in their intention to replace the principles of the Constitution with new principles more suitable for the administrative state.

"Progressive" or "liberal" thought was greatly influenced by the doctrines of relativism and historicism—the former a denial that there exists any objective truth to be discovered by the human mind, and the latter shorthand for the idea that moral "values" evolve with time and are largely a product of the age in which they are held.[1] The impact on American political thought engendered by these two ideas is only now beginning to be appreciated. If morality and principles of political right evolve over time, there is little reason to be concerned with the moral authorities from the past, including classical moral and political philosophy as well as the Bible. This was given expression by Woodrow Wilson, a leading light in the Progressive movement in his 1913 essay "What Is Progress?":

> Progress! Did you ever reflect that that word is almost a new one? No word comes more often or more naturally to the lips of modern man, as if the thing it stands for were almost synonymous with life itself, and yet men through many thousand years never talked or thought of progress. They thought in the other direction. Their stories of heroism and glory were tales of the past. The ancestor wore the heavier armor and carried the larger spear. "There were giants in those days." Now all that has altered. We think of the future, not the past, as the more glorious time in comparison with which the present is nothing.[2]

The emphasis on progress reflected a confidence that government could solve social problems scientifically. Historicism and relativism together with the new accent on progress meant that politics could no longer be understood in light of self-evident and unchanging truths, as the Founders thought; rather, politics should be understood in terms of a perceived direction that history is taking.

The progressive rejection of the Founders' understanding of self-evident truths occurred on both sides of the political spectrum.[3] As Professor Thomas West and Douglas Jeffrey have explained:

> On the right, for example, William Graham Sumner wrote that, "There are no dogmatic propositions of political philosophy which are universally and always true; there are views which prevail, at a time, for a while, and then fade away and give place to other views." On the left, Woodrow Wilson, pretending to agree with the Declaration, but in fact rejecting it, wrote that the Declaration's unalienable rights to life, liberty, and the pursuit of happiness mean that "each generation of men [may determine] what they will do with their lives, what they will prefer as the form and object of their liberty, in what they will seek their happiness." In Wilson's 1913 book *The New Freedom*, the newly elected president openly criticized the Declaration as outdated bunkum, complaining that "some citizens of this country have never got beyond the Declaration of Independence, signed in Philadelphia, July 4, 1776."[4]

The political principles of the Founders, Wilson continued, "do not fit the present problems; they read now like documents taken out of a forgotten age." Specifically, he argued, the Declaration reflected the worldview of Newtonian theory—the Declaration assumed there are unchanging moral and political principles, just as there are unchanging principles of physics—and the Founders had designed the nation to function as if it were a machine. Progressives, on the other hand, rightly understand politics in terms of history and evolution. They aim "to interpret the Constitution according to the Darwinian principle," thus establishing the progressive view of the Constitution as a "living" or "evolving" document. "All they ask," explained Wilson, "is recognition of the fact that a nation is a living thing and not a machine."[5] As progressive political scientist Charles Merriam summarized in 1903, the "natural law and natural rights" of the Founders had been discarded by intellectuals "with practical unanimity."[6]

More recently, again on both the political right and the left, the rejection

of natural rights in favor of evolution is almost universal among intellectuals. As West and Jeffrey write in their survey of American political
thought:

> Alasdair MacIntyre, for example, a conservative defender of tradi-
> tion, scorned the idea of natural rights in his [1984] book, *After
> Virtue*: "I mean those rights which are alleged to belong to hu-
> man beings as such and which are cited as a reason for holding
> that people ought not to be interfered with in their pursuit of life,
> liberty, and happiness....There are no such rights, and belief in
> them is one with belief in witches and unicorns." And prominent
> liberal Richard Rorty, one of the most influential philosophy pro-
> fessors in America, dismisses the Declaration's natural law
> argument as a "language game" that is no more true than another
> "language game" that would promote slavery over freedom.[7]

Nor is this bias restricted to intellectuals. The liberal critique of the
Constitution has been repeated so long and with such intensity that it has
become orthodoxy in our law schools, courtrooms, and legislative halls.
By 1986, liberal Supreme Court Justice William Brennan could easily dismiss the Constitution out of hand because it belonged "to a world that is
dead and gone." And before Anita Hill took the spotlight, the most controversial part of Clarence Thomas' confirmation hearings for his
nomination to the Supreme Court in 1991 stemmed from allegations that
he had invoked the "n-word"—the *natural* law. Members of the Senate
Judiciary Committee hardly knew how to respond, so alien was the vo-
cabulary of the Founders.

The rejection of the idea of natural rights in favor of history or
"progress" was necessary for the formulation of a new understanding of
human nature, and human society; it was also necessary for a redefinition
of the purpose of government and its relationship to the people who live
under it. This new understanding became the basis of modern liberalism
and its redefinition of equality, rights, and morality. Just as the ground
of the Founders' natural rights theory was a conception of human nature, the ground of the modern rejection of natural rights was a denial
of human nature. Historian Richard Hofstadter's outright dismissal of

nature as a standard of moral and political right was typical of thinkers who had studied the modern theory of evolution. "[N]o man who is as well abreast of modern science," Hofstadter wrote in the 1940s, "as the Fathers were of eighteenth-century science believes any longer in unchanging human nature."[8] For Carl L. Becker, writing in 1922 about the Declaration of Independence, there was no point to asking whether the Founders' appeal to natural rights and higher law was true; one could only attempt to explain their actions as an inevitable consequence of their historical circumstances:

> To ask whether the philosophy of the Declaration of Independence is true or false *is essentially a meaningless question* [emphasis added]. When honest men are impelled to withdraw their allegiance to the established law or custom of the community, still more when they are persuaded that such law or custom is too iniquitous to be longer tolerated, they seek for some principle more generally valid, some "law" of higher authority, than the established law or custom of the community. To this higher law or more generally valid principle they then appeal in justification of actions which the community condemns as immoral or criminal. They formulate the law or principle in such a way that it is, or seems to them to be, rationally defensible. To them it is "true" because it brings their actions into harmony with a rightly ordered universe, and enables them to think of themselves as having chosen the nobler part, as having withdrawn from a corrupt world in order to serve God or Humanity or a force that makes for the highest good.[9]

John Dewey, one of the twentieth century's most influential American liberal thinkers and an intellectual godfather of modern liberalism—who also worked with Roger Baldwin in founding the ACLU in 1920[10]—constructed perhaps the most comprehensive modern liberal political philosophy, building that philosophy on the complete rejection of human nature.

According to Dewey, there simply is no such thing as immutable human nature. Rather, human nature is a product of changing historical contexts and social institutions:

Social arrangements, laws, institutions are made for man, rather
than that man is made for them; that they are means and agencies
of human welfare and progress. But they are not means for obtaining something for individuals, not even happiness. They are
means of creating individuals....Individuality in a social and moral
sense is something to be wrought out.[11]

Human nature itself possesses nothing of intrinsic worth. Intelligence,
talents, and virtue are "wrought out" or produced by the social order; they
are not possessions of individual human beings because they are neither
products of human nature nor are they developed and refined by individual human effort.

Dewey rejected completely the idea that fixed principles grounded in
unchanging human nature can provide the foundation for a political regime. The new understanding of "progress" had exposed the very idea of
unchanging truths about human nature as a fraud. "No longer will views
generated in view of special situations be frozen into absolute standards
and masquerade as eternal truths."[12] The idea of fixed principles for any
polity he regarded as dangerous: "The belief in political fixity, of the sanc-
tity of some form of state consecrated by the efforts of our fathers and
hallowed by tradition, is one of the stumbling blocks in the way of orderly
and directed change; it is invitation to revolt and revolution."[13] On another occasion, Dewey offered the following criticism of the principles of
the Founding:

The fundamental defect [in the principles of the Founding] was
lack of perception of historic relativity. This lack is expressed in
the conception of the individual as something given, complete in
itself, and of liberty as a ready-made possession of the individual,
only needing the removal of external restrictions in order to manifest itself.[14]

But modern liberalism, argued Dewey, "is committed to the idea of
historic relativity."

It knows that the content of the individual and freedom change with time; that this is as true of social change as it is of individual development from infancy to maturity. The positive counterpart of opposition to doctrinal absolutism is experimentalism. The connection between historic relativity and experimental method is intrinsic. Time signifies change. The significance of individuality with respect to social policies alters with change of the conditions in which individuals live. The earlier liberalism in being absolute was unhistoric.

The Progressive theory reverses the relationship between the people and the government as understood by the Founders: Rather than the people delegating power to the government, the government has to empower the people. It is not enough, as the Founders thought, for government to leave people alone and protect their rights by requiring others—including government itself—to leave them alone. Dewey viewed people as essentially needy or disabled, and it is precisely when government leaves them alone that this need or disability is greatest. The government of the New Deal in the 1930s worried about the needs and disabilities of workers, whereas today's government has expanded its roster of dependents to include racial minorities, homosexuals, women, farmers, the elderly, the disabled, and the poor. According to the new liberal view, the American people are to be divided into groups based on needs and victimization and the new role of government is to offer entitlements and preferences to some at the expense of others. Measuring the complicated and changing demographics of the American people, and determining which groups are in need of what kind of government assistance, can only be accomplished through the work of a large bureaucratic class of "experts." The unprecedented exercise of political power by this bureaucratic class, while unconstitutional, is nonetheless indispensable for achieving evolving standards of liberal "social justice" and erecting the kind of administrative-welfare state that can dispense it.[15]

In short, the denial of human nature leads from an understanding of equality in terms of natural rights toward an understanding of equality as something to be produced by government through unequal treatment. This requires a large, active government, one which is not limited in power or scope. Dewey made clear the connection between historic relativity and the new view that government must be limitless:

> I pass now to what the social philosophy of liberalism becomes when its inheritance of absolutism is eliminated. In the first place such liberalism knows that an individual is nothing fixed, given ready-made. It is something achieved, and achieved not in isolation, but the aid and support of conditions, cultural and physical, including in "cultural" economic, legal, and political institutions as well as science and art. Liberalism knows that social conditions may restrict, distort, and almost prevent the development of individuality. It therefore takes an active interest in the working of social institutions that have a bearing, positive or negative, upon the growth of individuals who shall be rugged in fact and not merely in abstract theory. It is as much interested in the positive construction of favorable institutions, legal, political, and economic, as it is in the work of removing abuses and overt oppressions.[16]

When Dewey writes that government must take "an active interest in the working of social institutions," and that government "is as much interested in the positive construction of favorable institutions, legal, political, and economic," he means that no institution, and therefore no form of human behavior, can be outside the reach of government regulation.

"The commitment of liberalism to experimental procedure carries with it the idea of continuous reconstruction of the ideas of individuality and of liberty in intimate connection with changes in social relations." It follows, Dewey explained, "that there is no opposition in principle between liberalism as social philosophy and radicalism in action, if by radicalism is signified the adoption of policies that bring about drastic instead of piece-meal social changes."[17]

As Charles Merriam explained further, "the state ... is the creator of liberty." Bigger government, therefore, means *more* liberty, not less. "It is denied," Merriam concluded, "that *any* limit can be set to governmental activity," and therefore the Constitution's original intent, which limited government power, "no longer seems sufficient."[18] In precisely the same spirit, President Lyndon Johnson officially announced this new conception in a speech at Howard University in 1965: "We seek ... not just equality as a right and a theory but equality as a fact and equality as a result."[19]

✠·✠·✠

Under the Framers' Constitution, moral education was publicly promoted and public decency upheld in numerous ways. Under today's "living constitution" this is much less the case. There are two reasons why this is so.

First, the citizen character necessary for constitutional government—combining the virtues of self-restraint, self-reliance, civic knowledge, and liberty-loving self-assertiveness—is quite different from the character that gets along in the welfare state. The latter would be non-assertive about defending rights, and inclined to seek special treatment and government preferences based on needs or disabilities and an incapacity for self-reliance.

Second, the denial of human nature at the root of the progressive "living constitution" has an amoral implication: absent a common and unchanging human nature, there is no rational basis for an objective understanding of unchanging right and wrong. In this view, moral principles are simply prejudices and all "lifestyles" must be understood as equal. This explains the aversion of modern liberals toward any hint of government promotion of traditional morality or religion. It has filtered down into popular culture and public education in the general admonition that one ought never to make "value judgments."

The U.S. Supreme Court gave voice to this understanding of liberalism in the Court's opinion in the 1992 case, *Planned Parenthood v. Casey*: "At the heart of liberty is the right to define one's own concept of existence, of meaning, of the universe, and of the mystery of human life." If one has the right to define the meaning of the universe and the meaning of life, one certainly must also have the right to define right and wrong. This is the basis of the doctrine of "value relativism," which states that all moral judgments of right and wrong are "values," and all values are subjective and relative, nothing more than personal preferences. The opposition to the Founders' view could not be clearer. As Thomas Jefferson, author of the Declaration of Independence, once wrote, human beings "are inherently independent of all *but moral law*," an unchanging moral law of right and wrong grounded in self-evident truths about an unchanging human nature.

How does progressivism—which provides the foundation for modern day liberalism and powerfully informs the ACLU's work—impact public expression of religion in America? From the perspective of religion, which by definition is built upon faith in God, progressivism may be described as an unbounded faith in man and his works. For it holds that human beings are able to advance not only in terms of their comprehension of science and application of that comprehension to technology, but its moral and political application as well. Just as technological advances allow human beings to improve their health and material comfort (and few will dispute that human ingenuity so employed is a good thing), progressivism holds that humans are able through the social sciences to improve their societal and political well-being. In other words, human beings are evolving not only in physical terms but in moral and political terms as well. Religion, representing permanent, eternal, unchanging truths, and a perfect Being against which imperfect humans are judged, stands in the way of progress.

Religion and the principles of the American Founding are inimical to progressivism, since both represent absolute truth and eternal, unchanging principles. The Judeo-Christian religions hold that human beings are free and equal in the eyes of God, while good government, as understood by the Founders, holds that human beings are free and equal in the eyes of the law. Both ideas from the progressive point of view are relics of a self-deluded age and stand in the way and must be discredited and replaced, so that the idea of progress itself can become the new foundation for America. In American progressive thought, and the modern liberalism that takes its bearings from it, we see the most formidable challenge to the American Founding. We are able to turn from this point to see how this movement gave birth to the American Civil Liberties Union, with its hostility toward religion in the public square.

Endnotes

1. Tellingly, it was during the 1920s that the word "value" began to be used in its modern sense (e.g. "What are your values?"), gradually displacing the previously used "principle" (e.g. "She abides by certain principles"), and the sense of universal truths that the latter word carries with it.

2. Woodrow Wilson, "What is Progress?" in *The New Freedom* (New York: Doubleday, Page and Company, 1918), 42. See also, Ronald J. Pestritto, "Woodrow Wilson, the Organic State, and American Republicanism," in *History of American Political Thought*, Bryan-Paul Frost and Jeffrey Sikkenga, eds. (Lanham, Md.: Lexington Books, 2003), 549-568; and Charles R. Kesler, "Woodrow Wilson and the Statesmanship of Progress," in *Natural Right and Political Right: Essays in Honor of Harry V. Jaffa*, Thomas B. Silver and Peter W. Schramm, eds. (Durham, N.C.: Carolina Academic Press, 1984), 103-127.

3. This will be easily verified today by noting the extent to which the rhetoric of progress predominates in our political speech. It is not unlikely that the most frequently heard phrase in Congress is some variation of: "We must move forward, not back." A proposed law is promoted as "a step forward for the nation," or at least, "a useful first step." A bad bill in Congress is decried as one that "holds the nation back," or, worst of all, "would turn back the clock."

4. The authors have relied heavily on the excellent summary of progressive political thought in Thomas G. West and Douglas Jeffrey, *The Rise and Fall of Constitutional Government in America* (Claremont: The Claremont Institute: 2004). See also, Thomas G. West's essay, "Progressivism and the Transformation of American Government" in *The Progressive Revolution in Politics and Political Science: Transforming the American Regime*, John Marin and Ken Masugi, eds. (Lanham, Md.: Rowman and Littlefield, 2005).

5. Woodrow Wilson, *The New Freedom* (New York: Doubleday, Page and Company, 1913), 48.

6. Charles Edward Merriam, *A History of American Political Theories* (New York: The MacMillan Company, 1903, 1936), 308-309.

7. West and Jeffrey, *The Rise and Fall of Constitutional Government*, 32.

8. Richard Hofstadter, *The American Political Tradition* (New York: Knopf, 1949), 16.

9. Carl L. Becker, *The Declaration of Independence: A Study in the History of Political Ideas* (New York: Harcourt Brace, 1922), 277. Two decades later, as Nazism spread throughout Europe, Becker may have had

second thoughts, writing in a new introduction to the 1942 edition of the same book: "The incredible cynicism and brutality of Adolph Hitler's ambitions, made every day more real by the servile and remorseless activities of his bleak-faced, humorless Nazi supporters, have forced men everywhere to re-appraise the validity of half-forgotten ideas, and enabled them once more to entertain convictions as to the substance of things not evident to the senses. One of these convictions is that 'liberty, equality, fraternity,' and 'the inalienable rights of men' are phrases, glittering or not, that denote the fundamental realities that men will always fight for rather than surrender." Carl Becker, *The Declaration of Independence* (New York: Vintage Books, 1942), xviii.

10. Robert B. Westbrook, *John Dewey and American Democracy* (Ithaca, N.Y.: Cornell University Press, 1991), 278.

11. John Dewey, *Reconstruction in Philosophy* (Boston: Beacon, 1920), 193-194.

12. John Dewey, *The Public and its Problems*, (New York: Holt, 1927), 203.

13. Ibid., 34.

14. John Dewey, "The Future of Liberalism," *The Journal of Philosophy* 22, no. 9 (1935), 30.

15. West, "Progressivism and the Transformation of American Government," 16-17.

16. Dewey, "The Future of Liberalism," 31.

17. Ibid., 33.

18. Merriam, *A History of American Political Theories*, 313, 319. See also Dennis J. Mahoney, *Politics and Progress: The Emergence of American Political Science* (Lanham, Md.: Rowman and Littlefield, 2004).

19. Lyndon Johnson, "To Fulfill These Rights," June 4, 1965, in *Public Papers of the Presidents of the United States: Lyndon B. Johnson* (Washington D.C.: Government Printing Office, 1966), 2: 636.

CHAPTER FIVE

THE BIRTH OF THE ACLU AND THE RISE OF MODERN LIBERALISM

*Do steer away from making it look like a Socialist enterprise. Too many
people have gotten the idea that it is nine-tenths a Socialist movement....
We want to look like patriots in everything we do. We want to get a lot of
flags, talk a good deal about the Constitution and what our forefathers
wanted to make of this country, and to show that we are really the folks
that really stand for the spirit of our institutions.*
—*ACLU Founder Roger Nash Baldwin*, Memo on Strategy, *1917*

The American Civil Liberties Union is nationally regarded as the champion of individual rights and liberties, generally celebrated by the Left
and criticized by the Right. From its modest beginnings in 1920, it has
grown into an internationally recognized organization with over 2000
volunteer lawyers, affiliates in all 50 states, a membership of 400,000 as of
2005, and involvement in close to 6,000 cases nationally each year.[1] How
did this come to pass, and how should the ACLU be understood by Americans, particularly with respect to its efforts to remove religion from the
public square?

In this chapter we consider the events and personalities that led to
the founding of the ACLU, and the organization's place within modern

liberalism. As we will see, while the ACLU has always used the language of the American Founding—and to this day proclaims its allegiance to the idea of liberty, including religious liberty—it is an organization informed not by the idea of natural rights and the "laws of nature and Nature's God" from which those rights are derived, but upon the idea of human progress derived from the doctrines of progressivism. It is dedicated to reform, but not reform that is consistent with the principles of equality and liberty as understood by the American Founders.

Reform movements and debate about the direction the country is taking are as old as American politics itself. But "reform" begins from some moral-political reference point. The best and most successful reform efforts in American history have been those that were able to argue that a particular practice was not in keeping with the principles of the Founding—equal rights and liberty—and therefore in need of change. This was Lincoln's strategy in dealing with slavery. It was what animated the best of the labor reform movements of a century ago. When women demanded the right of suffrage, that change was successfully accomplished with reference to the Declaration of Independence and the universal natural rights that all human beings possess.[2]

Reform, as it manifested itself during the Progressive era, and even more so during the transformation of progressivism into modern liberalism, is different altogether. Highly ideological, progressive reform was understood and promoted by its advocates as movement away from the injustices of the past, which they regarded as inherent in the principles of the Founding. The Constitution of 1787 and the Bill of Rights might be adapted to the future to some extent, but were ultimately due for replacement. The principal thrust of progressivism was a debunking of the Founding as preparation for radical reform. One of the culminating achievements of the Progressive era was the publication in 1913 of Charles Beard's *An Economic Interpretation of the Constitution of the United States* which, as described by Professor Edward Erler, was little more than "a thinly veiled Marxist analysis of the Constitution":

> According to Beard, the Constitution, like every other human endeavor, was the product of class struggle. What made the class

struggle for the American Constitution different was the fact that it was waged largely in secret and by indirection. Instead of viewing the Framers of the Constitution as genuinely public-spirited patriots, Beard preferred to see them as members of the propertied elite who created the Constitution merely to aggrandize their own class interests at the expense of the political rights of the majority.[3]

From a progressive view, Erler writes, the Constitution, "while presenting a democratic façade, is in reality an elaborate scheme that allowed predatory minorities (the propertied, the wealthy, the holders of public securities, speculators) to dominate and effectively disenfranchise the majority." This view was stated succinctly by progressive theorist J. Allen Smith, who wrote:

[T]he Constitution was in form a political document, but its significance was mainly economic. It was the outcome of an organized movement on the part of a class to surround themselves with legal and constitutional guarantees which would check the tendency toward democratic legislation.[4]

As Erler concludes:

The debunking of the Constitution was intended to be a prelude to radical reform—a conscious effort to change the Constitution from one of limited government to one of unlimited government. The explicit goal of this reform was not greater protection of the rights and liberties of individuals, but a newly discovered sense of justice based on the redistribution of wealth. In practical terms it was necessary to reform the Constitution to reflect the priority of the welfare of the community (or the state) over the rights of individuals. One lamentable result of this project was that Beard and the Progressives made the rhetoric of class politics respectable for the first time in American history. Although the details of Beard's economic thesis have long ago been refuted, [the continuing] appeal to class envy as the mainstay of the welfare state is witness to the fact that the rhetorical power of Beard's work remains undiminished.[5]

✦·✦·✦

The ACLU was founded in January 1920, as successor to the National Civil Liberties Bureau (NCLB). The NCLB had come into being in 1917 as a spin-off from the American Union Against Militarism (AUAM), founded by communist activist Louis Lochner. The AUAM was one of a number of progressive, secular peace groups that had sprung up on the political Left as Americans contemplated involvement in the First World War.

Chosen to lead the ACLU was Roger Nash Baldwin (1884-1981), the Harvard-educated son of a wealthy Boston businessman, who had first received public notoriety for his reform efforts in St. Louis in 1910. Energetic and eager to see progressive ideas advance in America, Baldwin quickly became associated with the entire spectrum of the American Left—from liberal reformers and socialists to anarchists and radical communists, including such luminaries as Jane Addams, Emma Goldman, Max Eastman and Norman Thomas.[6] His reading and study ranged from standard leftist writers to the anarchist writings of Russian Prince Peter Kropotkin. This ideological attraction would hold true for the rest of his life, and, according to his biographer Robert C. Cottrell, "enabled him to consider himself at the cutting edge of the reform and radical movements that flourished before World War I."[7] Several of these prominent figures—Addams and Thomas, as well as Clarence Darrow, Felix Frankfurter, and Arthur Garfield Hays—would assist with the founding of the ACLU.

During World War I, the NCLB had set to work defending anti-war activists who found themselves in violation of the Selective Service Act and wartime legislation. It won several cases, although the ACLU was unable to keep Baldwin himself from a prison sentence. After the war, the ACLU moved to new offices in New York's fashionable Greenwich Village. In the nation's intellectual capital, Baldwin and his wife, Madeline Doty, became acquainted with birth-control and eugenics advocate Margaret Sanger, socialist writer Dorothy Day, radical journalists John Reed and Floyd Dell and future American Communist Party leader "Mother" Ella Reeve Bloor. All were part of an intellectual milieu that questioned traditional social institutions and political arrangements, and advocated fundamental political change.[8] Two original members of the ACLU's National Committee, William Z. Foster and Elizabeth Gurley Flynn, would go on to become prominent members of the Communist Party USA—the former serving as chairman in 1945, and the latter in the same position from 1961 until her death in Moscow in 1964.[9]

While Baldwin and the ACLU leadership did not consider themselves Communists in the strict sense, they rightly perceived that they shared the same Marxist ideology. They agreed that religion and the principles of the American Founding were outdated relics that now served only propertied interests and that history and progress were the new path to be followed. They were convinced that only a small cadre of intellectual leaders were capable of leading the masses out of the darkness of religion, limited constitutional government, and private property, and into the light of progressive socialism. Accordingly, they were great admirers of the newly established Soviet regime, which they were confident would prove the rightness of the progressive cause.

This ideological foundation is apparent in the ACLU's first annual report, published in 1921, which argued that the United States was firmly in the control of "the property interests," and that "political democracy as conceived by many of America's greatest leaders, does not exist, except in a few communities." Americans had been "drugged by propaganda" to "accept the dictatorship of property in the name of patriotism." The key tool for this "orderly progress" was complete freedom of opinion. The ACLU's work would be to provide assistance to any "who are prosecuted, or mobbed, or whose rights are restricted inside and outside the law." This assistance would "make a common cause that would lead "the friends of progress to a new social order." The new common cause would put "no limit on the principle of free speech."[10] This would become the standard operating procedure for the organization—limitless protection for the principle of free speech, not for the sake of protecting and preserving the principle itself or the regime that provided security for free speech, but for the sake of "orderly progress."

Baldwin was a prominent example of an American "intellectual" enamored with radical leftist thought. This predilection was confirmed further in an interview with *World Tomorrow* in April 1922, where he argued that true freedom for any society is impossible "until we are rid of this competitive struggle for property. We readily accept in theory the ethics of a communist society, 'to each according to his need, from each according to his ability.'"[11]

Like many on the American Left, Baldwin and the fledgling ACLU maintained for many years thereafter their openly stated respect and admiration for the new Soviet regime, even as its brutality under Lenin and more so under Stalin was becoming increasingly clear. It took a healthy dose of criticism in the early 1920s from Emma Goldman, who had come to realize the extent to which the Leninist regime was using brutality and terror to control the Russian population, before Baldwin toned down his advocacy of the Soviet Union.[12] Nonetheless, his support for the Soviet regime continued, with Baldwin making dubious distinctions in his 1928 apology, *Liberty Under the Soviets*. Civil liberties, he argued, must be understood in context: "Repression in Western democracies are violations of professed constitutional liberties and I condemn them as such. Repressions in Soviet Russia are weapons of struggle in a transition period to Socialism."[13]

During the 1930s the old Progressive movement began to transform itself into the modern-day liberalism of the Democratic Party, manifested most clearly in Franklin D. Roosevelt's presidency and the New Deal. But Baldwin and the ACLU retained during this time an attachment to radical Leftist thought, and to the Soviet regime. An article in *Soviet Russia Today* from 1934 includes Baldwin asserting:

> All my associates in the struggle for civil liberties take a class position, though many don't know it....I, too, take a class position. It is anti-capitalist and pro-revolutionary ... When that power of the working class is once achieved, as it has been only in the Soviet Union, I am for maintaining it by any means whatever.... The Soviet Union has already created liberties far greater than exist elsewhere in the world....It is genuine, and it is the nearest approach to freedom that the workers have ever achieved....If American workers, with no real liberties save to change masters or, rarely, to escape from the working class, could understand

their class interest, Soviet "workers' democracy" would be their goal.[14]

Similarly, in 1935, responding to a questionnaire sent by a representative of the Harvard class of 1905, Baldwin stated flatly:

> I have been to Europe several times, mostly in connection with international radical activities and have traveled in the United States to areas of conflict over workers' rights to strike and organize. My chief aversion is the system of greed, private profit, privilege and violence which makes up the control of the world today, and which has brought it to the tragic crisis of unprecedented hunger and unemployment. Therefore, I am for Socialism, disarmament and ultimately, for the abolishing of the State itself. I seek the social ownership of property, the abolition of the propertied class and sole control of those who produce wealth. Communism is the goal.[15]

Such remarkable statements would receive great attention in later years. In 1938, U.S. Representative Martin Dies assumed leadership of the recently created House Committee on Un-American Activities (HUAC), offering aggressive criticism of the ACLU for its Leftist credentials.[16] As Baldwin himself would admit later, "the Nazi-Soviet Pact exploded the myth that the Communists were a democratic ally."[17] Stung by the intensely negative publicity, and to avoid an internal schism, the organization purged itself of Elizabeth Gurley Flynn in 1940, an action which ACLU scholar and critic William Donohue assesses as "the most dramatic internal dispute in the history of the ACLU."[18] The event marked a true turning point for the organization and for Baldwin. It was the beginning of the ACLU's attempt to distance itself from the radical Left.

If Baldwin was frank during the 1930s about the organization's sympathies for Leftist political thought, he was similarly open about his understanding of civil liberties and why they should be defended. In the same article from *Soviet Russia Today* cited above, Baldwin noted, "I champion civil liberties as the best non-violent means of building the power on which worker's rule must be based."[19] In a letter to the *Christian Science*

Monitor a year earlier, he had written, "civil liberties, like democracy, are useful only as tools for social change. Political democracy as such a tool is obviously bankrupt throughout the world. Dictatorship in one form or another is rapidly replacing it."[20]

As the nation edged closer to the Second World War, and again at the start of the Cold War and the congressional investigations of Communist activities in the early 1950s, Baldwin and the ACLU would have their hands full explaining these comments—and distancing themselves from the Soviet Union. But the significance of Baldwin's comments about civil liberties early in the ACLU's history is this: Here we have in plain terms the impetus that drives the ACLU in its work from its founding to the present. Stated simply, the progressive social change that the Left desires cannot be achieved through democratic means. It requires what Lenin had called "democratic centralism," which, of course, does not rest on the "consent of the governed." Revolution, on the other hand, which would surely bring the Left to power as it had in Russia, is altogether too destructive and violent. That leaves the Left in search of other means to achieve its goals, and the rigorous defense of civil liberties through the courts, as the ACLU learned in its first eighty years, will serve as the best means for establishing "democratic centralism."

That the ACLU is solidly constructed around liberalism today cannot be in any doubt, as the organization has been selective in the constitutional rights it defends. The right to own and accumulate private property, for example, is one of the rights protected by government and most extensively discussed at the Founding, but it is utterly foreign to the liberal Left, and receives almost no attention by the ACLU in its work. Similarly, one of the hallmarks of modern American liberalism is opposition to the idea of privately owned firearms as guaranteed in the Second Amendment and solidly supported by modern scholarship. And yet the ACLU has never yet defended this important civil liberty and the organization is firmly opposed to private ownership of arms, advocating the view that alone among the rights guaranteed in the Bill of Rights, the Second Amendment is a collective right guaranteeing only the agents of government to keep and bear arms.

Americans should understand that advancing the agenda of modern liberalism is the primary work of the ACLU, not protecting the Bill of Rights. Its leadership learned early in its existence of a particularly effective strategy for achieving progressive-liberal goals. That strategy might be described as political *jiu-jitsu*, using the regime's own strengths against itself. In the next chapter we turn to one tactic the ACLU has learned over the past sixty years within this larger strategy, namely the tactic of challenging public expressions of faith as violations of the Establishment Clause.

Endnotes

1. Despite its clear liberal credentials, the ACLU has had no trouble attracting political conservatives and libertarians who are willing to make common cause with the organization on one or more issues. See Nicholas Confessore, "In Bed with Bob Barr: How Conservatives Became the ACLU's Best Friends," *The American Prospect* (Nov. 5, 2001), and Naftali Bendavid, "ACLU Membership Among Republicans Up Since Sept. 11, 2001," *Chicago Tribune*, June 6, 2003.

2. For more on these subjects, see Thomas G. West, *Vindicating the Founders: Race, Sex, Class, and Justice in the Origins of America* (Lanham, Md.: Rowman and Littlefield, 1997).

3. Edward J. Erler, "The Progressive Income Tax and the Progressive Attack on the Founding," in *Moral Ideas for America*, Larry P. Arnn and Douglas A. Jeffrey, eds. (Claremont: The Claremont Institute: 1993), 39-40.

4. As quoted in Edward Erler, *Moral Ideas for America*, 40.

5. Ibid., 41-42.

6. Robert C. Cottrell, *Roger Nash Baldwin and the American Civil Liberties Union* (New York: Columbia University Press, 2000), 30.

7. Ibid., 32.

8. This sentiment would not last long. Baldwin's wife, Madeline, explained their separation after only three years of marriage by noting, "I no longer thought the world was evolving and gradually growing better; that material advancement was improving mankind." As quoted in Robert Cottrell, *Roger Nash Baldwin and the American Civil Liberties Union*, 114.

9. Foster, who remained a committed defender of Stalin until his death, developed the idea of "boring from within," that is, weakening the political structure of democratic-capitalist regimes from the inside.

10. As quoted in Cottrell, *Roger Nash Baldwin and the American Civil Liberties Union*, 128-129.

11. Ibid.

12. One of Goldman's letters includes this reproach: "Now, listen, dear boy: We sent you a list of a thousand names of Soviet victims in prisons, concentration camps and exile. This list is only a very small part of the many thousands who have been incarcerated, starved, tortured, or even shot." Nov. 6, 1924, as reproduced in Cottrell, 177.

13. Quoted in William Donohue, *The Politics of the American Civil Liberties Union* (New Brunswick, N.J.: Transaction Inc., 1985), 230.

14. As quoted in William Donohue, *The Politics of the American Civil Liberties Union*, 138.

15. Baldwin would later claim, not very persuasively, that he meant by this final sentence communism "in its ordinary dictionary sense to designate the common ownership of property, not the political movement of Communism." Cottrell, *Roger Nash Baldwin and the American Civil Liberties Union*, 259.

16. On January 17, 1931, the Special House Committee to Investigate Communist Activities in the United States issued a report assessing the organization as follows: "The American Civil Liberties Union is closely affiliated with the communist movement in the United States, and fully 90% of its efforts are on behalf of Communists who have come into conflict with the law. It claims to stand for free speech, free press, and free assembly; but it is quite apparent that the main function of the ACLU is to attempt to protect the communists in their advocacy of force and violence to overthrow the Government, replacing the American flag with a red flag and erecting a Soviet Government in place of the republican form of government guaranteed to each State by the Federal Constitution. Roger N. Baldwin, its guiding spirit, makes no attempt to hide his friendship for the communists and their principles."

17. *New York Times*, "Obituary for Roger Baldwin," August 27, 1981, D18.

18. Donohue, *The Politics of the American Civil Liberties Union*, 138.

19. Quoted in Donahue, *The Politics of the American Civil Liberties Union*, 138.

20. Quoted in Cottrell, *Roger Nash Baldwin and the American Civil Liberties Union*, 212-213.

CHAPTER SIX

BUILDING THE WALL OF SEPARATION: THE ACLU TAKES RELIGION TO COURT

And can the liberties of a nation be thought secure when we have removed their only firm basis, a conviction in the minds of the people that these liberties are of the gift of God? That they are not to be violated but with his wrath?
—*Thomas Jefferson*, Notes on the State of Virginia

We have seen the ideas that lie behind the ACLU's energetic efforts to remove all vestiges of religion from the public square. We have also seen that the organization's birth and rise accompany the birth and rise of modern liberalism from its Progressive era roots. In this chapter we will examine the landmark Establishment Clause court cases and the arguments presented by the ACLU in their *amicus* briefs as well as briefs filed by petitioners or respondents in which the ACLU acted as counsel or co-counsel for the record. In particular, we will demonstrate how the ACLU's liberalism—rather than any loyalty to the American Founding—drives its interpretation of the First Amendment. We say again that the ultimate objective of progressivism and liberalism is not to defend but to discredit religion, and to replace the principles of the Founding—which are tied intimately and necessarily to the Judeo-Christian conception of human beings and their relation to God—with the wholly secular principles of modern liberalism.

Claiming that its *raison d'etre* is protection of the Bill of Rights, it was natural that the ACLU would choose to act primarily through the courts. The organization saw litigation rather than legislation as the best means for achieving its aims. It was through a series of important Supreme Court decisions that the ACLU has gained the ground that it has held and continues to hold to this day. This in itself is significant, as it circumvents the ordinary means of changing law through Congress and the state legislatures. In his history of the organization, Samuel Walker writes that "[i]n the Supreme Court, the ACLU gradually moved toward an 'absolutist' position on the First Amendment, eventually insisting, for example, on … a complete separation of church and state."[1] With this new interpretation of the First Amendment so far removed from its traditional meaning, it is not surprising that the ACLU found it easier to change the opinions of a few judges rather than trying to change the opinions of a majority of elected legislators, to say nothing of the opinions of the American people.

The ACLU's *Briefing Paper* on Church and State notes that: "Although the Bill of Rights was ratified in 1791, it took two centuries for a body of law on the church/state relationship to evolve. Indeed, the Supreme Court did not begin to develop modern Establishment Principles until the 1940s."[2] The American Founding, in this view, was inadequate, if not defective, with respect to civil liberties in general and religious liberties in particular; the true meaning of these liberties would become complete over time. Moreover, this view implies that the present understanding of church-state relations was inevitable, and solely a matter of political evolution.

It was, of course, not inevitable, but the result of decisions and actions taken by individuals and advocacy groups such as the ACLU. The "wall of separation" as it is understood by many judges and ACLU lawyers was indeed constructed over time, built on the new "modern Establishment Principles" referenced by the ACLU in its documents. It was not by coincidence that the construction of the wall of separation coincided with the great expansion of the size and scope of the federal government that occurred during the 1940s as the result of New Deal programs and the progressive view of politics represented by those programs. The ACLU's bizarre transformation of the Establishment Clause was at complete odds with the idea of "nonpreferentialism" toward religion laid down in James Madison's *Memorial and Remonstrance*, perhaps the most accurate and complete statement of the Founders' principles on the subject of religion. Quoting the Virginia Declaration of Rights, Madison argued that it is a "fundamental and undeniable truth" that "[r]eligion or the duty which we owe to our Creator and the Manner of discharging it, can be directed only by reason and conviction, not by force or violence." Madison continued:

> The Religion then of every man must be left to the conviction and conscience of every man; and it is the right of every man to exercise it as these may dictate. This right is in its nature an unalienable right. It is unalienable; because the opinions of men, depending only on the evidence contemplated by their own minds, cannot follow the dictates of other men: It is unalienable also, because what is here a right towards men, is a duty towards the Creator. It is the duty of every man to render to the Creator such homage, and such only, as he believes to be acceptable to him. This duty is precedent both in order of time and degree of obligation, to the claims of Civil Society.[3]

Madison concluded that "in matters of Religion, no man's right" is to be "abridged by the institution of Civil Society," and that Religion should be "wholly exempt from its cognizance." Madison's single-minded goal was to prevent religious establishments while at the same time protecting and promoting the free exercise of religion. Madison indicates the importance of this goal by entreating the help of the Almighty: "earnestly praying, as we are in duty bound, that the Supreme Lawgiver of the Universe, by illuminating those to whom it is addressed, may on the one hand, turn their councils from every act which would affront his holy prerogative, or violate the trust committed to them: and on the other, guide them into every measure which may be worthy of His blessing, may redound to their own praise, and may establish more firmly the liberties, the prosperity, and the Happiness of the Commonwealth."[4]

✛✛✛

An early and important victory for the ACLU was a case decided by the Supreme Court in 1925, *Gitlow v. New York*. This case was significant because it introduced the Incorporation Doctrine into modern jurisprudence, the constitutional theory that allows the limits on government expressed in the Bill of Rights to be applied not only against the federal government, but against the states by means of the Fourteenth Amendment. The decision, described on the ACLU website as "our first Supreme Court landmark," extended protection of the First Amendment's guarantee of free speech to the laws of New York, thereby opening the door to cases at the state level involving the "no establishment" and "free exercise" clauses.[5]

The same year, in Dayton, Tennessee, the landmark trial of John Thomas Scopes attracted national attention. This was the case which propelled the ACLU into the role of arbiter of modern civil liberties. Upon learning of the Tennessee legislature's Butler Act—a law making illegal the teaching of evolution or any theory that "denies" Divine Creation—the ACLU Board of Directors advertised to encourage violation of the law, promising to provide legal defense. The trial with its colorful lawyers, William Jennings Bryan arguing for the state of Tennessee and Clarence Darrow defending Scopes, brought the ACLU notoriety, even though it lost the case. The case remains one that the ACLU describes with pride in its public literature, and it continues to attract attention as evidenced by its dramatic and skewed portrayal in *Inherit the Wind*—both a stage play (1955) and a movie (1960).

In 1940, the Supreme Court brought the new "incorporation" doctrine of the Fourteenth Amendment to bear directly on the question of religion in *Cantwell v. Connecticut*. Jesse Cantwell and his sons were Jehovah's Witnesses, proselytizing a predominantly Catholic neighborhood in Connecticut. The Cantwells were distributing religious materials door-to-door and by approaching people on the street. After hearing an anti-Catholic message on the Cantwells' portable phonograph, two pedestrians reacted angrily. The Cantwells were subsequently arrested for violating a local ordinance requiring a permit for solicitation and for inciting a breach of the peace. The Supreme Court struck down the ordinance, arguing that it violated the First Amendment's Free Exercise Clause as incorporated against states as an aspect of "liberty" protected by the "due process" clause of the Fourteenth Amendment: "The First Amendment declares that Congress shall make no law respecting an establishment of religion or prohibiting the free exercise thereof. The Fourteenth Amendment has rendered the legislatures of the states [and local governments as agents of the state as well] as incompetent as Congress to enact such laws."[6]

The 1947 case, *Everson v. Board of Education*, served as the first of a series of Establishment Clause cases argued by the ACLU that provided the foundation for the rigid and inflexible separation of church and state doctrine that we see today. The case concerned a New Jersey state law allowing boards of education to reimburse parents—including parents of Catholic school students—for costs related to busing their students to and from school. In its amicus brief, the ACLU argued that "the use of public moneys to transport children attending parochial school is in aid and support of such schools and of religious institutions and tenets, and that the statute and resolution authorizing such expenditures violate the fundamental American principle of separation of church and state and the constitutional prohibition respecting an establishment of religion." The case, wrote the brief's authors, "presents a situation which, however innocent or plausible it may be made to appear, constitutes a definite crack in the wall of separation between church and state. Such cracks have a tendency to widen beyond repair unless promptly sealed up."

In its 5-4 decision, the Court upheld the New Jersey law, with Justice Hugo Black arguing that striking down the law would amount not to government neutrality toward religion, but hostility toward Catholics who would be barred from receiving a public benefit solely because of their religion. But it was here that Justice Black famously employed a phrase borrowed from Thomas Jefferson's January 1802 Letter to the Danbury Baptist Association where he spoke of a high wall of separation that must exist between church and state. "The First Amendment," Black wrote, "has erected a wall between church and state. That wall must be kept high and impregnable. We could not approve the slightest breach. New Jersey has not breached it here."[7] Justice Stanley F. Reed, who agreed with the majority's decision in *Everson*, was nevertheless puzzled by his colleague's use of the "wall" metaphor. In a dissenting opinion the following year in *McCullom v. Board of Education*, Reed objected to "drawing a rule of law from a figure of speech."[8]

If the language was not new, the argument about the meaning of the First Amendment used by the ACLU was. Clearly Jefferson's reference to the "wall of separation"—a phrase appearing in none other of his writings—points to protections against government intrusion on religion: "I contemplate with sovereign reverence *that act of the whole American people which declared that their legislature should make no law* respecting an establishment of religion, or prohibiting the free exercise thereof, thus building a wall of separation between church and state" (emphasis added). Further, Jefferson, writing in his capacity as President of the United States, closed his letter with a prayer: "I reciprocate your kind prayers for the protection and blessing of the common Father and Creator of man, and tender you for yourselves and your religious association, assurances of my high respect and esteem." As Professor Thomas G. West has noted, if the purpose of Jefferson's letter to the Danbury Baptists was to establish a wall preventing government from advancing religion, he would have been violating his own rule in the very document in which he pronounced it.[9] One must conclude, therefore, that either Jefferson was so confused that he contradicted himself, or the interpretation of Jefferson's words offered by the Supreme Court and the ACLU is grossly mistaken.

The Court included the full text of Madison's *Memorial and Remonstrance* at the end of its written opinion and Justice Black cited Madison's essay as evidence supporting his argument.[10] But as we saw above, Madison was no less concerned with prohibiting government establishments of religion than he was with protecting the right of religious free exercise. It is ironic that the Court cited Madison's *Memorial and Remonstrance* in the *Everson* case as *Everson* became the foundation of a jurisprudence, assisted by the ACLU, that eventually sought to use government power to stop any public affirmation or endorsement of religious belief, thus using the Establishment Clause to infringe on Free Exercise of religion!

While the immediate effect of *Everson* was to uphold payments of state funds for church-related schools, and hence a short-term loss for the ACLU, the longer-term significance of the case resided in the fact that the Court accepted application of the First Amendment's Establishment Clause to the states, thus continuing the logic of *Gitlow* and *Cantwell*.

More importantly, the Supreme Court accepted the ACLU's assertion of a "separation of church and state," and the *Everson* case, with its stark "wall" imagery, became the foundation for the ACLU's subsequent Establishment Clause cases. But perhaps the best measure of the ACLU's success came with the media, which gradually but steadily through the 1950s and 1960s began to refer to "the Constitution's separation of church and state," leaving many Americans with the mistaken impression that the words are part of our fundamental law.

❖❖❖❖

In the 1948 case, *McCollum v. Board of Education*, the Supreme Court put the "wall of separation" doctrine to use, ruling against the Champaign, Illinois, Board of Education's policy of allowing Wednesday classes for either the Protestant, Catholic, or Jewish faith. The classes were limited to students whose parents authorized their attendance, with other students required to attend "meaningful secular studies." As Justice Black wrote in his decision for the Court:

> Here not only are the State's tax-supported public school buildings used for the dissemination of religious doctrines. The State also affords sectarian groups an invaluable aid in that it helps to provide pupils for their religious classes through use of the State's compulsory public school machinery. This is not separation of Church and State.[11]

Two landmark cases would follow a decade later, both listed on the ACLU's "Greatest Hits" website: *Engel v. Vitale* and *Abington School District v. Schempp*. The two cases would come at a time of intense internal debate in the ACLU. On the one side were those who were willing to leave the religious questions alone in order to focus on what they regarded as more pressing civil liberties concerns; the other more numerous faction was more strident in its determination to advance the cause against religion. Thus in 1962, the ALCU formulated, in the words of historian Samuel Walker, "its strongest statement yet, opposing in-school prayers, Bible reading, and the observance of Christmas, Hanukkah, or Easter as religious holidays."[12] In *Engel*, the Court determined that recitation of a government-drafted prayer in New York classrooms violated the First Amendment. The prayer's authors had made every effort to make the prayer generic: "Almighty God, we acknowledge our dependence upon Thee, and we beg Thy blessings upon us, our parents, our teachers and our Country."[13] The *Engel* case, combined with the *Schempp* decision in 1963, which ruled against a Pennsylvania requirement that public school students read ten verses from the Bible each morning, virtually rendered all religious exercises in public schools to be unconstitutional. The "wall of separation" argument launched by the ACLU, and accepted by Justice Black in *Everson*, had suddenly grown to become a significant barrier to previously accepted public expressions of religion and religious teaching.

The *Schempp* decision is of special interest because of the Court's emphasis on the requirement of government *neutrality* toward religion as the foundation for its interpretation of the First Amendment. Justice Tom C. Clark's opinion, echoed by the concurring justices, argued:

> The place of religion in our society is an exalted one, achieved through a long tradition of reliance on the home, the church and the inviolable citadel of the individual heart and mind. We have come to recognize through bitter experience that it is not within the power of government to invade that citadel, whether its purpose or effect be to aid or oppose, to advance or retard. In the relationship between man and religion, the State is firmly committed to a position of neutrality.[14]

The next major development in constitutional law came in 1971, with what is probably the best-known of the ACLU-related cases, *Lemon v. Kurtzman*. The 7-0 decision concerned the Rhode Island Salary Supplement Act of 1969 and Pennsylvania's Non-Public Elementary and Secondary Education Act of 1968. Both laws permitted states to support directly the salaries of teachers of secular subjects in parochial and religious schools.[15] In its decision, the Court articulated a three pronged test for determining when the Establishment Clause has been violated. Any statute must:

1) have a secular purpose, neither endorsing nor disapproving of religion;
2) have an effect that neither advances nor inhibits religion;
3) not entangle the government in the regulation of religion.

Based on this newly adopted standard, the Court ruled that the two laws under review did indeed violate parts of this three-pronged test, and were therefore unconstitutional.

With the *Lemon* decision, the ACLU had succeeded in establishing a constitutional doctrine that had the effect of making religion's presence in the public square inherently tenuous. In *Wallace v. Jaffree* (1985), the ACLU further buttressed its wall of separation with an important high-profile victory, successfully helping to persuade the Court that an Alabama law requiring a moment of silence "for meditation or voluntary prayer" was an unconstitutional violation of the Establishment Clause. A majority of the Court determined in *Wallace* that the law violated the *Lemon* test inasmuch as it was an affirmative endorsement of religion, and therefore lacked a secular purpose.[16] The First Amendment was now read, in effect, as forbidding any government action that favored religion over irreligion.

In his dissenting opinion, Justice William Rehnquist questioned whether it could be possible that the First Amendment's authors intended "that the government be absolutely neutral as between religion and irreligion." Indeed, he continued:

> It would come as much of a shock to those who drafted the Bill of Rights as it will to a large number of thoughtful Americans today to learn that the Constitution, as construed by the majority, prohibits the Alabama Legislature from "endorsing" prayer. George Washington himself, at the request of the very Congress which passed the Bill of Rights, proclaimed a day of "public thanksgiving

and prayer, to be observed by acknowledging with grateful hearts the many and signal favors of Almighty God." History must judge whether it was the Father of his Country in 1789, or a majority of the Court today, which has strayed from the meaning of the Establishment Clause.[17]

Perhaps the most important aspect of the *Wallace* case lay in the doctrine that was included in Justice Sandra Day O'Connor's concurring opinion, holding to the idea that the Establishment Clause should be read as forbidding any "endorsement of religion."[18] This doctrine, utterly contrary to the Founders' thinking about religion's proper place in the republic, was the ACLU's real victory, and laid the groundwork for the further removal of expressions of faith in years ahead. And, it may be noted, the impact of this aspect of the *Wallace* decision has become quite visible. As noted above, after the *Everson* case, the media began referring to "the Constitution's separation of church and state." Since *Wallace*, one is increasingly likely to hear media references to "the Constitution's ban on preference for religion," a significant advance for the ACLU's underlying propaganda efforts.

In *Westside Community Schools v. Mergens* (1990), the Supreme Court upheld a Court of Appeals ruling that allowed public high school students to meet on school grounds for Bible study. Justice O'Connor wrote that "there is a crucial difference between government speech endorsing religion, which the Establishment Clause forbids, and private speech endorsing religion, which the Free Speech and Free Exercise clauses protect."[19]

Two years later, in 1992, the Court held in *Lee v. Weisman* that nonsectarian invocations and benedictions at public school graduation ceremonies violated the Establishment Clause. The decision also introduced the theory of "psychological coercion" as new doctrine. Students were now understood in need of protection from any acknowledgement of God. As Justice Anthony Kennedy wrote for the majority, "prayer exercises in public schools carry a particular risk of indirect coercion. The concern may not be limited to the context of schools, but it is most pronounced there." Kennedy acknowledged that "[w]hat to most believers may seem nothing more than a reasonable request that the nonbeliever respect their religious practices, in a school context may appear to the nonbeliever or dissenter to be an attempt to employ the machinery of the State to enforce a religious orthodoxy." He continued:

> The undeniable fact is that the school district's supervision and control of a high school graduation ceremony places public pressure, as well as peer pressure, on attending students to stand as a group or, at least, maintain respectful silence during the Invocation and Benediction. This pressure, though subtle and indirect, can be as real as any overt compulsion.[20]

Kennedy acknowledged that the Court was being asked "to recognize the existence of a practice of nonsectarian prayer ... prayer which is more acceptable than one which, for example, makes explicit references to the God of Israel, or to Jesus Christ, or to a patron saint," something not unlike a "civic religion" which might be "tolerated when sectarian exercises are not." But the First Amendment's Establishment Clause, Kennedy asserted, prohibits government from allowing mention of any "ethic and a morality which transcend human invention," because the appeal to a transcendent (i.e., having a non-human origin) morality is the essence of religion.[21] By the logic of this remarkable and sweeping statement, reading the Declaration of Independence—which begins by appealing to the transcendent "laws of nature and of nature's God"—at a public school graduation ceremony would be unconstitutional![22] Kennedy's argument presents a clear example of the moral relativism that informs modern liberalism: If any "morality which transcends human invention" is constitutionally suspect, then only subjective moral "values" invented or created by human will are worth constitutional protection.

In the 2000 case of *Santa Fe Independent School District v. Doe*, the Court gave further consideration to the question of prayer in public schools, again aided by ACLU briefs. Prior to 1995, the Santa Fe School District in Texas had allowed a student council chaplain to deliver a prayer over the public address system at varsity football games. After this practice was challenged in federal court, the District made the prayer voluntary, initiated and led by a student at home games. And in keeping with the Court's demand, the prayer was made non-sectarian and non-proselytizing. But a Federal Court of Appeal, followed by the U.S. Supreme Court determined that even this revised practice amounted to an unconstitutional establishment. The Court noted in its decision that it agreed with the distinction between government speech and private speech, "but we are not persuaded that the pre-game invocations should be regarded as 'private speech.'" The Court reasoned that since the student leading the prayer would be elected by the student body, "minority candidates will never prevail and ... their views will be effectively silenced."[23]

If the ACLU enjoyed a victory in this case, it was dealt a defeat the same year in *Mitchell v. Helms,* a case in which the Supreme Court ruled constitutional Louisiana's application of a federal school aid program that permitted private religious schools to receive educational and computer materials. The opinion, written by Justice Clarence Thomas, held that in giving consideration to such cases, the Court should no longer attempt to determine whether the aid is going to a "pervasively sectarian" school. "This doctrine, born of bigotry," wrote Justice Thomas, "should be buried now." He continued by noting that, "nothing in the Establishment Clause requires the exclusion of pervasively sectarian schools from otherwise permissible aid programs."[24]

Good News Club v. Milford Central School ruled on by the Court in 2001, with Justice Thomas again writing the majority opinion, required the Court to consider "whether Milford Central School violated the free speech rights of the Good News Club when it excluded the Club from meeting after hours at the school. The second question is whether any such violation is justified by Milford's concern that permitting the Club's activities would violate the Establishment Clause." The Court concluded that "Milford's restriction violates the Club's free speech rights and that no Establishment Clause concern justifies that violation."[25]

Another setback for the ACLU came in 2002 with the Court's decision in *Zelman v. Simmons-Harris* which ruled that Ohio's pilot program, giving school vouchers to families with children in the chronically underperforming Cleveland City School District, did not offend the First Amendment:

In sum, the Ohio program is entirely neutral with respect to religion. It provides benefits directly to a wide spectrum of individuals, defined only by financial need and residence in a particular school district. It permits such individuals to exercise genuine choice among options public and private, secular and religious. The program is therefore a program of true private choice. In keeping with an unbroken line of decisions rejecting challenges to similar programs, we hold that the program does not offend the Establishment Clause.[26]

The case was cause for much hand-wringing in liberal circles, and appeared as a defeat for the ACLU. But interestingly, as V. Phillip Muñoz points out, the case was decided on the basis of the Endorsement Test laid down by Justice O'Connor in the 1985 *Wallace v. Jaffree* decision. In this respect, while a tactical victory for school choice advocates, it was no real defeat for the ACLU, as the Court yet again accepted in principle that government may not endorse religion over irreligion.[27]

Given Supreme Court jurisprudence over the last fifty years, the Ninth Circuit Court of Appeal's 2002 decision in *Newdow v. U.S. Congress* should come as no surprise. Here the Ninth Circuit ruled that the Pledge of Allegiance's phrase "under God," added in 1954, was a violation of the Establishment Clause. Indeed, in the light of Supreme Court precedents, the decision was almost inevitable. At each step of the way, the ACLU has been close at hand to encourage the Court on to the next level of restriction. The Ninth Circuit Court decision in 2002, prompted professions of shock even on the political left. "Embarrassing at best," commented Democratic Senator Diane Feinstein, and Senate Minority Leader Tom Daschle described it as "just nuts."

More revealing are the ACLU's comments on the decision. "In our system of government," wrote ACLU Attorney Margaret Crosby, "fundamental rights come from the Constitution. The Ninth Circuit took those rights seriously in *Newdow*."[28] This idea, of course, stands in stark contrast to the Founders' view, for whom "fundamental" or natural rights were understood to come from human nature, not the Constitution or any other document. Crosby argued that in the years after 1954 the country was not ready to consider banishing God from the Pledge, the courts having "not yet recognized the rights of minority faiths to be free of religious coercion in public schools." "But 50 years later," Crosby wrote, "a law requiring school children to pledge allegiance to a nation 'under God' cannot be reconciled with the Supreme Court's strict constitutional precedents on religion in public school." In other words, progress toward complete secularization is inevitable, and will come step by step by virtue of precedent.

The Supreme Court's most recent Establishment Clause pronouncements came in two cases decided in June, 2005—*McCreary County v. ACLU of Kentucky* and *Van Orden v. Perry*. The *McCreary* case, in which the ACLU was one of the litigants, struck down two displays of the Ten Commandments in two Kentucky county courthouses, while the Court in *Van Orden* ruled that a monument of the Ten Commandments on the grounds of the Texas State Capitol was constitutionally permissible. In both decisions the Court was badly divided and the exchange between the justices was often heated. The *McCreary* decision was 5-4 with Justice Souter writing for the majority. In *Van Orden*, Chief Justice Rehnquist wrote an opinion which announced the judgment of the Court joined only by Justices Scalia, Kennedy and Thomas. The contradictory holdings in the two decisions are a telling sign of the unprincipled and largely arbitrary Establishment Clause jurisprudence that has developed over the last half century.

The controversy in the *McCreary* case arose when executives in two Kentucky counties (McCreary County and Pulaski County) posted wall displays of the Ten Commandments in their respective county courthouses and were then sued by the ACLU to force their removal. Responding to the legal challenges—and hoping to dilute any merely sectarian message that might be implied by only displaying the Ten Commandments—both counties expanded the displays to include other documents related to the American Founding which also demonstrate an acknowledgement of God, including the Declaration of Independence. The purpose of the display, according to the respective counties, was "to demonstrate that the Ten Commandments were part of the foundation of American Law and Government" and "to educate the citizens of the county regarding some of the documents that played a significant role in the foundation of our system of law and government."[29]

Justice Souter, writing for the majority in *McCreary*, relied upon an expanded version of the *Lemon* test to determine whether the Kentucky displays of the Ten Commandments violated the Establishment Clause. The first prong of the *Lemon* test examines whether government action has "a secular legislative purpose." But Justice Souter expanded the prohibitive reach of the first prong of the *Lemon* test from "a" secular purpose to a "predominant" secular purpose. In effect this requires all government action to be done with no religious purpose whatsoever. Drawing from the earlier *Everson* case as well, Souter wrote: "The touchstone for our analysis is the principle that the 'First Amendment mandates governmental neutrality between religion and religion, and between religion and nonreligion.'"[30]

The Court's emphasis on determining the purpose of government action—rather than simply judging whether a government policy or action amounts to an "establishment of religion" according to the original meaning of the term—requires that the justices inquire into the motives of government actors, an often difficult and imprecise endeavor. As Souter wrote, "scrutinizing purpose does make practical sense, as in Establishment Clause analysis, where an understanding of official objective emerges from readily discoverable fact, without any judicial psychoanalysis of a drafter's heart of hearts."[31] But, one might ask, what about cases where "an understanding of official objective" does not emerge from "readily discoverable fact?" Will such cases require "judicial psychoanalysis of a drafter's heart of hearts?" However they are determined, the Court must concern itself with the purpose and intent of legislation so long as it follows the principle of government neutrality between religion and nonreligion, a principle unknown to the original Establishment Clause but created and enlarged by the Court itself. Court-enforced neutrality demands that the Court be able to distinguish "a sham secular purpose from a sincere one," a problem that could be avoided completely if the Court confined itself to the constitutional question of whether a particular law or government action amounted to an establishment of religion as originally understood by the framers of the First Amendment. From the point of view of the original meaning of the Establishment Clause, it matters not whether government intends to promote or acknowledge religion; it matters only if government power is used to coerce religious beliefs or practices or to violate the rights of citizens on the basis of religious discrimination.

After stating the expanded *Lemon* test to be used in determining whether or not the purpose of the Kentucky counties' displays of the Ten Commandments was neutral both with respect to all religions as well as nonreligion, Souter spends considerable time recounting the legislative history of the case:

> When the government acts with the ostensible and predominant purpose of advancing religion, it violates that central Establishment Clause value of official religious neutrality, there being no neutrality when the government's ostensible object is to take sides….Manifesting a purpose to favor one faith over another, or adherence to religion generally, clashes with the "understanding, reached … after decades of religious war, that liberty and social stability demand a religious tolerance that respects the religious views of all citizens." By showing a purpose to favor religion, the government "sends the … message to … nonadherents 'that they are outsiders, not full members of the political community, and an accompanying message to adherents that they are insiders, favored members.'"[32]

Originally, McCreary and Paluski Counties displayed the Ten Commandments alone, which on its face, according to Souter, demonstrated a "predominantly religious purpose." After the initial lawsuits filed by the ACLU, the counties then added other historical documents in an obvious attempt to dilute the religious appeal of the display. Souter commented as follows:

> In this second display, unlike the first, the Commandments were not hung in isolation, merely leaving the Counties' purpose to emerge from the pervasively religious text of the Commandments themselves. Instead, the second version was required to include

the statement of the government's purpose expressly set out in the county resolutions, and underscored it by juxtaposing the Commandments to other documents with highlighted references to God as their sole common element. The display's unstinting focus was on religious passages, showing that the Counties were posting the Commandments precisely because of their sectarian content. That demonstration of the government's objective was enhanced by serial religious references and the accompanying resolution's claim about the embodiment of ethics in Christ. Together, the display and resolution presented an indisputable, and undisputed, showing of an impermissible purpose.[33]

Tracing the development of the displays through their third and final form, Souter concluded that the counties had never abandoned their original "predominantly religious purpose," attempting merely to disguise that purpose in an effort to pass Establishment Clause scrutiny. A "reasonable observer," Souter argued, would have to "suspect that the Counties were simply reaching for any way to keep a religious document on the walls of courthouses constitutionally required to embody religious neutrality." The displays, therefore, fail the first (revised) prong of the *Lemon* test and stand in violation of the Establishment Clause.

Of particular interest is the Court's assertion that the Ten Commandments have no bearing on and provide no background for the Declaration of Independence, one of the documents displayed alongside the Commandments. This should be obvious to a "reasonable observer," the Court majority argued, because "the Commandments are sanctioned as divine imperatives, while the Declaration of Independence holds that the authority of government to enforce the law derives 'from the consent of the governed.'"[34] Here the Court is echoing the assertions made by the ACLU in its brief for the respondents, which stated that "the Declaration of Independence and the Decalogue address distinct concepts—one, the relation of individuals to a deity and each other, the other, the relation of individuals to government."[35]

But the Court's and the ACLU's account of the political teaching of the Declaration is only half the story and only partially true. As discussed above in chapters two and three, the Declaration of Independence argues that legitimate governments derive "their just powers from the consent of the governed" *because* "all men are created equal" and "endowed by their Creator with certain unalienable rights." The natural rights with which man has been endowed by his Creator are antecedent to and remain the standard of judgment for all governments. Individual natural rights authorize men to consent to government, and natural human equality requires the consent of the governed. Absent natural human equality and individual natural rights, there is no justification for government by consent.

Further, the principle of human equality in the Declaration is emphatically a moral no less than a political principle: because all men are created equal and are endowed by their Creator with equal rights by nature, it is therefore morally wrong for one man to rule over another without the other's consent. The Declaration recognizes the American people in their moral as well as their political capacity, speaking of the Americans as "one people," "a free people," and "the good people." The American argument for independence from British rule and union among themselves rests on the claim that Americans possess the capacity of being free and good.

Contrary to the ACLU's brief in *McCreary*, therefore, which asserts that "the foundation of the law of the United States ... [and] the consent of the governed ... needs no external or divine authority for its support," the entire political argument of the Declaration rests on the equal relation of all men to the Creator. Thus while the ACLU insists that "other than the mention of a Creator, no link is apparent" between the political theology of the Declaration and the Biblical theology emanating from the Ten Commandments, the parallels between the Creator of the Declaration and the monotheistic, Creator God of the Ten Commandments are unmistakable and undeniable.

In his dissenting opinion in *McCeary*, Justice Scalia took occasion to emphasize the contrived and arbitrary meaning of the Court's Establishment Clause jurisprudence dating back to the *Everson* case. Scalia rightly noted that most of the recent Establishment Clause cases have little if any relationship to the purpose of the First Amendment as well as the entire Bill of Rights, which is to protect the rights of individuals. Mere acknowledgement of God or religion by government does not violate the rights of any citizens, including those who may not believe in the monotheistic God of the American political tradition:

> The beliefs of those citizens are entirely protected by the Free Exercise Clause, and by those aspects of the Establishment Clause that do not relate to government acknowledgment of the Creator. Invocation of God despite their beliefs is permitted not because nonmonotheistic religions cease to be religions recognized by the religion clauses of the First Amendment, but because *governmental invocation of God is not an establishment.*[36]

Scalia also took aim at the majority's argument that religious displays might pass Establishment Clause muster if they are done in the absence of religious purpose or endorsement:

> This inconsistency may be explicable in theory, but I suspect that the "objective observer" with whom the Court is so concerned will recognize its absurdity in practice. By virtue of details familiar only to the parties to litigation and their lawyers, McCreary and Pulaski Counties, Kentucky, and Rutherford County, Tennessee, have been ordered to remove the same display that appears in courthouses from Mercer County, Kentucky to Elkhart County, Indiana....Displays erected in silence (and under the direction of good legal advice) are permissible, while those hung after discussion and debate are deemed unconstitutional. Reduction of the Establishment Clause to such minutiae trivializes the Clause's protection against religious establishment; indeed, it may inflame religious passions by making the passing comments of every government official the subject of endless litigation.[37]

The arbitrariness of the Court's position regarding religion makes it impossible to apply any consistent principle or standard of review. Recalling the many instances when the Court upheld government promotions or endorsements of religion, Scalia remarked, "when the government relieves churches from the obligation to pay property taxes, when it allows students to absent themselves from public school to take religious classes, and when it exempts religious organizations from generally applicable prohibitions of religious discrimination, it surely means to bestow a benefit on religious practice—*but we have approved it* [emphasis added]." He continued:

> Indeed, we have even approved (post-*Lemon*) government-led prayer to God. In *Marsh* v. *Chambers*, the Court upheld the Nebraska State Legislature's practice of paying a chaplain to lead it in prayer at the opening of legislative sessions. The Court explained that "[t]o invoke Divine guidance on a public body entrusted with making the laws is not ... an 'establishment' of religion or a step toward establishment; it is simply a tolerable acknowledgment of beliefs widely held among the people of this country." (Why, one wonders, is not respect for the Ten Commandments a tolerable acknowledgment of beliefs widely held among the people of this country?)
>
> The only "good reason" for ignoring the neutrality principle set forth in any of these cases was the antiquity of the practice at issue....That would be a good reason for finding the neutrality principle a mistaken interpretation of the Constitution, but it is hardly a good reason for letting an unconstitutional practice continue.[38]

By adopting an *ad hoc* method of judging Establishment Clause challenges, the Court not only creates confusion over the meaning of the Constitution and its requirements, but it threatens the very idea of the rule of law: "What distinguishes the rule of law from the dictatorship of a shifting Supreme Court majority is the absolutely indispensable requirement that judicial opinions be grounded in consistently applied principle. That is what prevents judges from ruling now this way, now that—thumbs up or thumbs down—as their personal preferences dictate."

The unprincipled and confused state of Establishment Clause jurisprudence is perhaps best demonstrated by the fact that on the very same day that the Court struck down the Ten Commandments in Kentucky courthouses in the *McCreary* case, it delivered a second decision in *Van Orden v. Perry* approving a monument of the Ten Commandments located on the grounds of the Texas State Capitol. Writing a plurality decision, Chief Justice Rehnquist ruled that the monument did not violate the Establishment Clause. In direct contradiction of the majority opinion in *McCreary*, the Chief Justice openly acknowledged that "[o]ur institutions presuppose a Supreme Being," emphasizing that the responsibility of the Court is to "maintain a division between church and state" while not evincing "hostility to religion by disabling the government from in some ways recognizing our religious heritage."[39] He also acknowledged that while past Courts "have sometimes pointed to *Lemon v. Kurtzman*" as the authority, several subsequent opinions argued that *Lemon* served "as no more than helpful signposts" and that "[m]any of our recent cases simply have not applied the *Lemon* test." "Whatever may be the fate of the *Lemon* test in the larger scheme of Establishment Clause jurisprudence," Rehnquist concluded, "we think it not useful in dealing with the sort of passive monument that Texas has erected on its Capitol grounds."[40]

Ignoring the requirement of discerning "sincere" from "sham" purposes urged by the ACLU and employed by the majority in *McCreary*, Rehnquist wrote forthrightly that "of course, the Ten Commandments are religious—they were so viewed at their inception and so remain. The monument, therefore, has religious significance." But, Rehnquist argued, "simply having religious content or promoting a message consistent with a religious doctrine does not run afoul of the Establishment Clause."

In a remarkable concurring opinion, from which we will quote at length, Justice Thomas urged the Court to "abandon the inconsistent guideposts it has adopted for addressing Establishment Clause challenges" and return to the Clause's original meaning.[41] As he has done before, Justice Thomas reminded the Court that the Establishment Clause was principally a means of protecting federalism. With its restriction of power directed solely at Congress ("Congress shall make no law respecting an establishment of religion"), it was intended to provide wide latitude to the states in matters of religion and therefore by its nature and purpose it "resists incorporation against the states."

But even if the Court continues in its misguided approach of applying the Establishment Clause to state and local governments, Justice Thomas argued, the "task would be far simpler if we returned to the original meaning of the word 'establishment' than it is under the various approaches this Court now uses." The Founders' understanding of "establishment," Thomas pointed out, necessarily involved legal coercion regarding religious beliefs and practices. If this original understanding could be recovered, challenges such as the one to the Texas monument would rarely if ever arise:

> There is no question that, based on the original meaning of the Establishment Clause, the Ten Commandments display at issue here is constitutional. In no sense does Texas compel petitioner Van Orden to do anything. The only injury to him is that he takes offense at seeing the monument as he passes it on his way to the Texas Supreme Court Library. He need not stop to read it or even to look at it, let alone to express support for it or adopt the Commandments as guides for his life. The mere presence of the monument along his path involves no coercion and thus does not violate the Establishment Clause.[42]

Chastising the Court for wandering so far from the original intent of the Constitution it is charged with upholding, Thomas argued persuasively that a return to the original meaning "would do more than simplify our task"— it would also "avoid the pitfalls present in the Court's current approach to such challenges."

> This Court's precedent elevates the trivial to the proverbial "federal case," by making benign signs and postings subject to challenge. Yet even as it does so, the Court's precedent attempts to avoid declaring all religious symbols and words of longstanding tradition unconstitutional, by counterfactually declaring them of little religious significance. Even when the Court's cases recognize that such symbols have religious meaning, they adopt an unhappy compromise that fails fully to account for either the adherent's or the nonadherent's beliefs, and provides no principled way to choose between them. Even worse, the incoherence of the Court's decisions in this area renders the Establishment Clause impenetrable and incapable of consistent application. All told, this Court's jurisprudence leaves courts, governments, and

believers and nonbelievers alike confused—an observation that is hardly new.[43]

Sounding an alarm similar to that provided by Scalia in his *McCreary* dissent, Thomas warned the Court that it is on the path of replacing the rule of law with the rule of arbitrary judgments of the Court: "The unintelligibility of this Court's precedent raises the further concern that, either in appearance or in fact, adjudication of Establishment Clause challenges turns on judicial predilections. The outcome of constitutional cases ought to rest on firmer grounds than the personal preferences of judges."

Justice Thomas' closing words should serve as a clarion call to judges, lawyers, court observers and citizens who believe that the Court should always be mindful of the fact that it is charged with expounding the Constitution and does not sit as a "continuing constitutional convention":

> Much, if not all, of this would be avoided if the Court would return to the views of the Framers and adopt coercion as the touchstone for our Establishment Clause inquiry. Every acknowledgment of religion would not give rise to an Establishment Clause claim. Courts would not act as theological commissions, judging the meaning of religious matters. Most important, our precedent would be capable of consistent and coherent application. While the Court correctly rejects the challenge to the Ten Commandments monument on the Texas Capitol grounds, a more fundamental rethinking of our Establishment Clause jurisprudence remains in order.[44]

✢✢✢✢

In surveying the major cases involving the Establishment Clause, and the ACLU's involvement, several points become clear. First, the ACLU, beginning with the Scopes Trial, has spearheaded many of the landmark cases. Second, the organization has effectively and intentionally brought modern liberal principles of government to bear against religion's long-accepted presence in the American public square, arguing that the First Amendment must be read to forbid not only any connection with government, but any public expression of religion or any indication that government favors religion over irreligion. In the course of offering a new and expansive reading of the Establishment Clause, the Supreme Court has effectively adopted the position that the Establishment Clause is in conflict with the Free Exercise and Free Speech clauses of the First Amendment. In order to prevent an establishment of religion, American government must restrict the religious speech of citizens, such as voluntary prayers delivered at high school graduations and football games.

It may be said that now there are not one but rather two walls separating church and state. The original wall, built to protect religious liberty from the encroachment of a government establishment of religion, is the First Amendment as understood by its authors. The second wall was erected in opposition to the first. It rests on the foundation of the radical new liberalism that emerged after World War II. This new, radically secularized vision of the Establishment Clause was first articulated in the ACLU's amicus brief in the *Everson* case, a view that was adopted in its entirety by Justice Black's opinion for the Court. The years since 1947, as we have seen, have given us a series of decisions in which that second wall has been steadily strengthened and reinforced, ever more completely segregating religion from government and the public square.

Endnotes

1. Samuel Walker, *In Defense of American Liberties: A History of the ACLU* (Carbondale, Illinois: Southern Illinois University Press, 1990), 218.

2. ACLU *Briefing Paper*, Summer 1999.

3. The full text of Madison's *A Memorial and Remonstrance* is provided in the appendix.

4. Appendix, 200.

5. Note that throughout the history of "incorporating" the Bill of Rights' limits on government power to apply to state and local governments, the application of "incorporation" has always been selective. The ACLU, for example, has never attempted to apply the 2nd Amendment guarantee of the right to bear arms to state governments.

6. 310 U.S. 296, 303 (1940).

7. 330 U.S. 1, 18 (1947).

8. 333 U.S. 203, 247 (1948).

9. Thomas G. West, "Religious Liberty: The View from the Founding," in *On Faith and Free Government,* Daniel C. Palm, ed. (Lanham, Md.: Rowman and Littlefield, 1997), 5.

10. We thank Professor Edward Erler for bringing this to our attention.

11. 333 U.S. 203, 212 (1948).

12. Samuel Walker, *In Defense of American Liberties,* 223.

13. 370 U.S. 421, 422 (1962).

14. 374 U.S. 203, 226 (1963).

15. 403 U.S. 602 (1971).

16. 472 U.S. 38, 40 (1985).

17. 472 U.S. 38, 113 (1985).

18. Ibid., 67-71.

19. 496 U.S. 226, 250 (1990).

20. 505 U.S. 577, 593 (1992).

21. Ibid., 589.

22. See Edward J. Erler, "The First Amendment and the Theology of Republican Government," *Interpretation: A Journal of Political Philosophy* 27, no. 3 (Spring 2000), 252.

23. 530 US 290, 304 (2000).

24. 530 U.S. 793, 828 (2000).

25. 533 U.S. 98, 160 (2001).

26. 536 U.S. 639, 662 (2002). See also the amicus brief submitted by the Claremont Institute, authored by John Eastman and Edwin Meese III (Claremont: The Claremont Institute, 2002).

27. See V. Philip Muñoz, "James Madison's Principle of Religious Liberty," *American Political Science Review* 97, no. 1 (February 2003).

28. Margaret Crosby, "The Values of the Pledge of Allegiance," *Daily Journal,* September 3, 2002, available online at: http://www.aclunc.org/opinion/020903-pledge.html.

29. Quoted at 545 U.S. ___ (2005).

30. Ibid.

31. Ibid.

32. Ibid.

33. Ibid.

34. 1bid.

35. ACLU brief for respondent, 2003 U.S. Briefs 1693.

36. 545 U.S. ___ (2005), emphasis added.

37. Ibid.

38. Ibid.

39. Ibid.

40. Ibid.

41. Ibid.
42. Ibid.
43. Ibid.
44. Ibid.

CHAPTER SEVEN

IMMORAL RELIGION? THE ACLU'S SELECT DEFENSE OF RELIGIOUS FREE EXERCISE

A revelation, pretending to be from God, that contradicts any part of natural law, ought immediately to be rejected as an imposture.
—Samuel West, *Sermon before the Massachusetts Legislature, 1776*

The ACLU is best known for fighting its battles on Establishment Clause grounds, but it has made ample use of the Free Exercise Clause as well. The ACLU booklet on First Amendment issues involving religion is called *The Right to Religious Liberty*. The book's response to the query "What is the purpose of the Free Exercise Clause?" opens with the proclamation that "the purpose of the Establishment Clause and the Free Exercise Clause is to guarantee religious liberty." On this point, both progressive organizations like the ACLU and Americans loyal to the principles of the Founding will agree. Richard J. Neuhaus has written that the First Amendment's two Religion Clauses are really one, and that they need not be "balanced" against each other. "Each is in the service of the other....the free exercise of religion requires the non-establishment of religion. The positive good is free exercise, to which non-establishment is instrumental."[1] That view is echoed by V. Phillip Muñoz, who notes that "[r]eligious free exercise,

93

including the right not to exercise a religion, is the end; no-establishment is a means toward fulfilling that end."[2] In this section, we will see cases where the ACLU has accomplished some good in protecting or advancing the cause of religious liberty. Indeed, several of the organization's most renowned cases have transformed the manner in which Americans now understand the meaning of religious liberty. And, at first glance, ACLU efforts on behalf of religious free exercise might seem inconsistent with its rigorous efforts to remove all religious reference from the public square. On closer inspection, however, its work can be seen for what it is—fully consistent with its larger underlying goal to reconstruct the American regime on a progressive foundation.

To understand how this is so, we must first recall how the American Founders understood free exercise. As we have noted above, the first principle of the American regime was the idea that "all men are created equal," that is to say the principle of equal rights before law. In world-historical terms, religion has only relatively recently come to operate with the sense of a common humanity consistent with the idea of human equality. Primitive religions often permitted or even required human sacrifice, murder or enslavement of captive enemies, cannibalism, subjugation of women, polygamy, and were emphatically not built on ideas of a common humanity. As we discussed above in chapter two, each ancient city had its own law-giving gods. The fates of a city, its laws, and its gods were intrinsically bound together. The military defeat of a city, for example, meant the death of its civic gods and the destruction of its laws. Furthermore, the pagan gods of the ancient world were understood as gods of particular people, not all humankind.

In the West, the concept of a single God for humankind is not introduced until the establishment of Judaism. Later, Christianity builds on that same premise and from these monotheistic faiths, with their understanding of God and his relationship to all human beings, would arise the idea of true religious liberty, as opposed to mere toleration. Founded in the seventh century, Islam too is a monotheistic religion, although there remains serious debate among theologians and scholars whether Islam is compatible with the idea of religious liberty.³ Michael Novak has pointed out that,

> [i]t is the special virtue of the Jewish and Christian conception of God that it allows us to make a twofold claim: to recognize in public the beliefs on which our rights are founded, and to refuse to mandate for others that they must hold the same beliefs.⁴

In our time, co-existing with Judeo-Christian faiths are other doctrines that are radically inconsistent with the concept of equality. For example, one of the most widely followed belief systems in the world, Hinduism, is to this day understood by some to require social stratification by caste alongside a belief in reincarnation. Another, Islam, is understood by some of its adherents to place severe limits on the legal rights of women, to require the assassination of heretics, and to encourage suicide attacks on its perceived enemies. And of course while Hindus or Muslims can immigrate and become perfectly good Americans, none of these particular practices are legal in the United States because religious free exercise is limited to those religious practices that are consistent with reason and the idea of equal natural rights. Clearly there is opposition between a government "dedicated to the proposition that all men are created equal," in the words of Abraham Lincoln, and religious practices informed by the stark denial of that proposition. Thus Hinduism, Islam or any other faith may be freely practiced in the United States, provided its followers have abandoned those practices inconsistent with American law.

This idea was clear from the United States' colonial origins, in which there was never any doubt that religious liberty was understood as limited to those practices that were both legal and consistent with public order. Typical of this view was New York's 1777 Constitution, which provided "that the liberty of conscience, hereby granted, shall not be construed as to excuse acts of licentiousness, or justify practices inconsistent with the peace or safety of the state."⁵ Similarly, as Justice Morrison Waite wrote in the Supreme Court's unanimous decision in *Reynolds v. U.S.*, the 1878 Supreme Court case that confirmed the constitutionality of the federal ban on Mormon polygamy:

> Laws are made for the government of actions, and while they cannot interfere with mere religious belief and opinions, they may with practices. Suppose one believed that human sacrifices were a necessary part of religious worship, would it be seriously contended that the civil government under which he lived could not interfere to prevent a sacrifice? Or if a wife religiously believed it was her duty to burn herself upon the funeral pile of her dead husband, would it be beyond the power of the civil government to prevent her carrying her belief into practice? ... Can a man excuse his practices to the contrary because of his religious belief? To permit this would be to make the professed doctrines of religious belief superior to the law of the land, and in effect to permit every citizen to become a law unto himself. Government could exist only in name under such circumstances.[6]

The free exercise of religion in the United States, then, is not unlimited. For the ACLU, however, the free exercise of religion is understood in radical or absolute terms, in keeping with its expansive understanding of other forms of expression. Just as the organization holds and promotes the view that all forms of speech and expression, no matter how inconsistent with the principle of equality and public order, are protected by the First Amendment, so it promotes the view that government is to be wholly neutral with respect to religious beliefs and practices, regardless of their consistency with the principle of human equality.

The reason for this, again, is simple. The ACLU has replaced the idea of equal rights before law as set forth in the Founding with something else, namely, the unfettered expression of the human will. This explains why, for the ACLU, all forms of expression—from obscene speech to nude dancing—are equally protected by the First Amendment. The ACLU frequently cites with approval Supreme Court Justice John M. Harlan's comment from the 1971 decision in *Cohen v. California*, that "one man's vulgarity is another's lyric." If there is no objective standard of moral truth, if morality is merely a relativistic matter of personal preference, then there is no principled ground upon which an objective distinction can be made between beauty and vulgarity, virtue and vice, right and wrong—every vulgarity is at the same time a lyric, and every lyric is a vulgarity. Even the most base moral preferences are equally legitimate because they share the same groundless foundation of all moral preferences: human will unrestrained by reason or any kind of deliberation. All forms of political protest, therefore—from a labor union strike to Nazis marching in Skokie, Illinois—are equally protected. And all forms of religious expression—whether Judaism, Roman Catholic, Protestantism, paganism, atheism or Satanic worship—are equally protected. Since there is no higher truth than the individual will, no religious expression has any greater value than its value as expression. And it should come as no surprise to us that the Supreme Court has begun to treat cases involving religious expression as First Amendment free speech questions rather than what they actually are—questions concerning one's First Amendment right to free exercise of religion.[7]

Since 1940, ACLU efforts respecting the Free Exercise Clause have focused on two points: First, broadening protections for those religious faiths outside what was the Judeo-Christian mainstream, and secondly, extending the idea of free exercise to include atheism. Both aims have been pursued by the ACLU rigorously since 1947, ostensibly for the purpose of achieving a fuller realization of the free exercise of religion. And again, in some instances the organization's efforts have been laudable. Yet due to the ideas that inform their efforts, others have had the effect of undermining the principles of government laid down in 1776. In particular, the ACLU tends to defend religious liberty when the religious exercise in question is one that challenges or rejects the tenets of Judeo-Christian religion and morality. As William Donahue has written:

> It is always fascinating to watch how vigilant the ACLU is about religious liberty when it comes to witches and Satanists. In the 1990s, ACLU affiliates were particularly active in defending Wicca, the religion of witches. The case that drew the most attention was in Virginia. There the ACLU asked a Fairfax County judge to allow a Wiccan priestess to perform a marriage ceremony. The case bounced around quite a bit until the Norfolk Circuit Court issued

a minister's certificate to Wiccan high priestess Rosemary Kooiman. Richard Ferris, who represented the witch, invoked Thomas Jefferson's legacy upon victory, saying that if the ruling had gone the other way, Jefferson's principles and religious liberty would be "in deep trouble in the very state where they were born."[8]

The first substantial ACLU efforts on behalf of religious expression concerned the Jehovah's Witnesses, a sect launched by Charles Taze Russell in 1879, with beliefs significantly at odds with Protestantism and Catholicism. From 1937 to 1955, the Supreme Court heard no fewer than forty-five cases concerning at first the free speech and press rights, and later the religious liberty of Jehovah's Witnesses, with numerous victories for the sect. The ACLU filed amicus briefs in many of these cases, properly arguing that the religious liberty clause protected the Witnesses' right to practice their faith freely.[9]

The ACLU's best remembered work with the Jehovah's Witnesses—and perhaps especially indicative of the organization's politics—concerns the flag salute cases during the 1940s, especially *Minersville School District v. Gobitis* and *West Virginia v. Barnette*.[10] In the former case, the U.S. Supreme Court upheld in an 8-1 decision Pennsylvania's public school flag salute requirement. Justice Frankfurter reasoned that the Court ought not make itself "the school board for the country," and that the state had a clear interest in promoting "national unity" which, wrote Frankfurter, "is the basis of national security." The promotion of national unity among school children was important enough to trump religious freedom, and the required daily salute to the flag would help "promote in the minds of children who attend the common schools an attachment to the institutions of their country."[11]

But the Court's decision, delivered in June 1940, prompted a wave of violent attacks against not only members of the Gobitis family, but of sect members in forty-four states, causing U.S. Solicitor General Francis Biddle to appeal in a nationwide broadcast for calm, and FBI Director J. Edgar Hoover to "outlaw the vigilantes."[12] *West Virginia v. Barnette*, decided only a short time later in 1943, reversed *Gobitis*, upholding the right of the Witnesses and their children to opt out of the Pledge of Allegiance. Here the Court reasoned not on the basis of religious liberty, but freedom of speech, including the right not to be compelled to express belief. "The very purpose of the Bill of Rights," wrote Justice Robert Jackson,

> was to withdraw certain subjects from the vicissitudes of political controversy, to place them beyond the reach of majorities ... One's right to life, liberty, and property, to free speech, a free press, freedom of worship and assembly, and other fundamental rights may not be submitted to vote....If there is any fixed star in our constitutional constellation, it is that no official, high or petty, can prescribe what shall be orthodox in politics, nationalism, religion, or other matters of opinion or force citizens to confess by word or act their faith therein.[13]

The ACLU's participation in this case is rightly regarded as one of its finest moments, ending the wave of violence directed at Jehovah's Witnesses and their children. More importantly, it set a new standard for tolerance for dissenters in America. In so doing, however, *Barnette* resolved an immediate and ugly problem by replacing it with a subtler and more complex one—how is it constitutionally possible to instill in children in a public setting a respect and reverence for their country, without that civic education training becoming subject to charges of unconstitutional coercion?

In *Employment Division of Oregon v. Smith* (1990), the Supreme Court made considerable progress in restoring the original and true intent of the First Amendment's Religion Clauses. The Court ruled that the Free Exercise Clause did not protect two Native American counselors for a drug rehabilitation program who argued that their use of hallucinogenic peyote deserved constitutional protection. The Court was not persuaded of this, rejecting the idea that a guarantee of religious liberty implies license to disobey drug laws. As Justice Antonin Scalia wrote in the decision:

> It is a permissible reading of the [free exercise clause] ... to say that if prohibiting the exercise of religion ... is not the object of the [law] but merely the incidental effect of a generally applicable and otherwise valid provision, the First Amendment has not been

offended....To make an individual's obligation to obey such a law contingent upon the law's coincidence with his religious beliefs, except where the State's interest is "compelling"—permitting him, by virtue of his beliefs, "to become a law unto himself," contradicts both constitutional tradition and common sense.[14]

The ACLU understood the *Smith* decision as a defeat. Interestingly, many conservatives opposed the *Smith* decision as well, concerned that the case represented hostility to religion. Instead of drawing a distinction between religious practices that conform to the laws and principles necessary for the public good and maintenance of public order versus religious practices that do not (such as ingesting peyote and other narcotics), many conservative Republicans joined the ACLU and liberal Democrats in support of the Religious Freedom Restoration Act (RFRA), passed almost unanimously by Congress in 1993 and signed into law by President Bill Clinton. The Act prohibited government from "substantially burdening" an individual's free exercise of religion, even if the burden placed on that individual resulted from a law of "general applicability"—a law that applies to everyone equally. Only if government could demonstrate that its burden was for the sake of a compelling interest, and was the least restrictive means to achieve that interest, could the burden on an individual's free exercise be permitted. The Act was essentially a return to the standards laid down in the *Sherbert v. Verner* and *Wisconsin v. Yoder* decisions, both of which carved free exercise exceptions from otherwise generally applicable laws. RFRA mandated a return to strict scrutiny as the test for all free exercise claims.

But in 1997 the Supreme Court rightly struck down RFRA in *City of Boerne v. Flores*, arguing that Congress had exceeded its constitutional powers under Section 5 of the Fourteenth Amendment, which provides that "The Congress shall have power to enforce, by appropriate legislation, the provisions of this article." Congress had erred in writing the law, wrote Justice Kennedy, in two ways. First, congressional power is "limited to remedial or preventive legislation," in other words, "legislation which deters or remedies constitutional violations." The RFRA went beyond this. Secondly, and of greater importance, the law violated the separation of powers doctrine, with Congress effectively altering the Court's standards for interpreting the Fourteenth Amendment. For the past half-century, the Supreme Court has assumed that the Constitution means whatever the Court says it means.[15] This is clearly wrong. Upon this supposition the Constitution is transformed from the rule of law into the rule of judges. But it is no less wrong for Congress to assert that the Constitution means whatever *it* says the Constitution means. The very purpose of a written constitution is that all branches of government are subordinate to the Constitution and possess only those powers delegated to it by the Constitution.

Later incarnations of the law, the Religious Liberty Protection Act (RLPA) and the Religious Land Use and Institutionalized Persons Act (RLUIPA) of 2000 were passed by Congress, this time relying, not on Section 5 of the Fourteenth Amendment, but on the Commerce Clause and Spending Clause (constitutional provisions liberals have long used to expand the scope of congressional power). RLUIPA provided in part that: "No government shall impose a substantial burden on the religious exercise of a person residing in or confined to an institution" unless the burden advanced "a compelling government interest" and did so by "the least restrictive means." In effect this restated the purpose of the earlier Religious Freedom Restoration Act. But whereas the Supreme Court struck down RFRA in the 1997 *Boerne* case, the Court upheld RLUIPA in a unanimous decision in the 2005 case, *Cutter v. Wilkinson*.[16] The central question raised in *Boerne*, as discussed above, was whether Congress possessed constitutional authority to pass RFRA under Section 5 of the Fourteenth Amendment. The Court rightly concluded that contrary to the claims of Congress, the Fourteenth Amendment did not empower Congress to define the substance of rights or to determine which constitutional standards were applicable to the resolution of free exercise cases. These were matters reserved to the Supreme Court. In *Cutter*, however, the Court focused on whether RLUIPA amounted to an establishment of religion. Justice Ruth Bader Ginsburg, writing for the Court, described RLUIPA as "the latest of long-running congressional efforts to accord religious exercise heightened protection from government-imposed burdens."[17] Since RLUIPA sought to protect free exercise on a neutral basis—not preferring any religion—the Court concluded that the act "fits within the corridor between the Religion Clauses: On its face, the Act qualified as a permissible legislative accommodation of religion that is not barred by the Establishment Clause."[18] This "corridor"—a product of the constitutional demand for neutrality—is occupied by "adherents of 'nonmainstream' religions: the Satanist, Wicca, and Asatru" as well as members of the "Church of Jesus Christ Christian."

When the Supreme Court handed down the *Cutter* decision in May, 2005, some advocates of original intent were hopeful that it represented the death knell of the poorly contrived three-pronged *Lemon* test. Justice Ginsburg's majority opinion rejected the argument of the Court of Appeals for the Sixth Circuit, which had argued that RLUIPA failed the *Lemon* test because it "impermissibly advanced religion by giving greater protection to religious rights than to other constitutionally protected rights."[19] As Justice Thomas wrote in a concurring opinion,

> The Court properly declines to assess RLUIPA under the discredited test of *Lemon* v. *Kurtzman* ... *Lemon* held that, to avoid invalidation under the Establishment Clause, a statute "must have a secular legislative purpose," "its principal or primary effect must be one that neither advances nor inhibits religion," and it "must not foster an excessive government entanglement with religion." Under the first and second prongs, RLUIPA—and, indeed, any accommodation of religion—might well violate the Clause. Even laws *disestablishing* religion might violate the Clause. Disestablishment might easily have a religious purpose and thereby flunk the first prong, or it might well "strengthen and revitalize" religion and so fail the second.[20]

As we saw in the previous chapter, however, the *Lemon* test survived *Cutter*. A month after the *Cutter* decision, in June 2005, the Court employed the *Lemon* test in *McCreary County v. ACLU of Kentucky*, indicating that it is not yet willing to give *Lemon* the burial it properly deserves. That the Court would discard *Lemon* in *Cutter* only to resuscitate it a month later is indicative of the arbitrariness of the Court's Religion Clauses jurisprudence.

The *Cutter* decision, however, was disappointing for more than its failure to kill the old *Lemon* test. The majority opinion did not address the incredibly expansive reading of the Commerce and Spending Clauses that Congress offered as justification for RLUIPA. Only Justice Thomas in his concurring opinion noted that while RLUIPA might be consonant with the Establishment Clause, "it may well exceed Congress' authority under either the Spending Clause or the Commerce Clause."

Since the New Deal, Congress and the Supreme Court have used the Commerce Clause to justify massive expansions of federal regulatory power over states and individuals, power that could never be justified by any common sense reading of the Constitution. Article I, Section 8 of the Constitution authorizes Congress to "regulate Commerce with foreign Nations, and among the several States." Beginning with *Wickard v. Filburn* in 1947, a case turning on the question of whether Congress possessed constitutional power to regulate the amount of wheat a farmer could grow for his own private consumption, the Supreme Court has argued that any activity that affects commerce or the economy, however indirect or remote the influence might be, can be regulated by Congress because it falls within the jurisdiction of "regulat[ing] commerce among the several states."[21] And Congress has been all too willing to oblige. In the case of *Wickard*, the Court argued that while the domestic production and consumption of wheat is neither "commerce" nor "interstate," a farmer who consumes produce grown on his farm is less likely to purchase food at grocery markets, which will have an indirect effect on interstate commerce and the economy, and therefore Congress can regulate the domestic production and consumption of wheat or other produce under the Commerce Clause. By this reading, *any* human activity can be regulated by Congress because *any* human activity can be shown to have some kind of economic effect.

The holding in *Wickard* remained a critical and unchallenged premise for the expanding regulatory powers excised by Congress for the next fifty years, until the 1995 case of *United States v. Lopez*. In *Lopez* and a similar case in 2000, *United States v. Morrison*, the Supreme Court finally argued that the Commerce Clause does not justify any exercise of federal legislative or regulatory power, suggesting that the Interstate Commerce Clause should be limited to "commerce" that is "interstate."[22] Some constitutionalists were hopeful that these cases represented a return to the original and much more limited scope of power granted by the Commerce Clause. But that hope may have been overly optimistic.

In *Gonzales v. Raich,* a 6-3 decision handed down only a week after the Court ruled on RLUIPA in the *Cutter* case, the Supreme Court reinforced the unprincipled *Wickard* interpretation of the Commerce Clause, arguing that Congress can regulate the medicinal use of marijuana, an activity that should be regulated by the police powers of the states under the original Constitution and its distribution of powers between the states and the federal government. In his dissenting opinion in the *Gonzales* case, Justice Thomas pointed out that Congress simply "declared that state policy would disrupt federal law enforcement," but that "Congress presented no evidence in support of its conclusion, which are not so much findings of fact as assertions of power." "Congress," Justice Thomas wrote, "cannot define the scope of its own power [under the Commerce Clause] merely by declaring the necessity of its enactments." He concluded that:

> Respondents Diane Monson and Angel Raich use marijuana that has never been bought or sold, that has never crossed state lines, and that has had no demonstrable effect on the national market for marijuana. If Congress can regulate this under the Commerce Clause, then it can regulate virtually anything—and the Federal Government is no longer one of limited and enumerated powers.[23]

The *Cutter* and *Gonzales* cases are related in that they both reinforce the view that the Commerce Clause offers unprincipled and unlimited power to Congress. Many conservatives applauded RLUIPA and the Court's decision to uphold it in *Cutter* because they saw it as a defense of religion. But at what cost? The Court's opinion in *Cutter* regarding the Establishment Clause is certainly better and closer to a jurisprudence of original intent than the earlier Establishment cases such as *Lemon,* although the Court has yet to fully embrace the original meaning of the First Amendment's Religion Clauses. But *Cutter* is a loss, not a victory, in the larger battle to restore the Constitution to American politics and law. It is probably no coincidence that in its amicus brief in *Cutter*, the ACLU argued in support of the RLUIPA solely on the ground that it does not violate the Establishment Clause, while remaining silent as to whether Congress possesses any power under the Constitution to pass a law such as RLUIPA.[24] By conceding a tactical loss in affording religion slightly greater protection—and we ought not forget that the religions for which protection was sought in the *Cutter* case included Satanism, Wiccaism, and other "nonmainstream" religions—liberal advocates of big, unconstitutional government such as the ACLU actually won a great victory. For our purposes, the important point is that the ACLU joins here with liberal and many conservative organizations in tinkering with constitutional procedures, ostensibly to protect religious freedom, while forgetting or ignoring the larger and more important constitutional principles of limited government and separation of powers. As Edward J. Erler has noted, "a Constitution divorced from these principles—and ultimately [these] are moral principles—will give no guidance" to questions concerning the free exercise of religion.[25]

In a 2001 case that might otherwise have been handled by its Drug Policy Litigation Project, the ACLU found a free exercise argument for a Rastafarian citizen of Guam. Nelson Tebbe of the ACLU insisted that "Rastafarianism is a legitimate religion. Our client … is a devout adherent to this religion, and the use of marijuana as a sacrament is necessary for the practice of this faith….We must be careful to not allow the hysteria caused by the ongoing war on drugs to impinge upon religious freedoms."[26] Here again the ACLU has failed to distinguish between religious faith and the actions that are supported by that faith. The beliefs of Rastafarians, and their right to promote them, are protected by the Free Exercise Clause, but their actions—including the use of illegal or regulated drugs—are subject to the same regulations as everyone else. Religious belief does not make an individual exempt from the otherwise valid laws.

Another one of the ACLU"s proclaimed "Great Victories" was the Supreme Court's ruling in *Church of Lukumi Babalu Aye, Inc. v. Hialeah* (1993). In this case, the Court decided against the city of Hialeah, Florida, and its restrictions against ritual animal sacrifice, as practiced by the followers of Santeria, a syncretic religion originating in the Carribean.[27] The Court reaffirmed the standard it set forth in the earlier *Smith* case, that "[i]n addressing the constitutional protection for free exercise of religion, our cases establish the general proposition that a law that is neutral and of general applicability need not be justified by a compelling governmental interest even if the law has the incidental effect of burdening a particular religious practice."[28] Justice Kennedy argued in his majority opinion that both the text of city ordinances and the legislative history preceding the adoption of the ordinances evidenced a desire to limit the exercise of certain Santeria religious rituals involving animal sacrifice. Indeed, the Hialeah city council, prior to passing the ordinance prohibiting religious animal sacrifices, adopted a resolution declaring that "the City reiterates its commitment to a prohibition against any and all acts *of any and all religious groups* which are inconsistent with public morals, peace or safety."[29] In this respect the ordinance was not a law of general applicability and was passed with the express purpose of suppressing the free exercise right of one particular religion. The Court therefore declared the ordinance unconstitutional based on *Smith* standards. The Court quoted the city ordinance to the effect that:

> It prohibits the sacrifice of animals, but defines sacrifice as "to unnecessarily kill ... an animal in a public or private ritual or ceremony not for the primary purpose of food consumption." The definition excludes almost all killings of animals except for religious sacrifice, and the primary purpose requirement narrows the proscribed category even further, in particular by exempting kosher slaughter ... We need not discuss whether this differential treatment of two religions is itself an independent constitutional violation....It suffices to recite this feature of the law as support for our conclusion that Santeria alone was the exclusive legislative concern.[30]

Two observations about the ACLU's involvement in this case deserve mention. On the one hand, the ACLU was right to point to the *Smith* standard, arguing in its amicus brief that "[l]aws that burden religious exercise must be neutral and generally applicable." It was not contended that the surreptitious disposal of animal carcasses, sometimes in public places, as practiced by Santeria members is not a public health concern. But as the ACLU pointed out, if the Hialeah city council was primarily interested in the safe disposal of animal carcasses, it should have written a law prohibiting animal disposal practices that are harmful to public health. Such a law would be applicable to restaurants, grocery stores, and even private individuals who consume meat at home, no less than members of a religious sect. Thus the ACLU concluded its amicus brief by noting:

> The City cannot distinguish animal sacrifice from other killings of animals or other disposal of meat scraps. It forbids animal sacrifice not because it values animal rights over human rights, but because it places no value on petitioners' free exercise of religion. These ordinances are not neutral and generally applicable ... They violate the Free Exercise Clause as interpreted in *Smith*.[31]

On the other hand, it should not pass without notice that the Hialeah case is typical of the ACLU's select defense of the right of religious free exercise. While rarely defending that right when exercised by members of mainstream Christian religions, the ACLU employs considerable time, energy, and strategy whenever they can defend the free exercise of non-Judeo-Christian religions or quasi-Judeo-Christian religions such as Santeri that feature the ritualistic sacrifice and slaughter of animals, something most Americans today find barbaric.

The ACLU also filed an amicus brief in *Lamb's Chapel v. Center Moriches Union Free School District*.[32] Lamb's Chapel, a private New York Christian organization, sued a school district because of its restrictions that disallowed the use of public school facilities to exhibit for public viewing, outside of school hours, a six-part film series dealing with family and child-rearing issues and advocating Christian morality. The Supreme Court ruled against the school district, explaining in a 9-0 decision that Lamb's Chapel had a right to use school facilities for showing their film before a public audience. But interestingly, the Court decided the case on the basis of free speech, rather than free exercise of religion, and religious groups for the past decade have turned to the free speech argument, virtually ignoring the Free Exercise Clause as a losing proposition. As the Court argued, "the principle that has emerged from our cases 'is that the First Amendment forbids the government to regulate speech in ways that favor some viewpoints or ideas at the expense of others.'"[33] The Court concluded "that the interest of the State in avoiding an Establishment Clause violation 'may be [a] compelling' one justifying an abridgment of free speech otherwise protected by the First Amendment; but ... that permitting use of university property for religious purposes under the open access policy involved there would not be incompatible with the Court's Establishment Clause cases."[34] Commenting on this trend, V. Philip Munoz writes that *Lamb's Chapel* and the cases that followed appeared to be victories for religious freedom, but from a constitutional perspective, their impact on free exercise has been devastating: "[R]eligious free exercise has lost its independent value. The Court has transformed religion into a subspecies of speech."[35]

By transforming free exercise into free speech, contemporary jurisprudence has in effect set the provisions of the First Amendment at odds against one another. The 1995 case of *Rosenberger v. University of Virginia* is typical in its framing of the question as free exercise and free speech on the one hand versus establishment of religion on the other. At issue in *Rosenberger* was whether the University could fund a student group, Wide Awake Productions, and the publishing of its student newspaper, *Wide Awake*. The purpose of the publication was "to challenge Christians to live, in word and deed, according to the faith they proclaim and to encourage students to consider what a personal relationship with Jesus Christ means." As the ACLU stated succinctly in its amicus brief offered in defense of the University's decision not to provide funding, "[t]his case presents a conflict between free speech and Establishment Clause principles."[36] Writing for the majority, Justice Kennedy rejected the argument of the ACLU, that funding a student newspaper which presents a Christian view is tantamount to an unconstitutional establishment of religion. Instead, argued Kennedy, the decision to withhold funding "was a denial of the right of free speech and would risk fostering a pervasive bias or hostility to religion, which could undermine the very neutrality the Establishment Clause requires. There is no Establishment Clause violation in the University's honoring its duties under the Free Speech Clause."[37]

The *Rosenberger* case reveals the strange conclusions drawn from the Court's changing interpretations of the Constitution. First, the authors of the First Amendment never intended the Establishment Clause to be in conflict with the Free Exercise Clause or the Free Speech Clause. Only by expanding "establishment" beyond its original meaning to include any government support for or mention of religion and morality is such a conflict possible. And, indeed, if the Court holds to its current view of the Establishment Clause we should expect to see many more challenges on Free Speech grounds, because nothing less than government restriction of speech will be necessary to comply with the Court's new liberal and contrived definition of what constitutes an "establishment of religion." Second, *Rosenberger* and other cases show the complete acceptance of the progressive view that rights or entitlements come from government. From the point of view of the original intent of the Constitution, any university, public or private, can choose to not fund any activities it wishes. By withholding funds from a student newspaper, no one's right to the free exercise of religion is trammeled; students would still be free to hold any religious beliefs they want and raise money from other sources and publish those views. In words used by the Founders, students are neither "harmed" nor "molested" on account of their religious opinions simply because a university chooses not to fund their organization. Only if we believe that rights are entitlements that should be given to us by an administrative-welfare state can one argue that withholding funding for a student group is a violation of the right to free speech or any other right.

Nonetheless, it is interesting that the ACLU, while leaping to the defense of non-Judeo-Christian religious practices, and while claiming to be a stalwart defender of free speech regardless of content, refuses to defend the free speech of students when their speech is used to advocate Christianity. The contradiction is caused mostly by its own liberal reinterpretation of the Constitution: claiming unqualified protection for all speech while claiming all government involvement with religion and morality to be an unconstitutional establishment. But when these two liberal principles come into conflict and when the speech in question is Christian speech, the ACLU comes down squarely on the side of no-establishment. It is fair to ask what position the ACLU might have taken if the student publication in the *Rosenberger* case was one that advocated voodooism, witchcraft or atheism.

Significantly, the ACLU has had little to say on this question, remaining in the background on these cases and the organization is apparently unconcerned about the need to defend religious liberties of Christians, even when the argument is posed on free speech grounds.[38] As William Donahue has cogently argued, on some rare occasions the ACLU and its state affiliates have risen to the defense of traditional Christianity or Judaism. For example:

> In a 1989 policy statement, the ACLU agreed that freedom of religion protected privileged communications with the clergy. And in a case that had real repercussions, the Connecticut Civil Liberties Union in 1986 defended the right of William P. Nichols, a painting contractor, to hold prayer meetings in his home in Stratford, Connecticut. Stratford's anti-religious zoning ordinance required a permit for any religious purpose, even if the activity took place in the privacy of one's own home. (Tupperware parties, the ACLU pointed out in court, required no such permits.)

But these few examples, Donahue observes, "though frequently cited by the ACLU as demonstrative of its balanced approach to the subject, represent the exception, not the rule, to its basic position."[39] And, we might note, in the cases where the ACLU defends the right of free exercise for members of the Christian or Jewish faiths, these efforts form part of an overall design to make religion radically private, remaining consistent to its desire to drive the influence of Christianity and Judaism out of the public square.

But the ACLU is apparently willing to make exceptions for public profession of religion—if that religion serves to promote liberal political correctness. In 2002, the ACLU reversed its usual opposition to religious instruction in public education settings, coming to the defense of the University of North Carolina when it distributed selections from the Koran as required reading for incoming freshmen. The irony was not lost on the *Wall Street Journal*, which carried an editorial essay with the subtitle: "The ACLU finally finds a religion it can tolerate. Surprise—it's Islam." The University of North Carolina sent students excerpts from the Koran as well as a CD offering recitals in Arabic, including chants that call faithful Muslims to prayer. According to University Chancellor James Moeser, the purpose of the exercise was "to seek understanding and bring home to students the reasons Islam has a billion followers across the globe." Most surprising, noted the *Wall Street Journal's* editorial board, was "the acquiescent response of those civil liberties watchdogs usually ever alert to the danger that somebody, somewhere, might be sneaking a prayer into some school program or graduation ceremony. The American Civil Liberties Union, normally busy saving the nation's schools from the smallest whiff of religious influence, has leapt to university's defense. Finally, it seems, the ACLU has found a religion it can tolerate."[40]

True to its own foundations, the ACLU has become in our time a stalwart defender of the free exercise of religion, but in the main for progressive-liberal causes, quick to defend drug use or other religious practices skirting the edge of the law. It is strangely silent, however, when the civil rights and liberties of Christian and Jewish organizations are in question. Thus it is no surprise that the organization is popularly understood as a supporter of liberal causes. What the ACLU supports ultimately is modern liberalism, and like its extensive work with the Establishment Clause, its efforts utilizing the Free Exercise Clause serve that same ultimate purpose—to replace constitutional government and traditional morality with a progressive state and progressive morality.

Endnotes

1. Richard J. Neuhaus, "Constitution Protects Religion and Free Practice Thereof," *Sunday Republican* (Waterbury, Conn.), July 5, 1987.

2. Vincent Phillip Muñoz, "Establishing Free Exercise," *First Things*, December 2003, 15.

3. For a succinct analysis of Islam and its political implications, see Paul Marshall, Roberta Green, and Lela Gilbert, *Islam at the Crossroads: Understanding Its Beliefs, History, and Conflicts* (Grand Rapids, Mi.: Baker Books, 2002).

4. Michael Novak, "The Ten Commandments Controversy," lecture delivered Oct. 11, 2003 as reprinted in Hillsdale College, *Imprimis* 32, no. 12 (December 2003), 6.

5. As cited in Thomas G. West, "Religious Liberty: The View from the Founding," in Daniel C. Palm, ed., *On Faith and Free Government* (Lanham, Md.: Rowman and Littlefield, 1997), 15. See also Justice Scalia's concurring opinion in *City of Boerne v. Flores*, 117 S.Ct. 2157, 138 L.Ed.2d 624 (1997).

6. Reynolds v. United States 98 U.S. 145, 166 (1878).

7. Munoz, 16.

8. William A. Donahue, *Twilight of Liberty: The Legacy of the ACLU* (New Brunswick: Transaction Publishers, 2001), 340.

9. Samuel Walker, *In Defense Of American Liberties: A History of the ACLU* (Carbondale, Illinois: Southern Illinois University Press, 1990), 107.

10. Minersville School District v. Gobitis 310 U.S. 586 (1940) and West Virginia State Board of Education v. Barnette, 319 U.S. 624 (1943).

11. 310 U.S. 586, 599 (1940).

12. Walker, 109.

13. 319 U.S. 624, 642 (1943).

14. 494 U.S. 872, 890 (1990).

15. See *Cooper v. Aaron*, in which the Supreme Court asserted "that the federal judiciary is supreme in the exposition of the law of the Constitution, and that principle has ever since been respected by this Court and the Country as a permanent and indispensable feature of our constitutional system. It follows that the interpretation of the Fourteenth Amendment [and by extension the entire Constitution] enunciated by this Court ... is the supreme law of the land," 358 U.S. 1, 19 (1958).

16. 544 U.S. ___ (2005).

17. Ibid.

18. Ibid.

19. Ibid.

20. Ibid.

21. Wickard v. Filburn, 317 U.S. 111 (1942).

22. United States v. Lopez, 514 U.S. 549 (1995); United States v. Morrison, 529 U.S. 598 (2000). In *Lopez*, the Supreme Court struck down the Gun Free School Zones Act and in *Morrison* the Court struck down parts of the Violence Against Women Act, arguing in part in both cases that Congress lacked authority under the Commerce Clause to pass the respective statutes.

23. 545 U.S. ___ (2005).

24. Americans United for Separation of Church and State and ACLU amicus brief in *Cutter v. Wilkinson*, 544 U.S. ___ (2005).

25. Edward J. Erler, "Religious Freedom After Boerne: Has the Supreme Court Usurped Democracy?" American Political Science Association Annual Conference, Sept. 3-6, 1998.

26. "ACLU Asks U.S. Appeals Court to Defer to Guam High Court on Rastafarian's Right to Use Marijuana for Religious Purposes," ACLU Press Release, Nov. 2, 2001. Available online at: http://www.aclu.org/DrugPolicy/DrugPolicy.cfm?ID + 10236& = 228.

27. "The ACLU and the Supreme Court: 77 Years, 77 Great Victories," available online at: http://archive.aclu.org/library/75hits.html.

28. 508 U.S. 520, 531 (1993).

29. Ibid., 526, emphasis added.

30. Ibid., 535-536.

31. ACLU amicus brief in *Church of Lukumi Babalu Aye, Inc. v. Hialeah,* 20.

32. 508 U.S. 384

33. Ibid., 394, quoting *City Council of Los Angeles v. Taxpayers for Vincent,* 466 U.S. 789, 804 (1984).

34. Ibid., 395.

35. Munoz, "Establishing Free Exercise," 17.

36. ACLU amicus brief in *Rosenberger v. University of Virginia,* 515 U.S. 819.

37. 515 U.S. 819, 845-46.

38. Donahue, *Twilight of Liberty,* 120.

39. Ibid., 98.

40. Wall Street Journal "Mandating the Koran," August 13, 2002 available at http://opinionjounal.com/editorial/feature.html.

CONCLUSION

If we could first know where *we are, and* whither *we are tending,
we could better judge* what *to do, and* how *to do it.*
—Abraham Lincoln, 1858

Let us review what we have learned about the ACLU and its consistent efforts to restrict religious expression in America. We believe that we can with confidence say the following: First, although the ACLU seems to many people to be loyal to the principles of the American Founding, its progressive origins and its close association with modern liberalism belie this first impression. It is not an organization loyal to the founding principles of the nation, but takes its bearings from the progressive rejection of those principles in its attempt to re-create the nation.

Second, in aiming to reinvent America by selective interpretations of the Bill of Rights, the ACLU should be understood as not merely a liberal organization but a radical one, in the same sense that its early contemporary allies were radicals—pacifists, anarchists, socialists, and communists. Because of its radical objectives, the ACLU must reject the moderation of the American Founding as outdated, a relic of a past that is dead and gone

115

and cannot be revived even if it were desirable to do so.

The ACLU is right to oppose establishment of religion, but gravely mistaken in identifying virtually every public expression of religion as an establishment. It is likewise mistaken in holding—as most liberals do— that morality and religion have no place in American public discourse. During the Revolution and the early years of the Republic on through the Civil War and Reconstruction, America's greatest statesmen and political thinkers recognized the importance of religion in public affairs. And they understood that this could be accomplished without offense to the First Amendment's Establishment Clause. It is only with the intrusion of progressivism and modern liberalism that the foundations are laid for a new and expanded skepticism about religion. Mainstream Judeo-Christian religions and the morality that flows from them are anathema to the administrative state and its goal of reducing citizens to subservience. The spiritedness and fierce sense of independence inculcated by religion— especially the religion witnessed during the American Founding—stands over and against the principal purposes of the administrative state.

It suits the ACLU's efforts in our time to portray the United States as a nation divided between Bible-thumping fundamentalists intent on creating a Christian America and a progressive ACLU boldly holding the line for the sake of secular Americans and the Bill of Rights. In truth the lines are not so clearly drawn. Common sense, however, tells us that there are very few Christians in America who would want to impose their beliefs on others, if such a thing was even possible. Most Christians, like persons of other faiths, recognize that a regime characterized by an established religion is seldom an appealing atmosphere in which to live. Moreover, for those who wish to further the cause of "true" religious faith in the world, an established religion will do little to achieve their purpose. The European nations with established faiths do not rank high in terms of religious character, regular church attendance, or other measures of faith.

As Jefferson wrote in his Virginia Statute for Religious Liberty, "all attempts to influence [religious belief] by temporal punishments, or burthen, or by civil incapacitations"—all established religions, in other words—"tend only to beget habits of hypocrisy and meanness, and are a departure from the plan of the holy author of our religion." Jefferson, of course, is famous for asking, "can the liberties of a nation be thought secure when we have removed their only firm basis, a conviction in the minds of the people that these liberties are of the gift of God? That they are not to be violated but with his wrath?"[1] But as Edward J. Erler has pointed out:

> Here the atheist could not properly be a citizen, although presumably the adherents of "false religion" could be as long as they believed that natural rights, including the right to freedom of conscience, had a divine source. But Jefferson is also famous for his statement that "the legitimate powers of government extend to such acts only as are injurious to others. But it does no injury for my neighbor to say there are twenty gods, or no god." Here the atheist is to be tolerated along with the polytheist, even though both adhere to views that are not only false but harmful to republican government. From the point of view of the theology of the Declaration of Independence, atheism and polytheism are wholly irrational. Atheism would ultimately mean that all law is positive, having no transcendent source or ground; and as every reader of Plato's *Euthyphro* knows, polytheism leads to the untenable solution of fighting gods....Here rational monotheism and revealed monotheism are in complete agreement in rejecting both atheism and polytheism. Yet Jefferson's hatred of sectarian tyranny was so thoroughgoing that he believed that the only solution to atheism and polytheism in a republic is for the man of reason to persuade the atheist and the polytheist of the irrationality of their beliefs. As Jefferson concluded, "Reason and free inquiry are the only effectual agents against error. Give a loose to them, they will support the *true religion*."[2]

It is worth repeating Erler's true argument that "rational monotheism and revealed monotheism are in complete agreement in rejecting both atheism and polytheism" because the former results in legal positivism, while the latter necessarily leads to multiple and contradictory divine sources of law. In both instances, the will of the human lawmaker or the will of the human interpreter of the law becomes the source of legal and moral right. In a democratic or republican form of government, that source is ultimately the majority of the people; it is to say that right is whatever the majority says is right, that might makes right. Stripped of its legalisms and sophistry, this is nothing but radical moral relativism. It is nihilism. Politically, nothing can be more dangerous because it categorically denies the moral framework of natural law and natural rights which provide the only defense and sound basis for free society and constitutional govern-ment.[3]

But according to the modern Supreme Court and the ACLU, the rela-tivism and nihilism inherent in atheism and polytheism are protected by the First Amendment's Religion Clauses. In his majority opinion in the *McCreary* case, discussed in chapter six, Justice Souter argued that be-cause the Establishment Clause requires government to remain neutral among competing religions and between religion and irreligion, govern-ment therefore may not distinguish between monotheistic and polytheistic religions. In his dissenting opinion in *McCreary*, Justice Scalia argued that while many of the Founders' proclamations and endorsements of religion were non-sectarian, they were emphatically monotheistic. "Historical prac-tices thus demonstrate," Scalia concluded, "that there is a distance between the acknowledgement of a single Creator and the establishment of a reli-gion.[4] Justice Souter's response was one of almost disbelief, asserting "[t]his is truly a remarkable view." Souter rejects the original intent of the Estab-lishment Clause on two grounds: first, original intent is difficult if not impossible to ascertain because there were conflicting views among some of the Founders; and second, he argued that the original intent of the Establishment Clause, to the degree it can be discerned, sought to "ex-clude only rivalry among Christian sects," that it was only Christian monotheism that the Founders wanted to protect. According to Souter's originalist interpretation, Islam, Judaism, and other monotheistic religions were excluded, and therefore the narrow original intent of the Establish-ment Clause is inadequate for the religious pluralism and diversity that America now exhibits.

The principles of the Founding are so foreign to Souter, however, that he cannot imagine that "government should be free to approve the core beliefs of a favored religion over the tenets of others, a view that should trouble anyone who prizes religious liberty."[5] In other words, Justice Souter cannot imagine any principled reason why the moral conditions of free society should be preferred over moral relativism and nihilism. In the words of Jefferson, "reason and free inquiry," however, which are in the service of and the source of "true religion," are possible only in a regime where the rights of free speech and the free exercise of religion are protected. In other words, the rights of all citizens, including those claiming to be atheists or polytheists, are best protected, and the truth is best served, in a regime founded upon the idea that all men are created equal and possess equal natural rights, an idea that flows from the monotheistic premise of one God for all men and one transcendent authority for all law. And as Madison remarked in his *Memorial and Remonstrance*, where religious liberty has not been protected, "experience [has] witnessed that ecclesiastical establishments, instead of maintaining the purity and efficacy of Religion, have had a contrary operation....What have been its fruits? More or less in all places, pride and indolence in the Clergy; ignorance and servility in the laity; in both, superstition, bigotry and persecution."[6]

What does this mean for us today in thinking clearly about questions of religion and morality in America? It means that Americans should not hesitate to use in the public square the language of religious faith to the extent that the Founders did in their public papers and speeches. It means that while specifics of Christian doctrine cannot be demanded by government as a condition of citizenship or as a prerequisite to the exercise of civil and political rights, encouragement for religion over irreligion can be promoted and encouraged by government action. It means that solemn and respectful reference to a Creator, a Supreme Being, or God, cannot constitute a violation of the Establishment Clause because that same language is part of the Declaration of Independence, a document enshrined in our nation's organic law. And it means that public expressions of faith, like a cross in the Mojave Desert or a Biblical quotation in admiration of God's works at the Grand Canyon or a cross on the Los Angeles County seal, should be gratefully received and supported rather than discouraged by government.

Ironically, the progress Americans can make now respecting religion and politics is to return—yes, to go back!—to the Founders' moderate understanding. Calvin Coolidge noted in his July 5, 1926 speech at Philadelphia:

> It is often asserted that the world has made a great deal of progress since 1776, that we have had new thoughts and new experiences which have given us a great advance over the people of that day, and that we may therefore very well discard their conclusions for something more modern. But that reasoning can not be applied to the great charter. If all men are created equal, that is final. If they are endowed with inalienable rights, that is final....No advance, no progress can be made beyond these propositions.[7]

Writing only a few years after the ACLU's birth, Coolidge argued in this speech that whatever schemes to improve the American regime might be devised, if they departed from the natural law doctrine of equality of rights as understood in 1776, they would be returning to some form of inequality. By the same token, there is no room for progress from the Founders' understanding of religion's relation to political life in the American republic. The work of the ACLU has brought us "progress," or rather change, away from the principles of the Founding. It may be new, but the series of court cases pursued by the ACLU that have removed simple mention of God from public life are not an advance over the Founding; they represent steps backward, back to the days when citizens knew not of the divine origins of their rights or the limitations on government power implied by those rights.

And what of the future? In his famous "House Divided" speech on June 16, 1858, Lincoln argued that the agitation over slavery,

> will not cease, until a crisis shall have been reached and passed. "A house divided against itself cannot stand." I believe this government cannot endure permanently half slave and half free. I do not expect the Union to be dissolved—I do not expect the house to fall—but I do expect it will cease to be divided. It will become all

one thing, or all the other. Either the opponents of slavery will arrest the further spread of it, and place it where the public mind shall rest in the belief that it is in the course of ultimate extinction, or its advocates will push it forward, till it shall become alike lawful in all the States, old as well as new—North as well as South.[8]

Americans are not warring today over the question of slavery, thankfully, but we do find ourselves in the midst of a great national struggle over the meaning of liberty, rights, and the purpose of government. That struggle is nowhere more focused that in the dispute over religion in the public square—a dispute which clarifies and publicizes the controversy of competing doctrines. We can be certain that the future holds one of two things: either the nation will continue to follow the ACLU's path, or it will re-adopt the moral principles of the American Founding and offer constitutional protection to the public expression of religious beliefs and sentiments. The alternatives could not be more striking.

If the people of the United States and the policies they adopt continue to follow the ACLU's lead, Americans will find themselves further and further removed from the principles of the Founding. And it is not hyperbole to suggest that, at some point, if we continue on this path, the nation will eventually require a new constitution to reflect more accurately the principles of progressivism, and officially abandon the Founding belief in certain "self-evident truths" bound up in the "laws of nature and of nature's God." These are but the logical extension of points along the road upon which the ACLU currently marches.

As a practical matter, the ACLU has declared in its handbook series that the First Amendment does not preclude teaching about religion's importance as an influence in history, or the limited singing of Christmas carols along with other Christmas music during the holidays. But the result of the ACLU's ceaseless litigation is clear to any parent of elementary-age children: public school teachers and principals petrified of lawsuits simply refuse any acknowledgement of religion at all, as thoroughly secularized Christmas music programs and public ceremonies increasingly become the norm.

Alternatively, a critical mass of Americans will recognize the implications of modern liberalism, and its implications for religious expression in the public square. If this comes to pass, it means that a significant number of Americans will have rejected the idea of a new-world progressive utopia and they will return instead to the moderate and reasonable principles of the American Founding and the idea of freedom understood not as license, but as freedom within the confines of rational and revealed morality. They will have become able to accept scientific and technological progress that betters their individual lives while rejecting the misguided ideals of moral and political progressive evolution that can only lead to violations of their individual freedom, liberty and natural rights. They will have become able to recognize the ACLU's attempt to define as an establishment of religion any mention of God in the public square as a radical and preposterous notion.

At present the ACLU's project to secularize the nation may appear well advanced, even nearly complete. The misguided attraction many Americans on both sides of the political spectrum have to the organization and its progressive ideals remains strong. ACLU membership has grown significantly in the wake left by September 11, 2001. "Progress" remains still the watchword even among the people's representatives on Capitol Hill, and the modern liberalism of the welfare state—coupled with the public's routine acceptance of governmental intrusion into private lives—remains a dominant factor in America today.

On the other hand, it's not impossible that we may be turning the corner. A number of states have introduced legislation to create Religious Freedom Restoration Acts, with such bills having become state law in thirteen states since 1997.[9] At the popular level, Americans are displaying increasing skepticism and impatience for the ACLU's activities respecting religion, which appear either petty, or leading in a direction that will end with the Declaration of Independence itself being declared unconstitutional. The bronze plaques removed on July 14, 2003 from the South Rim of the Grand Canyon were ordered replaced ten days later by the Park Service Deputy Director Donald Murphy, and the Evangelical Sisterhood of Mary received a letter of apology. Attempts to have a creationist book removed from the Grand Canyon bookstore on First Amendment Establishment Clause grounds have so far failed, with several non-creationist authors rallying to its defense.[10] Nationally, it's no exaggeration to say that the Ninth Circuit Court of Appeals striking down the Pledge of Allegiance provoked a national outrage, indicating that many Americans are beginning to have grave doubts about an American public square devoid of religious expression. It may well take a future court decision declaring that the Declaration of Independence, with its references to God, may no longer be taught in public schools as a set of ideas about humanity, God, and the legitimate purpose of government, but only as an erroneous artifact from the distant past. Or perhaps it will be a future case requiring an end to the practice of hiring chaplains for military forces; or a demand that the fifty state constitutions with references to God be rewritten to expunge the offending language; or that "In God We Trust" be removed from coins; or that the Supreme Court be barred from opening its sessions with a prayer; or that Congress be prohibited from hiring chaplains and opening its sessions with a prayer. Whatever the case may be that triggers decisive public action, the cards are on the table, and the ACLU, which has labored long to earn a reputation as one of the nation's most "liberal" organizations, is increasingly regarded by more and more Americans as decidedly illiberal.

Within the academic world, there remains a viable alternative to the "strict separation" doctrine of the ACLU and the modern Supreme Court: James Madison's *Memorial and Remonstrance*, which outlined a doctrine that has been described as "non-preferentialism." According to that view, government recognizes the civic importance to religion in a republic, but stays aloof from religious matters. First Amendment scholar V. Philip Muñoz has written that:

> Although James Madison has been invoked by justices and judicial scholars for over 100 years, Madison's principle of religious liberty has never been fully recognized or adopted by the Supreme Court. Judges and scholars have failed to understand Madison's radical but simple teaching: Religion is not part of the social compact, and therefore, the state may not take religion within its

cognizance. A Madisonian interpretation of the Establishment Clause would prevent the state from supporting religion as an end in itself, but it also would prevent the state from excluding religious individuals and organizations from generally available benefits supporting a secular purpose. A Madisonian interpretation of the Free Exercise Clause would prevent the state from prohibiting religious individuals and organizations special exemptions from generally applicable laws that indirectly burden religious exercise.[11]

The United States has prospered in large measure because the American Founders offered an essentially moderate solution to the question of religion's place in the regime. The Founders wisely offered neither establishment of religion, on the one hand, nor a total absence of public religious expression on the other. They designed a regime that offered political stability, freedom and opportunity unequaled in human history. It allowed religious expression without the dangers inherent in established faith. The time may well be at hand for a return to the Founders' moderate understanding of religion's legitimate place in the public square.

Endnotes

1. *Notes on the State of Virginia*, Query 18.
2. Edward J. Erler, "The First Amendment and the Theology of Republican Government," *Interpretation: A Journal of Political Philosophy* 27, no. 3 (Spring 2000), 248-249.
3. Conservatives often make the mistake of assuming that the positivism, relativism, and nihilism we are describing are attributes of the political Left only. The same doctrines infect the scholarship of some of the most prominent conservative jurists and political thinkers. No one has examined this problem more thoroughly than Professor Harry Jaffa. See e.g. Jaffa's *Original Intent and the Framers of the Constitution: A Disputed Question* (Regnery Gateway, 1994) and *Storm Over the Constitution* (Lexington Books, 1999).
4. 545 U.S. ___ (2005).
5. Ibid.
6. See the appendix for the complete text of James Madison's *A Memorial and Remonstrance*, 193-200.

7. Calvin Coolidge, *Foundations of the Republic* (New York: Scribner's, 1926), 450-51.

8. Abraham Lincoln, *The Collected Works of Abraham Lincoln*, Roy P. Basler, ed. (New Brunswick: Rutgers University Press, 1953), 461.

9. Rhode Island, Connecticut, Florida, Illinois, Arizona, South Carolina, Texas, Idaho, New Mexico, Missouri, Pennsylvania and Oklahoma have passed their own state Religious Freedom Acts. Alabama made religious freedom even more secure by specifically amending their state constitution to recognize religious freedom as a fundamental right protected by the compelling interest test. See Christopher J. Kicka, Esq., "Religious Freedom Is Endangered but States are Fighting Back," viewed online May 12, 2005, at: http://www.hslda.org/docs/nche/000000/00000029.asp.

10. *Los Angeles Times*, "Religion, Geology Collide at the Grand Canyon," January 7, 2003, A13.

11. V. Philip Muñoz, "James Madison's Principle of Religious Liberty," *American Political Science Review* 97, no. 1 (Feb. 2003), 31.

APPENDIX:
DOCUMENTS FROM THE
FOUNDING ON RELIGION AND
RELIGIOUS LIBERTY

DECLARATION OF INDEPENDENCE IN CONGRESS, JULY 4, 1776

THE UNANIMOUS DECLARATION OF THE THIRTEEN UNITED STATES OF AMERICA

WHEN in the Course of Human Events, it becomes necessary for one People to dissolve the Political Bands which have connected them with another, and to assume, among the Powers of the Earth, the separate and equal Station to which the Laws of Nature and of Nature's God entitle them, a decent Respect to the Opinions of Mankind requires that they should declare the Causes which impel them to the Separation.

We hold these Truths to be self-evident, that all Men are created equal, that they are endowed by their Creator with certain unalienable Rights, that among these are Life, Liberty, and the Pursuit of Happiness—That to secure these Rights, Governments are instituted among Men, deriving their just Powers from the Consent of the Governed, that whenever any Form of Government becomes destructive of these Ends, it is the Right of the People to alter or to abolish it, and to institute new Government, laying its Foundation on such Principles, and organizing its Powers in such Form, as to them shall seem most likely to effect their Safety and Happiness. Prudence, indeed, will dictate that Governments long established should not be changed for light and transient Causes; and accordingly all Experience hath shewn, that Mankind are more disposed to suffer, while Evils are sufferable, than to right themselves by abolishing the Forms to which they are accustomed. But when a long Train of abuses and Usurpations, pursuing invariably the same Object, evinces a Design to reduce them under absolute Despotism, it is their Right, it is their Duty, to throw off such Government, and to provide new Guards for their future Security. Such has been the patient Sufferance of these Colonies; and such is now the Necessity which constrains them to alter their former Systems of Government. The History of the present King of Great-Britain is a History of repeated Injuries and Usurpations, all having in direct Object the Establishment of an absolute Tyranny over these States. To prove this, let Facts be submitted to a candid World.

HE has refused his Assent to Laws, the most wholesome and necessary for the public Good.

HE has forbidden his Governors to pass Laws of immediate and pressing Importance, unless suspended in their Operation till his Assent should be obtained; and when so suspended, he has utterly neglected to attend to them.

HE has refused to pass other Laws for the accommodation of large Districts of People, unless those People would relinquish the Right of Representation in the Legislature, a Right inestimable to them, and formidable to Tyranny only.

HE has called together Legislative Bodies at Places unusual, uncomfortable, and distant from the Depository of their Public Records, for the sole Purpose of fatiguing them into Compliance with his Measures.

HE has dissolved Representative Houses repeatedly, for opposing with manly Firmness his Invasions on the Rights of the People.

HE has refused for a long Time, after such dissolutions, to cause others to be elected; whereby the Legislative Powers, incapable of Annihilation, have returned to the People at large for their exercise; the State remaining, in the mean time, exposed to all the Dangers of Invasion from without, and Convulsions within.

HE has endeavored to prevent the Population of these States; for that

Purpose obstructing the Laws for Naturalization of Foreigners; refusing to pass others to encourage their Migrations hither, and raising the Conditions of new Appropriations of Lands.

HE has obstructed the Administration of Justice, by refusing his Assent to Laws for establishing Judiciary Powers.

HE has made Judges dependent on his Will alone, for the Tenure of their Offices, and the Amount and Payment of their Salaries.

HE has erected a Multitude of New Offices, and sent hither Swarms of Officers to harass our People, and eat out their Substance.

HE has kept among us, in Times of Peace, Standing Armies, without the Consent of our Legislatures.

HE has affected to render the Military independent of and superior to the Civil Power.

HE has combined with others to subject us to a Jurisdiction foreign to our Constitution, and unacknowledged by our Laws; giving his Assent to their acts of Pretended Legislation:

FOR quartering large Bodies of Armed Troops among us:

FOR protecting them, by a mock Trial, from Punishment for any Murders which they should commit on the Inhabitants of these States:

FOR cutting off our Trade with all Parts of the World:

FOR imposing Taxes on us without our Consent:

FOR depriving us, in many Cases, of the Benefits of Trial by Jury:

FOR transporting us beyond Seas to be tried for pretended Offences:

FOR abolishing the free System of English Laws in a neighboring Province, establishing therein an arbitrary Government, and enlarging its Boundaries so as to render it at once an example and fit Instrument for introducing the same absolute rule into these Colonies:

FOR taking away our Charters, abolishing our most valuable Laws, and altering fundamentally the Forms of our Governments:

FOR suspending our own Legislatures, and declaring themselves invested with Power to legislate for us in all Cases whatsoever.

HE has abdicated Government here, by declaring us out of his Protection, and waging War against us.

HE has plundered our Seas, ravaged our Coasts, burnt our Towns, and destroyed the Lives of our People.

HE is, at this Time, transporting large Armies of foreign Mercenaries to complete the Works of Death, Desolation and Tyranny, already begun with Circumstances of Cruelty and Perfidy scarcely paralleled in the most barbarous Ages, and totally unworthy the Head of a civilized Nation.

HE has constrained our Fellow Citizens taken Captive on the high Seas, to bear Arms against their Country, to become the Executioners of their Friends and Brethren, or to fall themselves by their Hands.

HE has excited domestic Insurrections amongst us, and has endeavored to bring on the Inhabitants of our Frontiers, the merciless Indian Savages, whose known Rule of Warfare, is an undistinguished Destruction of all Ages, Sexes and Conditions.

IN every stage of these Oppressions we have Petitioned for Redress in the most humble Terms: Our repeated Petitions have been answered only by repeated Injury. A Prince, whose Character is thus marked by every Act which may define a Tyrant, is unfit to be the Ruler of a free People.

NOR have we been wanting in Attention to our British Brethren. We have warned them, from time to time, of Attempts by their Legislature to extend an unwarrantable Jurisdiction over us. We have reminded them of the Circumstances of our Emigration and Settlement here. We have appealed to their native Justice and Magnanimity, and we have conjured them by the Ties of our common Kindred to disavow these Usurpations, which would inevitably interrupt our connections and correspondence. They too have been deaf to the Voice of Justice and of Consanguinity. We must, therefore, acquiesce in the Necessity, which denounces our Separation, and hold them, as we hold the Rest of Mankind, Enemies in War, in Peace Friends.

WE, therefore, the Representatives of the UNITED STATES OF AMERICA, in GENERAL CONGRESS, Assembled, appealing to the Supreme Judge of the World for the Rectitude of our Intentions, do, in the Name, and by Authority of the good People of these Colonies, solemnly Publish and Declare, That these United Colonies are, and of Right ought to be, FREE AND INDEPENDENT STATES; that they are absolved from all Allegiance to the British Crown, and that all political Connection between them and the State of Great-Britain, is, and ought to be, totally dissolved; and that as FREE AND INDEPENDENT STATES, they have full Power to levy War, conclude Peace, contract Alliances, establish Commerce, and to do all other Acts and Things which INDEPENDENT STATES may of Right do. And for the Support of this Declaration, with a firm Reliance on the Protection of DIVINE PROVIDENCE, we mutually pledge to each other our *Lives*, our *Fortunes* and our *sacred Honor*.

NORTHWEST ORDINANCE (1787)

Article I

No person, demeaning himself in a peaceable and orderly manner, shall ever be molested on account of his mode of worship, or religious sentiments, in the said territory.

Article III

Religion, morality, and knowledge being necessary to good government and the happiness of mankind, schools and the means of education shall forever be encouraged. The utmost good faith shall always be observed towards the Indians; their lands and property shall never be taken from them without their consent; and in their property, rights, and liberty they never shall be invaded or disturbed unless in just and lawful wars authorized by Congress; but laws founded in justice and humanity shall, from time to time, be made, for preventing wrongs being done to them, and for preserving peace and friendship with them.

✛✛✛

UNITED STATES CONSTITUTION (1787)

Preamble

We The People of the United States, in Order to form a more perfect Union, establish Justice, insure domestic Tranquility, provide for the common defense, promote the general Welfare, and secure the Blessings of Liberty to ourselves and our Posterity, do ordain and establish this Constitution for the United States of America.

Article VI

All Debts contracted and Engagements entered into, before the Adoption of this Constitution, shall be as valid against the United States under this Constitution, as under the Confederation.

This Constitution, and the Laws of the United States which shall be made in Pursuance thereof; and all Treaties made, or which shall be made, under the Authority of the United States, shall be the supreme Law of the Land; and the Judges in every State shall be bound thereby, any Thing in the Constitution or Laws of any State to the Contrary notwithstanding.

The Senators and Representatives before mentioned, and the Members of the several State Legislatures, and all executive and judicial Officers; both of the United States and of the several States, shall be bound by Oath or Affirmation, to support this Constitution; but no religious Test shall ever be required as a Qualification to any Office or public Trust under the United States.

Article VII

The Ratification of the Conventions of nine States, shall be sufficient for the Establishment of this Constitution between the States so ratifying the Same.

DONE in Convention by the Unanimous Consent of the States present the Seventeenth Day of September in the Year of our Lord one thousand seven hundred and Eighty seven and of the Independence of the United States of America the Twelfth In witness whereof We have hereunto subscribed our Names,

Attest William Jackson Secretary

Go: Washington—President and deputy from Virginia

First Amendment

Congress shall make no law respecting an establishment of religion, or prohibiting the free exercise thereof; or abridging the freedom of speech, or of the press; or the right of the people peaceably to assemble, and to petition the Government for a redress of grievances.

✚•✚•✚

STATE CONSTITUTIONS ACKNOWLEDGING GOD

ALABAMA

We, the people of the State of Alabama, in order to establish justice, insure domestic tranquility, and secure the blessings of liberty to ourselves and our posterity, invoking the favor and guidance of Almighty God, do ordain and establish the following Constitution and form of government for the State of Alabama.

Art. I, Sec. 3.

Religious freedom. That no religion shall be established by law; that no preference shall be given by law to any religious sect, society, denomination, or mode of worship; that no one shall be compelled by law to attend any place of worship; nor to pay any tithes, taxes, or other rate for building or repairing any place of worship, or for maintaining any minister or ministry; that no religious test shall be required as a qualification to any office or public trust under this state; and that the civil rights, privileges, and capacities of any citizen shall not be in any manner affected by his religious principles.

ALASKA

We the people of Alaska, grateful to God and to those who founded our nation and pioneered this great land, in order to secure and transmit to succeeding generations our heritage of political, civil, and religious liberty within the Union of States, do ordain and establish this constitution for the State of Alaska.

Art. I, Sec. 4.

No law shall be made respecting an establishment of religion, or prohibiting the free exercise thereof.

ARIZONA

We the people of the State of Arizona, grateful to Almighty God for our liberties, do ordain this Constitution.

Art. II, Sec. 12.

The liberty of conscience secured by the provisions of this Constitution shall not be so construed as to excuse acts of licentiousness, or justify practices inconsistent with the peace and safety of the State. No public money or property shall be appropriated for or applied to any religious worship, exercise, or instruction, or to the support of any religious establishment. No religious qualification shall be required for any public office or employment, nor shall any person be incompetent as a witness or juror in consequence of his opinion on matters of religion, nor be questioned touching his religious belief in any court of justice to affect the weight of his testimony.

ARKANSAS

We, the people of the State of Arkansas, grateful to Almighty God for the privilege of choosing our own form of government, for our civil and religious liberty, and desiring to perpetuate its blessings and secure the same to our selves and posterity, do ordain and establish this Constitution.

Art. II, Sec. 24.

Religious liberty. All men have a natural and indefeasible right to worship Almighty God according to the dictates of their own consciences; no man can, of right, be compelled to attend, erect or support any place of worship; or to maintain any ministry against his consent.

No human authority can, in any case or manner whatsoever, control or interfere with the right of conscience; and no preference shall ever be given, by law, to any religious establishment, denomination or mode of worship above any other.

Art. II, Sec. 25.

Protection of religion. Religion, morality and knowledge being essential to good government, the General Assembly shall enact suitable laws to protect every religious denomination in the peaceable enjoyment of its own mode of public worship.

Art. II, Sec. 26.

Religious tests. No religious test shall ever be required of any person as a qualification to vote or hold office, nor shall any person be rendered incompetent to be a witness on account of his religious belief; but nothing herein shall be construed to dispense with oaths or affirmations.

CALIFORNIA

We, the people of California, grateful to Almighty God for our freedom in order to secure and perpetuate its blessings, do establish this Constitution.

Art. I, Sec. 4.

Free exercise and enjoyment of religion without discrimination or preference are guaranteed. This liberty of conscience does not excuse acts that are licentious or inconsistent with the peace or safety of the State. The Legislature shall make no law respecting an establishment of religion. A person is not incompetent to be a witness or juror because of his or her opinions on religious beliefs.

COLORADO

We, the people of Colorado, with profound reverence for the Supreme Ruler of the Universe, in order to form a more independent and perfect government, establish justice, insure tranquility, provide for the common defense, promote the general welfare, and secure the blessings of liberty to ourselves and our posterity, do ordain and establish this constitution for the 'State of Colorado'.

Art. II, Sec. 4

That the free exercise and enjoyment of religious profession and worship, without discrimination, shall forever hereafter be guaranteed; and no person shall be denied any civil or political right, privilege, or capacity on account of his opinions concerning religion; but the liberty of conscience hereby secured shall not be construed to dispense with oaths or affirmations, excuse acts of licentiousness, or justify practices inconsistent with the good order, peace or safety of the state. No person shall be required to attend or support any ministry or place of worship, religious sect or denomination against his consent. Nor shall any preference be given by law to any religious denomination or mode of worship.

CONNECTICUT

The People of Connecticut acknowledging with gratitude, the good providence of God, in having permitted them to enjoy a free government; do, in order more effectually to define, secure, and perpetuate the liberties, rights and privileges which they have derived from their ancestors; hereby, after a careful consideration and revision, ordain and establish the following constitution and form of civil government.

Art. I, Sec. 3.

The exercise and enjoyment of religious profession and worship, without discrimination, shall forever be free to all persons in the state; provided, that the right hereby declared and established, shall not be so construed as to excuse acts of licentiousness, or to justify practices inconsistent with the peace and safety of the state.

DELAWARE

Through Divine goodness, all men have by nature the rights of worshipping and serving their Creator according to the dictates of their consciences, of enjoying and defending life and liberty, of acquiring and protecting reputation and property, and in general of obtaining objects suitable to their condition, without injury by one to another; and as these rights are essential to their welfare, for due exercise thereof, power is inherent in them; and therefore all just authority in the institutions of political society is derived from the people, and established with their consent, to advance their happiness; and they may for this end, as circumstances require, from time to time, alter their Constitution of government.

Art. I, Sec. 1.

Although it is the duty of all men frequently to assemble together for the public worship of Almighty God; and piety and morality, on which the prosperity of communities depends, are hereby promoted; yet no man shall or ought to be compelled to attend any religious worship, to contribute to the erection or support of any place of worship, or to the maintenance of any ministry, against his own free will and consent; and no power shall or ought to be vested in or assumed by any magistrate that shall in any case interfere with, or in any manner control the rights of conscience, in the free exercise of religious worship, nor a preference given by law to any religious societies, denominations, or modes of worship.

FLORIDA

We, the people of the State of Florida, being grateful to Almighty God for our constitutional liberty, in order to secure its benefits, perfect our government, insure domestic tranquility, maintain public order, and guarantee equal civil and political rights to all, do ordain and establish this constitution.

Art. I, Sec. 3.

Religious freedom. There shall be no law respecting the establishment of religion or prohibiting or penalizing the free exercise thereof. Religious freedom shall not justify practices inconsistent with public morals, peace or safety. No revenue of the state or any political subdivision or agency thereof shall ever be taken from the public treasury directly or indirectly in aid of any church, sect, or religious denomination or in aid of any sectarian institution.

Georgia

To perpetuate the principles of free government, insure justice to all, preserve peace, promote the interest and happiness of the citizen and of the family, and transmit to posterity the enjoyment of liberty, we the people of Georgia, relying upon the protection and guidance of Almighty God, do ordain and establish this Constitution.

Art. I, Sec. I, paragraphs III and IV.

Freedom of conscience. Each person has the natural and inalienable right to worship God, each according to the dictates of that person's own conscience; and no human authority should, in any case, control or interfere with such right of conscience.

Religious opinions; freedom of religion. No inhabitant of this state shall be molested in person or property or be prohibited from holding any public office or trust on account of religious opinions; but the right of freedom of religion shall not be so construed as to excuse acts of licentiousness or justify practices inconsistent with the peace and safety of the state.

Hawaii

We, the people of Hawaii, grateful for Divine Guidance, and mindful of our Hawaiian heritage and uniqueness as an island State, dedicate our efforts to fulfill the philosophy decreed by the Hawaii State motto, 'Ua mau ke ea o ka aina i ka pono.'

We reserve the right to control our own destiny, to nurture the integrity of our people and culture, and to preserve the quality of life that we desire.

We reaffirm our belief in a government of the people, by the people and for the people, and with an understanding and compassionate heart toward all the peoples of earth, do hereby ordain and establish this constitution for the State of Hawaii."

Art. I, Sec. 4.

No law shall be enacted respecting an establishment of religion, or prohibiting the free exercise thereof, or abridging the freedom of speech or of the press or the right of the people peaceably to assemble and to petition the government for a redress of grievances.

IDAHO

We, the people of the State of Idaho, grateful to Almighty God for our freedom, to secure its blessings and promote our common welfare do establish this Constitution.

Art. I, Sec. 4.

Guaranty of Religious Liberty. The exercise and enjoyment of religious faith and worship shall forever be guaranteed; and no person shall be denied any civil or political right, privilege, or capacity on account of his religious opinions; but the liberty of conscience hereby secured shall not be construed to dispense with oaths or affirmations, or excuse acts of licentiousness or justify polygamous or other pernicious practices, inconsistent with morality or the peace or safety of the state; nor to permit any person, organization, or association to directly or indirectly aid or abet, counsel or advise any person to commit the crime of bigamy or polygamy, or any other crime. No person shall be required to attend or support any ministry or place of worship, religious sect or denomination, or pay tithes against his consent; nor shall any preference be given by law to any religious denomination or mode of worship. Bigamy and polygamy are forever prohibited in the state, and the legislature shall provide by law for the punishment of such crimes.

ILLINOIS

We, the People of the State of Illinois—grateful to Almighty God for the civil, political and religious liberty which He has permitted us to enjoy and seeking His blessing upon our endeavors—in order to provide for the health, safety and welfare of the people; maintain a representative and orderly government; eliminate poverty and inequality; assure legal, social and economic justice; provide opportunity for the fullest development of the individual; insure domestic tranquility; provide for the common defense; and secure the blessings of freedom and liberty to ourselves and our posterity—do ordain and establish this Constitution for the State of Illinois.

Art. I, Sec. 3.

The free exercise and enjoyment of religious profession and worship, without discrimination, shall forever be guaranteed, and no person shall be denied any civil or political right, privilege or capacity, on account of his religious opinions; but the liberty of conscience hereby secured shall not be construed to dispense with oaths or affirmations, excuse acts of licentiousness, or justify practices inconsistent with the peace or safety of the State. No person shall be required to attend or support any ministry or place of worship against his consent, nor shall any preference be given by law to any religious denomination or mode of worship.

Indiana

To the end that justice be established, public order maintained, and liberty perpetuated, we, the people of the State of Indiana, grateful to Almighty God for the free exercise of the right to choose our own form of government, do ordain this constitution.

Art. I, Sec. 3.

No law shall, in any case whatever, control the free exercise and enjoyment of religious opinions, or interfere with the rights of conscience.

Art. I, Sec. 4.

No preference shall be given by law to any creed, religious society, or mode of worship; and no man shall be compelled to attend, erect, or support any place of worship, or to maintain any ministry against his consent.

Art. I, Sec. 5.

No religious test shall be required as a qualification for any office of trust or profit.

Iowa

We, the People of the State of Iowa, grateful to the Supreme Being for the blessings hitherto enjoyed, and feeling our dependence on Him for a continuation of those blessings, do ordain and establish a free and independent government, by the name of the State of Iowa, the boundaries whereof shall be as follows...

Art. I, Sec. 3.

The General Assembly shall make no law respecting an establishment of religion, or prohibiting the free exercise thereof; nor shall any person be compelled to attend any place of worship, pay tithes, taxes, or other rates for building or repairing places of worship, or the maintenance of any minister, or ministry.

Art. I, Sec. 4.

No religious test shall be required as a qualification for any office, or public trust, and no person shall be deprived of any of his rights, privileges, or capacities, or disqualified from the performance of any of his public or private duties, or rendered incompetent to give evidence in any court of law or equity, in consequence of his opinions on the subject of religion; and any party to any judicial proceeding shall have the right to use as a witness, or take the testimony of, any other person not disqualified on account of interest, who may be cognizant of any fact material to the case; and parties to suits may be witnesses, as provided by law.

KANSAS

We, the people of Kansas, grateful to Almighty God for our civil and religious privileges, in order to insure the full enjoyment of our rights as American citizens, do ordain and establish this constitution of the state of Kansas, with the following boundaries, to wit...

Bill of Rights, Sec. 7.

Religious liberty. The right to worship God according to the dictates of conscience shall never be infringed; nor shall any person be compelled to attend or support any form of worship; nor shall any control of or interference with the rights of conscience be permitted, nor any preference by given by law to any religious establishment or mode of worship. No religious test or property qualification shall be required for any office of public trust, nor for any vote at any election, nor shall any person be incompetent to testify on account of religious belief.

KENTUCKY

We, the people of the Commonwealth of Kentucky, grateful to Almighty

God for the civil, political and religious liberties we enjoy, and invoking the continuance of these blessings, do ordain and establish this Constitution.

Sec. 1

Rights of life, liberty, worship, pursuit of safety and happiness, free speech, acquiring and protecting property, peaceable assembly, redress of grievances, bearing arms. All men are, by nature, free and equal, and have certain inherent and inalienable rights, among which may be reckoned...

Second: The right of worshipping Almighty God according to the dictates of their consciences.

LOUISIANA

We, the people of Louisiana, grateful to Almighty God for the civil, political, economic, and religious liberties we enjoy, and desiring to protect individual rights to life, liberty, and property; afford opportunity for the fullest development of the individual; assure equality of rights; promote the health, safety, education, and welfare of people; maintain a representative and orderly government; endure domestic tranquility; provide for the common defense; and secure the blessings of freedom and justice to ourselves and our posterity, do ordain and establish this constitution.

Art. I, Sec. 8.

No law shall be enacted respecting an establishment of religion or prohibiting the free exercise thereof.

MAINE

Objects of government. We the people of Maine, in order to establish justice, insure tranquility, provide for our mutual defense, promote our common welfare, and secure to ourselves and our posterity the blessings of liberty, acknowledging with grateful hearts the goodness of the Sovereign Ruler of the Universe in affording us an opportunity so favorable to the design; and, imploring God's aid and direction in its accomplishment, do agree to form ourselves into a free and independent State, by the style and title of the State of Maine and do ordain and establish the following Constitution for the government of the same.

Art. I, Sec. 3.

All individuals have a natural and unalienable right to worship Almighty God according to the dictates of their own consciences, and no person shall be hurt, molested or restrained in that person's liberty or estate for worshipping God in the manner and season most agreeable to the dictates of that person's own conscience, nor for that person's religious professions or sentiments, provided that that person does not disturb the public peace, nor obstruct others in their religious worship;—and all persons demeaning themselves peaceably, as good members of the State, shall be equally under the protection of the laws, and no subordination nor preference of any one sect or denomination to another shall ever be established by law, nor shall any religious test be required as a qualification for any office or trust, under this State; and all religious societies in this State, whether incorporate or unincorporate, shall at all times have the exclusive right of electing their public teachers, and contracting with them for their support and maintenance.

MARYLAND

We, the People of the State of Maryland, grateful to Almighty God for our civil and religious liberty, and taking into our serious consideration the best means of establishing a good Constitution in this State for the sure foundation and more permanent security thereof, declare…

Art. 36

That as it is the duty of every man to worship God in such manner as he thinks most acceptable to Him, all persons are equally entitled to protection in their religious liberty; wherefore, no person ought by any law to be molested in his person or estate, on account of his religious persuasion, or profession, or for his religious practice, unless, under the color of religion, he shall disturb the good order, peace or safety of the State, or shall infringe the laws of morality, or injure others in their natural, civil or religious rights; nor ought any person to be compelled to frequent, or maintain, or contribute, unless on contract, to maintain, any place of worship, or any ministry; nor shall any person, otherwise competent, be deemed incompetent as a witness, or juror, on account of his religious belief, provided, he believes in the existence of God, and that under His dispensation such person will be held morally accountable for his acts, and be rewarded or punished therefor either in this world or in the world to come.

MASSACHUSETTS

The end of the institution, maintenance and administration of government, is to secure the existence of the body-politic, to protect it, and to furnish the individuals who compose it, with the power of enjoying in safety and tranquility their natural rights, and the blessings of life: And whenever these great objects are not obtained, the people have a right to alter the government, and to take measures necessary for their safety, prosperity and happiness.—The Body-Politic is formed by a voluntary association of individuals: It is a social compact, by which the whole people covenants with each Citizen, and each Citizen with the whole people, that all shall be governed by certain Laws for the Common good. It is the duty of the people, therefore, in framing a Constitution of Government, to provide for an equitable mode of making laws, as well as for an impartial interpretation, and a faithful execution of them; that every man may, at all times, find his security in them. WE, therefore, the people of Massachusetts, acknowledging, with grateful hearts, the goodness of the Great Legislator of the Universe, in affording us, in the course of his Providence, an opportunity, deliberately and peaceably, without fraud, violence or surprise, or entering into an Original, explicit, and Solemn Compact with each other; and of forming a New Constitution of Civil Government, for Ourselves and Posterity; and devoutly imploring His direction in so interesting a Design, DO agree upon, ordain and establish, the following Declaration of Rights, and Frame of Government, as the CONSTITUTION OF THE COMMONWEALTH OF MASSACHUSETTS.

Part I, Art. II.

It is the right as well as the Duty of all men in society publicly, and at stated seasons to worship the SUPREME BEING, the great Creator and preserver of the Universe. And no Subject shall be hurt, molested, or restrained, in his person, Liberty, or Estate, for worshipping God in the manner and season most agreeable to the Dictates of his own conscience, or for his religious profession or sentiments; provided he doth not Disturb the public peace, or obstruct others in their religious Worship

Part I, Art. III.

As the happiness of a people, and the good order and preservation of civil government, essentially depend upon piety, religion and morality; and as these cannot be generally diffused through a Community, but by the institution of the public Worship of God, and of public instructions in piety, religion and morality: Therefore, to promote their happiness and to secure the good order and preservation of their government, the people of this Commonwealth have a right to invest their legislature shall, from time to time, authorize and require, the several Towns, Parishes, precincts, and other bodies politic, or religious societies, to make suitable provision, at their own Expense, for the institution of Public worship of God, and for the support and maintenance of public protestant teachers of piety, religion and morality, in all cases where such provision shall not be made Voluntarily—And the people of this Commonwealth have also a right to, and do, invest their legislature with authority to enjoin upon all the Subjects an attendance upon the instructions of the public teachers aforesaid, at stated times and seasons, if there he any on whose instructions they can Conscientiously and conveniently attend—PROVIDED notwithstanding, that the several towns, parishes, precincts, and other bodies politic, or religious societies, shall, at all times, have the exclusive right of electing their public Teachers, and of contracting with them for their support and maintenance.—And all monies paid by the Subject to the Support of public worship, and of the public teachers aforesaid, shall, if he require it, be uniformly applied to the support of the public teacher or teachers of his own religious sect or denomination, provided there be any on whose instructions he attends: otherwise it may be paid towards the support of the teacher or teachers of the parish or precinct in which the said monies are raised— And every denomination of Christians, demeaning themselves peaceably, and as good Subjects of the Commonwealth, shall be equally under the protection of the Law: And no subordination of any one sect or denomination to another shall ever be established by law.

MICHIGAN

We, the people of the State of Michigan, grateful to Almighty God for the blessings of freedom, and earnestly desiring to secure these blessings undiminished to ourselves and our posterity, do ordain and establish this constitution.

Art. I, Sec. 4.

Every person shall be at liberty to worship God according to the dictates of his own conscience. No person shall be compelled to attend, or, against his consent, to contribute tot the erection or support of any place of religious worship, or to pay tithes, taxes or other rates for the support of any minister of the gospel or teacher of religion. No money shall be appropriated or drawn from the treasury for the benefit of any religious sect or society, theological or religious seminary; nor shall property belonging to the state be appropriated for any such purpose. The civil and political rights, privileges and capacities of no person shall be diminished or enlarged on account of his religious belief.

MINNESOTA

We, the people of the state of Minnesota, grateful to God for our civil and religious liberty, and desiring to perpetuate its blessings and secure the same to ourselves and our posterity, do ordain and establish this Constitution...

Art. I, Sec. 16.

Freedom of conscience; no preference to be given to any religious establishment or mode of worship. The enumeration of rights in this constitution shall not deny or impair others retained by and inherent in the people. The right of every man to worship God according to the dictates of his own conscience shall never be infringed; nor shall any man be compelled to attend, erect or support any place of worship, or to maintain any religious or ecclesiastical ministry, against his consent; nor shall any control of or interference with the rights of conscience be permitted, or any preference be given by law to any religious establishment or mode of worship; but the liberty of conscience hereby secured shall not be so construed as to excuse acts of licentiousness or justify practices inconsistent with the peace or safety of the state, nor shall any money be drawn from the treasury for the benefit of any religious societies or religious or theological seminaries.

Art. I, Sec. 17.

Religious tests and property qualifications prohibited. No religious test or amount of property shall be required as a qualification for any office of public trust in the state. No religious test or amount of property shall be required as a qualification of any voter at any election in this state; nor shall any person be rendered incompetent to give evidence in any court of law or equity in consequence of his opinion upon the subject of religion.

MISSISSIPPI

We, the people of Mississippi in convention assembled, grateful to Almighty God, and invoking his blessing on our work, do ordain and establish this constitution.

Art. III, Sec. 18.

No religious test as a qualification for office shall be required; and no preference shall be given by law to any religious sect or mode of worship; but the free enjoyment of all religious sentiments and the different modes of worship shall be held sacred. The rights hereby secured shall not be construed to justify acts of licentiousness injurious to morals or dangerous to the peace and safety of the state, or to exclude the Holy Bible from use in any public school of this state.

MISSOURI

We, the people of Missouri, with profound reverence for the Supreme Ruler of the Universe, and grateful for His goodness—do establish this Constitution for the better government of the State.

Art. I, Sec. 5.

Religious freedom—liberty of conscience and belief—limitations.—

That all men have a natural and indefeasible right to worship Almighty God according to the dictates of their own consciences; that no human authority can control or interfere with the rights of conscience; that no person shall, on account of his religious persuasion or belief, be rendered ineligible to any public office or trust or profit in this state, be disqualified from testifying or serving as a juror or be molested in his person or estate; but this section shall not be construed to excuse acts of licentiousness, nor to justify practices inconsistent with the good order, peace or safety of the state, or with the rights of others.

Art. 1, Sec. 6.

Practice and support of religion not compulsory—contracts therefor enforceable.—That no person can be compelled to erect, support or attend any place or system of worship, or to maintain or support any priest, minister, preacher or teacher of any sect, church, creed or denomination of religion; but if any person shall voluntarily make a contract for any such object, he shall be held to the performance of the same.

Montana

We, the people of Montana, grateful to God for the quiet beauty of our state, the grandeur of our mountains, the vastness •of our rolling plains, and desiring to improve the quality of life, equality of opportunity and to secure the blessings of liberty for this and future generations do ordain and establish this constitution.

Art. II, Sec. 5.

Freedom of religion. The state shall make no law respecting an establishment of religion or prohibiting the free exercise thereof.

Nebraska

We, the people, grateful to Almighty God for our freedom, do ordain and establish the following declaration of rights sand frame of government, as the Constitution of the State of Nebraska.

Art. I, Sec. 4.

All persons have a natural and indefeasible right to worship Almighty God according to the dictates of their own consciences. No person shall be compelled to attend, erect or support any place of worship against his consent, and no preference shall be given by law to any religious society, nor shall any interference with the rights of conscience be permitted. No religious test shall be required as a qualification for office, nor shall any person be incompetent to be a witness on account of his religious beliefs; but nothing herein shall be construed to dispense with oaths and affirmations. Religion, morality, and knowledge, however, being essential to good government, it shall be the duty of the Legislature to pass suitable laws to protect every religious denomination in the peaceable enjoyment of its own mode of public worship, and to encourage schools and the means of instruction.

NEVADA

We, the people of the State of Nevada, grateful to Almighty God for our freedom, in order to secure its blessings, insure domestic tranquility, and form a more perfect government, do establish this constitution.

Art. I, Sec. 4.

The free exercise and enjoyment of religious profession and worship, without discrimination or preference, shall forever be allowed in this State; an no person shall be rendered incompetent to be a witness on account of his opinions on matters of his religious belief; but the liberty of conscience hereby secured shall not be so construed as to excuse acts of licentiousness, or justify practices inconsistent with the peace or safety of this State.

NEW HAMPSHIRE

Part I, Art. 4.

Among the natural rights, some are, in their very nature unalienable, because no equivalent can be given or received for them. Of this kind are Rights of Conscience.

Part I, Art. 5.

Every individual has a natural and unalienable right to worship God according to the dictates of his own conscience, and reason: and no subject shall be hurt, molested, or restrained, in his person, liberty, or estate, for worshipping God in the manner and season most agreeable to the dictates of his own conscience: or for his religious profession, sentiments, or persuasion: provided he doth not disturb the public peace or disturb others in their religious worship.

Part I, Art. 6.

As morality and piety, rightly grounded on high principles, will give the best and greatest security to government, and will lay, in the hearts of men, the strongest obligations to due subjection: and as the knowledge of these is most likely to be propagated through a society, therefore, the several parishes, bodies, corporate, or religious societies shall at all times have the right of electing their own teachers, and of contracting with them for their support or maintenance, or both. But no person shall ever be compelled to pay towards the support of the schools of any sect or denomination. And every person, denomination or sect shall be equally under the protection of the law; and no subordination of any one sect, denomination or persuasion to another shall ever be established.

NEW JERSEY

We, the people of the State of New Jersey, grateful to Almighty God for the civil and religious liberty which He hath so long permitted us to enjoy, and looking to Him for a blessing upon our endeavors to secure and transmit the same unimpaired to succeeding generations, do ordain and establish this Constitution.

Art. I, Sec. 3.

No person shall be deprived of the inestimable privilege of worshipping Almighty God in a manner agreeable to the dictates of his own conscience; nor under any pretense whatever be compelled to attend any place of worship contrary to his faith and judgment; nor shall any person be obliged to pay tithes, taxes, or other rates for building or repairing any church or churches, place or places of worship, or for the maintenance of any minister or ministry, contrary to what he believes to be right or has deliberately and voluntarily engaged to perform.

Art. I, Sec. 4.

There shall be no establishment of one religious sect in preference to another; no religious or racial test shall be required as a qualification for any office or public trust.

Art. I, Sec. 5.

No person shall be denied the enjoyment of any civil or military right, nor be discriminated against in the exercise of any civil or military right, nor be segregated in the militia or in the public schools, because of religious principles, race, color, ancestry or national origin.

NEW MEXICO

We, the people of New Mexico, grateful to Almighty God for the blessings of liberty, in order to secure the advantages of a state government, do ordain and establish this Constitution.

Art. II, Sec. 11.

Every man shall be free to worship God according to the dictates of his own conscience, and no person shall ever be molested or denied any civil or political right or privilege on account of his religious opinion or mode of religious worship. No person shall be required to attend any place of worship or support any religious sect or denomination; nor shall any preference be given by law to any religious denomination or mode of worship.

NEW YORK

We The People of the State of New York, grateful to Almighty God for our Freedom, in order to secure its blessings, DO ESTABLISH THIS CONSTITUTION.

Art. I, Sec. 3.

The free exercise and enjoyment of religious profession and worship, without discrimination or preference, shall forever be allowed in this state to all mankind; and no person shall be rendered incompetent to be a witness on account of his opinions on matters of religious belief; but the liberty of conscience hereby secured shall not be so construed as to excuse acts of licentiousness, or justify practices inconsistent with the peace or safety of this state.

NORTH CAROLINA

We, the people of the State of North Carolina, grateful to Almighty God, the Sovereign Ruler of Nations, for the preservation of the American

Union and the existence of our civil, political and religious liberties, and acknowledging our dependence upon Him for the continuance of those blessings to us and our posterity, do, for the more certain security thereof and for the better government of this State, ordain and establish this Constitution.

Art. I, Sec. 13.

Religious Liberty. All persons have a natural and inalienable right to worship Almighty God according to the dictates of their own consciences, and no human authority shall, in any case whatever, control or interfere with the rights of conscience.

NORTH DAKOTA

We, the people of North Dakota, grateful to Almighty God for the blessings of civil and religious liberty, do ordain and establish this constitution.

Art. I, Sec. 3.

The free exercise and enjoyment of religious profession and worship, without discrimination or preference shall be forever guaranteed in this state, and no person shall be rendered incompetent to be a witness or juror on account of his opinion on matters of religious belief; but the liberty of conscience hereby secured shall not be so construed as to excuse acts of licentiousness, or justify practices inconsistent with the peace or safety of this state.

Ohio

We, the people of the State of Ohio, grateful to Almighty God for our freedom, to secure its blessings, and promote our common welfare, do establish this Constitution.

Art. I, Sec. 7.

All men have a natural and indefeasible right to worship Almighty God according to the dictates of their own conscience. No person shall be compelled to attend, erect, or support any place of worship, or maintain any form of worship, against his consent; and no preference shall be given, by law, to any religious society; nor shall any interference with the rights of conscience be permitted. No religious test shall be required, as a qualification for office, nor shall any person be incompetent to be a witness on account of his religious belief; but nothing herein shall be construed to dispense with oaths and affirmations. Religion, morality, and knowledge, however, being essential to good government, it shall be the duty of the general assembly to pass suitable laws to protect every religious denomination in the peaceable enjoyment of its own mode of public worship, and to encourage schools and the means of instruction.

OKLAHOMA

Invoking the guidance of Almighty God, in order to secure and perpetuate the blessing of liberty; to secure just and rightful government; to promote our mutual welfare and happiness, we, the people of the State of Oklahoma, do ordain and establish this Constitution.

Art. I, Sec. 2.

Perfect toleration of religious sentiment shall be secured, an no inhabitant of the State shall ever be molested in person or property on account of his or her mode of religious worship; and no religion test shall be required for the exercise of civil or political rights. Polygamous or plural marriages are forever prohibited.

OREGON

We the people of the State of Oregon to the end that Justice be established, order maintained, and liberty perpetuated, do ordain this Constitution.

Art. I, Sec. 2.

Freedom of worship. All men shall be secure in the Natural right, to worship Almighty God according to the dictates of their own consciences.

Art. I, Sec. 3.

Freedom of religious opinion. No law shall in any case whatever control the free exercise, and enjoyment of religious opinions, or interfere with the rights of conscience.

Art. I, Sec. 5.

No money to be appropriated for religion. No money shall be drawn from the Treasury for the benefit of any religious or theological institution, nor shall any money be appropriated for the payment of any religious services in either house of the Legislative Assembly.

We, the people of the Commonwealth of Pennsylvania, grateful to Almighty God for the blessings of civil and religious liberty, and humbly invoking his guidance, do ordain and establish this Constitution.

Art. I, Sec. 3.

All men have a natural and indefeasible right to worship Almighty God according to the dictates of their own consciences; no man can of right be compelled to attend, erect or support any place of worship, or to maintain any ministry against his consent; no human authority can, in any case whatever, control or interfere with the rights of conscience, an no preference shall ever be given by law to any religious establishments or modes of worship.

Art. I, Sec. 4.

No person who acknowledges the being of a God and a future state of rewards and punishments shall, on account of his religious sentiments, be disqualified to hold any office or place of trust or profit under this Commonwealth.

RHODE ISLAND

We, the people of the State of Rhode Island and Providence Plantations, grateful to Almighty God for the civil and religious liberty which He hath so long permitted us to enjoy, and looking to Him for a blessing upon our endeavors to secure and to transmit the same, unimpaired, to succeeding generations, do ordain and establish this Constitution of government.

Art. I, Sec. 3.

Whereas Almighty God hath created the mind free; and all attempts to influence it by temporal punishments or burdens, or by civil incapacitations, tend to beget habits of hypocrisy and meanness; and whereas a principal object of our venerable ancestors, in their migration to this country and their settlement of this state, was, as they expressed it, to hold forth a lively experiment that a flourishing civil state may stand and be best maintained with full liberty in religious concernments; we, therefore, declare that no person shall be compelled to frequent or to support any religious worship, place, or ministry whatever, except in fulfillment of such person's voluntary contract; nor enforced, restrained, molested, or burdened in body or goods; nor disqualified from holding any office; nor otherwise suffer on account of such person's religious belief; and that every person shall be free to worship God according to the dictates of such person's conscience, and to profess and by argument to maintain such person's opinion in matters of religion; and that the same shall in no wise diminish, enlarge, or affect the civil capacity of any person.

South Carolina

We, the people of the State of South Carolina, in convention assembled, grateful to God for our liberties, do ordain and establish this constitution for the preservation and perpetuation of the same.

Art. I, Sec. 2.

The General Assembly shall make no law respecting an establishment of religion or prohibiting the free exercise thereof, or abridging the freedom of speech or of the press; or the right of the people peaceably to assemble and to petition the government or any department thereof for a redress of grievances.

South Dakota

We, the people of South Dakota, grateful to Almighty God for our civil and religious liberties, in order to form a more perfect and independent government, establish justice, insure tranquility, provide for the common defense, promote the general welfare and preserve to ourselves and to our posterity the blessings of liberty, do ordain and establish this Constitution for the state of South Dakota.

Art. VI, Sec. 3.

The right to worship God according to the dictates of conscience shall never be infringed. No person shall be denied any civil or political right, privilege or position on account of his religious opinions; but the liberty of conscience hereby secured shall not be so construed as to excuse licentiousness, the invasion of the rights of others, or justify practices inconsistent with the peace or safety of the state.

No person shall be compelled to attend or support any ministry or place of worship against his consent nor shall any preference be given by law to any religious establishment or mode of worship. No money or property of the state shall be given or appropriated for the benefit of any sectarian or religious society or institution.

TENNESSEE

Art. I, Sec. 3.

That all men have a natural and indefeasible right to worship Almighty God according to the dictates of their own conscience; that no man can of right be compelled to attend, erect, or support any place of worship, or to maintain any minister against his consent; that no human authority can, in any case whatever, control or interfere with the rights of conscience; and that no preference shall ever be given, by law, to any religious establishment or mode of worship.

Art. I, Sec. 4.

That no political or religious test, other than an oath to support the Constitution of the United States and of this State, shall ever be required as a qualification to any office or public trust under this State.

TEXAS

Humbly invoking the blessings of Almighty God the people of the State of Texas do ordain and establish this Constitution.

Art. I, Sec. 4.

Religious Tests. No religious test shall ever be required as a qualification to any office, or public trust, in this State; nor shall any one be excluded from holding office on account of his religious sentiments, provided he acknowledge the existence of a Supreme Being."

Art. I, Sec. 5.

Witness not disqualified by religious beliefs; oaths and affirmations. No person shall be disqualified to give evidence in my of the Courts of this State on account of his religious opinions, or for the want of any religious belief, but all oaths or affirmations shall be administered in the mode most binding upon the conscience, and shall be taken subject to the pains and penalties of perjury.

Art. I, Sec. 6.

Freedom of Worship. All men have a natural and indefeasible right to worship Almighty God according to the dictates of their own consciences. No man shall be compelled to attend, erect or support any place of worship, or to maintain any ministry against his consent. No human authority ought, in any case whatever, to control or interfere with the rights of conscience in matters of religion, and no preference shall ever be given by law to any religious society or mode of worship. But it shall be the duty of the Legislature to pass such laws as may be necessary to protect equally every religious denomination in the peaceable enjoyment of its own mode of public worship.

UTAH

Grateful to Almighty God for life and liberty, we, the people of Utah, in order to secure and perpetuate the principles of free government, do ordain and establish this CONSTITUTION.

Art. I, Sec. 4.

The rights of conscience shall never be infringed. The State shall make no law respecting an establishment of religion or prohibiting the free exercise thereof; no religious test shall be required as a qualification for any office of public trust or for any vote at any election; nor shall any person be incompetent as a witness or juror on account of religious belief or the absence thereof. There shall he no union of Church and State, nor shall any church dominate the State or interfere with its functions. No public money or property shall be appropriated for or applied to any religious worship, exercise or instruction, or for the support of any ecclesiastical establishment. No property qualification shall be required of any person to vote, or hold office, except as provided in this Constitution.

Article 3rd.

That all men have a natural and unalienable right, to worship Almighty God, according to the dictates of their own consciences and understandings, as in their opinion shall be regulated by the word of God; and that no man ought to, or of right can be compelled to attend any religious worship, or erect or support any place of worship, or maintain any minister, contrary to the dictates of his conscience, nor can any man be justly deprived or abridged of any civil right as a citizen, on account of his religious sentiments, or peculiar mode of religious worship; and that no authority can, or ought to be vested in, or assumed by, any power whatever, that shall in any case interfere with, or in any manner control the rights of conscience, in the free exercise of religious worship. Nevertheless, ever sect or denomination of christians ought to observe the sabbath or Lord's day, and keep up some sort of religious worship, which to them shall seem most agreeable to the revealed will of God.

Art. I, Sec. 16.

That religion or the duty which we owe to our Creator, and the manner of discharging it, can be directed only by reason and conviction, not by force or violence; and, therefore, all men are equally entitled to the free exercise of religion, according to the dictates of conscience; and that it is the mutual duty of all to practice Christian forbearance, love, and charity towards each other. No man shall be compelled to frequent or support any religious worship, place, or ministry whatsoever, nor shall be enforced, restrained, molested, or burthened in his body or goods, nor shall otherwise suffer on account of his religious opinions or belief; but all men shall be free to profess and by argument to maintain their opinions in matters of religion, and the same shall in nowise diminish, enlarge, or affect their civil capacities. And the General Assembly shall not prescribe any religious test whatever, or confer any peculiar privileges or advantages on any sect or denomination, or pass any law requiring or authorizing any religious society, or the people of any district within this Commonwealth, to levy on themselves or others, any tax for the erection or repair of any house of public worship, or for the support of any church or ministry; but it shall be left free to every person to select his religious instructor, and to make for his support such private contract as he shall please.

Washington

We, the people of the State of Washington, grateful to the Supreme Ruler of the Universe for our liberties, do ordain this constitution.

Art. I, Sec. 11.

Religious Freedom. Absolute freedom of conscience in all matters of religious sentiment, belief and worship, shall be guaranteed to every individual, and no one shall be molested or disturbed in person or property on account of religion; but the liberty of conscience hereby secured shall not be so construed as to excuse acts of licentiousness or justify practices inconsistent with the peace and safety of the state. No public money or property shall be appropriated for or applied to any religious worship, exercise instruction, or the support of any religious establishment: *Provided, however,* That this article shall not be so construed as to forbid the employment by the state of a chaplain for such of the state custodial, correctional, and mental institutions, or by a county's or public hospital district's hospital, health care facility, or hospice, as in the discretion of the legislature may seem justified. No religious qualification shall be required for any public office or employment, nor shall any person be incompetent as a witness or juror, in consequence of his opinion on matters of religion, nor be questioned in any court of justice touching his religious belief to affect the weight of his testimony.

West Virginia

Since through Divine Providence we enjoy the blessings of civil, political and religious liberty, we, the people of West Virginia, in and through the provisions of this Constitution, reaffirm our faith in and constant reliance upon God and seek diligently to promote, preserve and perpetuate good government in the State of West Virginia for the common welfare, freedom, and security of ourselves and our posterity.

Art. III, Sec. 15.

No man shall be compelled to frequent or support any religious worship, place or ministry whatsoever; nor shall any man be enforced, restrained, molested or burthened, in his body or goods, or otherwise suffer, on account of his religious opinions or belief, but all men shall be free to profess and, by argument, to maintain their opinions in matters of religion; and the same shall, in nowise, affect, diminish or enlarge their civil capacities; and the Legislature shall not prescribe any religious test whatever, or confer any peculiar privileges or advantages on any sect or denomination, or pass any law requiring or authorizing any religious society, or the people of any district within this State, to levy on themselves, or others, any tax for the erection or repair of any house for public worship, or for the support of any church or ministry, but it shall be left free for every person to select his religious instructor, and to make for his support such private contracts as he shall please.

Art. III, Sec. 15.

Public schools shall provide a designated brief time at the beginning of each school day for any student desiring to exercise their right to personal and private contemplation, meditation or prayer. No student of a public school may be denied the right to personal and private contemplation, meditation or prayer nor shall any student be required or encouraged to engage in any given contemplation, meditation or prayer as a part of the school curriculum.

WISCONSIN

We, the people of Wisconsin, grateful to Almighty God for our freedom, in order to secure its blessings, form a more perfect government, insure domestic tranquility and promote the general welfare; do establish this constitution.

Art. I, Sec. 18.

The right of every person to worship Almighty God according to the dictates of conscience shall never be infringed; nor shall any person be compelled to attend, erect or support any place of worship, or to maintain any ministry, without consent; nor shall any control of, or

interference with, the rights of conscience be permitted, or any preference be given by law to any religious establishments or modes of worship; nor shall any money be drawn from the treasury for the benefit of religious societies, or religious or theological seminaries.

Art. I, Sec. 19.

No religious tests shall ever be required as a qualification for any office of public trust under the state, and no person shall be rendered incompetent to give evidence in any court of law or equity in consequence of his opinions on the subject of religion.

WYOMING

We, the people of the State of Wyoming, grateful to God for our civil, political and religious liberties, and desiring to secure them to ourselves and perpetuate them to our posterity, do ordain and establish this Constitution.

Art. I, Sec. 18.

Religious liberty. The free exercise and enjoyment of religious profession and worship without discrimination or preference shall be forever guaranteed in this state, and no person shall be rendered incompetent to hold any office of trust or profit, or to serve as a witness or juror, because of his opinion on any matter of religious belief whatsoever; but the liberty of conscience hereby secured shall not be so construed as to excuse acts of licentiousness or justify practices inconsistent with the peace or safety of the state.

Art. I, Sec. 19.

Appropriations for sectarian or religious societies or institutions prohibited. No money of the state shall ever be given or appropriated to any sectarian or religious society or institution.

✠✠✠

GEORGE WASHINGTON, FIRST INAUGURAL ADDRESS (1789)

Fellow Citizens of the Senate and of the House of Representatives:

Among the vicissitudes incident to life no event could have filled me with greater anxieties than that of which the notification was transmitted by your order, and received on the fourteenth day of the present month. On the one hand, I was summoned by my country, whose voice I can never hear but with veneration and love, from a retreat which I had chosen with the fondest predilection, and, in my flattering hopes, with an immutable decision, as the asylum of my declining years—a retreat which was rendered every day more necessary as well as more dear to me by the addition of habit to inclination, and of frequent interruptions in my health to the gradual waste committed on it by time. On the other hand, the magnitude and difficulty of the trust to which the voice of my country called me, being sufficient to awaken in the wisest and most experienced of her citizens a distrustful scrutiny into his qualifications, could not but overwhelm with despondence, one, who inheriting inferior endowments from nature and unpracticed in the duties of civil administration, ought to be peculiarly conscious of his own deficiencies. In this conflict of emotions all I dare aver, is, that it has been my faithful study to collect my duty from a just appreciation of every circumstance by which it might be affected. All I dare hope, is, that if, in executing this task, I have been too much swayed by a grateful remembrance of former instances, or by an affectionate sensibility to this transcendent proof of the confidence of my fellow-citizens, and have thence too little consulted my incapacity as well as disinclination for the weighty and untried cares before me, my *error* will be palliated by the motives which misled me, and its consequences be judged by my country with some share of the partiality in which they originated.

Such being the impressions under which I have, in obedience to the public summons, repaired to the present station, it would be peculiarly improper to omit in this first official act my fervent supplications to that Almighty Being who rules over the universe; who presides in the councils of nations; and whose Providential aid can supply every human defect; that His benediction may consecrate to the liberties and happiness of the People of the United States, a Government instituted by themselves for these essential purposes, and may enable every instrument employed in its administration to execute with success the functions allotted to his charge. In tendering this homage to the Great Author of every public and private good, I assure myself that it expresses your sentiments not less than my own, nor those of my fellow-citizens at large less than either. No people can be bound to acknowledge and adore the Invisible Hand which conducts the affairs of men more than those of the United States. Every step by which they have advanced to the character of an independent nation seems to have been distinguished by some token of Providential agency. And in the important revolution just accomplished in the system of their united government the tranquil deliberations and voluntary consent of so many distinct communities from which the event has resulted can not be compared with the means by which most governments have been established, without some return of pious gratitude, along with an humble anticipation of the future blessings which the past seem to presage. These reflections, arising out of the present crisis, have forced themselves too strongly on my mind to be suppressed. You will join with me, I trust, in thinking that there are none under the influence of which the proceedings of a new and free government can more auspiciously commence.

By the article establishing the Executive Department it is made the duty of the President "to recommend to your consideration such measures as he shall judge necessary and expedient." The circumstances under which I now meet you will acquit me from entering into that subject, further than to refer to the great constitutional charter under which you are assembled, and which, in defining your powers, designates the objects to which your attention is to be given. It will be more consistent with those circumstances, and far more congenial with the feelings which actuate me, to substitute, in place of a recommendation of particular measures, the tribute that is due to the talents, the rectitude, and the patriotism, which adorn the characters selected to devise and adopt them. In these honorable qualifications I behold the surest pledges that as on one side no local prejudices or attachments—no separate views, nor party animosities, will misdirect the comprehensive and equal eye which ought to watch over this great assemblage of communities and interests; so, on another, that the foundation of our national policy will be laid in the pure and immutable principles of private morality, and the pre-eminence of free government be exemplified by all the attributes which can win the affections of its citizens and command the respect of the world. I dwell on this prospect with every satisfaction which an ardent love for my country can inspire: since there is no truth more thoroughly established than that there exists in the economy and course of nature an indissoluble union between virtue and happiness; between duty and advantage; between the genuine maxims of an honest and magnanimous policy and the solid rewards of public prosperity and felicity; since we ought to be no less persuaded that the propitious smiles of Heaven can never be expected on a nation that disregards the eternal rules of order and right which Heaven itself has ordained: and since the preservation of the sacred fire of liberty and the destiny of the republican model of government are justly considered, perhaps, as *deeply*, perhaps as *finally*, staked on the experiment entrusted to the hands of the American people.

Besides the ordinary objects submitted to your care, it will remain with your judgment to decide how far an exercise of the occasional power delegated by the fifth article of the Constitution is rendered expedient at the present juncture, by the nature of objections which have been urged against the system, or by the degree of inquietude which has given birth to them. Instead of undertaking particular recommendations on this subject, in which I could be guided by no lights derived from official opportunities, I shall again give way to my entire confidence in your discernment and pursuit of the public good: for I assure myself, that, whilst you carefully avoid every alteration which might endanger the benefits of an united and effective government, or which ought to await the future lessons of experience, a reverence for the characteristic rights of freemen, and a regard for the public harmony, will sufficiently influence your deliberations on the question, how far the former can be impregnably fortified or the latter be safely and advantageously promoted.

To the preceding observations I have one to add, which will be most properly addressed to the House of Representatives. It concerns myself, and will therefore be as brief as possible. When I was first honored with a call into the service of my country, then on the eve of an arduous struggle for its liberties, the light in which I contemplated my duty required that I should renounce every pecuniary compensation. From this resolution I have in no instance departed. And being still under the impressions which produced it, I must decline, as inapplicable to myself, any share in the personal emoluments which may be indispensably included in a permanent provision for the Executive Department; and must accordingly pray that the pecuniary estimates for the station in which I am placed, may, during my continuance in it, be limited to such actual expenditures as the public good may be thought to require.

Having thus imparted to you my sentiments as they have been awakened by the occasion which brings us together, I shall take my present leave; but not without resorting once more to the benign Parent of the human race in humble supplication that, since he has been pleased to favor the American People with opportunities for deliberating in perfect tranquility, and dispositions for deciding with unparalleled unanimity on a form of government for the security of their union, and the advancement of their happiness, so his divine blessing may be equally *conspicuous* in the enlarged views, the temperate consultations, and the wise measures on which the success of this Government must depend.

GEORGE WASHINGTON, THANKSGIVING PROCLAMATION (1789)

Whereas it is the duty of all Nations to acknowledge the providence of Almighty God, to obey His will, to be grateful for His benefits, and humbly to implore His protection and favor, and whereas both Houses of Congress have by their joint Committee requested me "to recommend to the People of the United States a day of public thanksgiving and prayer to be observed by acknowledging with grateful hearts the many signal favors of Almighty God especially by affording them an opportunity peaceably to establish a form of government for their safety and happiness."

Now therefore I do recommend and assign Thursday the 26th day of November next to be devoted by the People of these States to the service of that great and glorious Being, who is the beneficent Author of all the good that was, that is, or that will be. That we may then all unite in rendering unto Him our sincere and humble thanks, for His kind care and protection of the People of this Country previous to their becoming a Nation, for the signal and manifold mercies, and the favorable interpositions of His Providence, which we experienced in the course and conclusion of the late war, for the great degree of tranquility, union, and plenty, which we have since enjoyed, for the peaceable and rational manner, in which we have been enabled to establish constitutions of government for our safety and happiness, and particularly the national one now lately instituted, for the civil and religious liberty with which we are blessed; and the means we have of acquiring and diffusing useful knowledge; and in general for all the great and various favors which He hath been pleased to confer upon us.

And also that we may then unite in most humbly offering our prayers and supplications to the great Lord and Ruler of Nations and beseech Him to pardon our national and other transgressions, to enable us all, whether in public or private stations, to perform our several and relative duties properly and punctually, to render our national government a blessing to all the people, by constantly being a Government of wise, just, and constitutional laws, discreetly and faithfully executed and obeyed, to protect and guide all Sovereigns and Nations (especially such as have shown kindness unto us) and to bless them with good government, peace, and concord. To promote the knowledge and practice of true religion and virtue, and the increase of science among them and us, and generally to grant unto all Mankind such a degree of temporal prosperity as He alone knows to be best.

Given under my hand at the City of New York the third day of October in the year of our Lord 1789.

Go: Washington

GEORGE WASHINGTON, LETTER TO THE HEBREWS AT NEWPORT (1790)

Gentlemen:

While I received with much satisfaction your address replete with expressions of esteem, I rejoice in the opportunity of assuring you that I shall always retain grateful remembrance of the cordial welcome I experienced on my visit to Newport from all classes of citizens.

The reflection on the days of difficulty and danger which are past is rendered the more sweet from a consciousness that they are succeeded by days of uncommon prosperity and security.

If we have wisdom to make the best use of the advantages with which we are now favored, we cannot fail, under the just administration of a good government, to become a great and happy people.

The citizens of the United States of America have a right to applaud themselves for having given to mankind examples of an enlarged and liberal policy—a policy worthy of imitation. All possess alike liberty of conscience and immunities of citizenship.

It is now no more that toleration is spoken of as if it were the indulgence of one class of people that another enjoyed the exercise of their inherent natural rights, for, happily, the Government of the United States, which gives to bigotry no sanction, to persecution no assistance, requires only that they who live under its protection should demean themselves as good citizens in giving it on all occasions their effectual support.

It would be inconsistent with the frankness of my character not to avow that I am pleased with your favorable opinion of my administration and fervent wishes for my felicity.

May the children of the stock of Abraham who dwell in this land continue to merit and enjoy the good will of the other inhabitants—while every one shall sit in safety under his own vine and fig tree and there shall be none to make him afraid.

May the father of all mercies scatter light, and not darkness, upon our paths, and make us all in our several vocations useful here, and in His own due time and way everlastingly happy.

✥ ✥ ✥

GEORGE WASHINGTON, FAREWELL ADDRESS (1796)

Friends, and Fellow-Citizens:

The period for a new election of a Citizen, to Administer the Executive government of the United States being not far distant, and the time actually arrived, when your thoughts must be employed in designating the person, who is to be clothed with that important trust, it appears to me proper, especially as it may conduce to a more distinct expression of the public voice, that I should now apprise you of the resolution I have formed, to decline being considered among the number of those, out of whom a choice is to be made.

I beg you, at the same time, to do me the justice to be assured that this resolution has not been taken, without a strict regard to all the considerations appertaining to the relation, which binds a dutiful citizen to his country, and that, in withdrawing the tender of service which silence in my situation might imply, I am influenced by no diminution of zeal for your future interest, no deficiency of grateful respect for your past kindness; but am supported by a full conviction that the step is compatible with both.

The acceptance of, and continuance hitherto in, the office to which your Suffrages have twice called me, have been a uniform sacrifice of inclination to the opinion of duty, and to a deference for what appeared to be your desire. I constantly hoped, that it would have been much earlier in my power, consistently with motives, which I was not at liberty to disregard, to return to that retirement, from which I had been reluctantly drawn. The strength of my inclination to do this, previous to the last Election, had even led to the preparation of an address to declare it to you; but mature reflection on the then perplexed and critical posture of our Affairs with foreign Nations, and the unanimous advice of persons entitled to my confidence, impelled me to abandon the idea.

I rejoice, that the state of your concerns, external as well as internal, no longer renders the pursuit of inclination incompatible with the sentiment of duty or propriety; and am persuaded, whatever partiality may be retained for my services, that in the present circumstances of our country, you will not disapprove my determination to retire.

The impressions, with which I first undertook the arduous trust, were explained on the proper occasion. In the discharge of this trust, I will only say, that I have, with good intentions, contributed towards the Organization and Administration of the government, the best exertions of which a very fallible judgment was capable. Not unconscious, in the outset, of the inferiority of my qualifications, experience in my own eyes, perhaps still more in the eyes of others, has strengthened the motives to diffidence of myself; and every day the increasing weight of years admonishes me more and more, that the shade of retirement is as necessary to me as it will be welcome. Satisfied that if any circumstances have given peculiar value to my services, they were temporary, I have the consolation to believe, that while choice and prudence invite me to quit the political scene, patriotism does not forbid it.

In looking forward to the moment, which is intended to terminate the career of my public life, my feelings do not permit me to suspend the deep acknowledgment of that debt of gratitude which I owe to my beloved country, for the many honors it has conferred upon me; still more for the steadfast confidence with which it has supported me; and for the opportunities I have thence enjoyed of manifesting my inviolable attachment, by services faithful and persevering, though in usefulness unequal to my zeal. If benefits have resulted to our country from these services, let it always be remembered to your praise, and as an instructive example in our annals, that, under circumstances in which the Passions agitated in every direction were liable to mislead, amidst appearances sometimes dubious, vicissitudes of fortune often discouraging, in situations in which not infrequently want of Success has countenanced the spirit of criticism, the constancy of your support was the essential prop of the efforts, and a guarantee of the plans by which they were effected. Profoundly penetrated with this idea, I shall carry it with me to my grave as a strong incitement to unceasing vows that Heaven may continue to you the choicest tokens of its beneficence; that your Union and brotherly affection may be perpetual; that the free constitution, which is the work of your hands, may be sacredly maintained; that its Administration in every department may be stamped with wisdom and Virtue; that, in fine, the happiness of the people of these States, under the auspices of liberty, may be made complete by so careful a preservation and so prudent a use of this blessing as will acquire to them the glory of recommending it to the applause, the affection, and adoption of every nation which is yet a stranger to it.

Here, perhaps, I ought to stop. But a solicitude for your welfare which cannot end but with my life, and the apprehension of danger, natural to that solicitude, urge me on an occasion like the present, to offer to your solemn contemplation, and to recommend to your frequent review, some sentiments which are the result of much reflection, of no inconsiderable observation, and which appear to me all important to the permanency of your felicity as a People. These will be offered to you with the more freedom, as you can only see in them the disinterested warnings of a parting friend, who can possibly have no personal motive to bias his counsel. Nor can I forget, as an encouragement to it, your indulgent reception of my sentiments on a former and not dissimilar occasion.

Interwoven as is the love of liberty with every ligament of your hearts, no recommendation of mine is necessary to fortify or confirm the attachment.

The Unity of Government which constitutes you one people is also now dear to you. It is justly so; for it is a main Pillar in the Edifice of your real independence, the support of your tranquility at home; your peace abroad; of your safety; of your prosperity; of that very Liberty which you so highly prize. But as it is easy to foresee, that from different causes and from different quarters, much pains will be taken, many artifices employed, to weaken in your minds the conviction of this truth; as this is the point in your political fortress against which the batteries of internal and external enemies will be most constantly and actively (though often covertly and insidiously) directed, it is of infinite moment that you should properly estimate the immense value of your national Union to your collective and individual happiness; that you should cherish a cordial, habitual and immoveable attachment to it; accustoming yourselves to think and speak of it as of the Palladium of your political safety and prosperity; watching for its preservation with jealous anxiety; discountenancing whatever may suggest even a suspicion that it can in any event be abandoned, and indignantly frowning upon the first dawning of every attempt to alienate any portion of our Country from the rest, or to enfeeble the sacred ties which now link together the various parts.

For this you have every inducement of sympathy and interest. Citizens by birth or choice, of a common country, that country has a right to concentrate your affections. The name of AMERICAN, which belongs to you, in your national capacity, must always exalt the just pride of Patriotism, more than any appellation derived from local discriminations. With slight shades of difference, you have the same Religion, Manners, Habits, and political Principles. You have in a common cause fought and triumphed together. The independence and liberty you possess are the work of joint councils, and joint efforts; of common dangers, sufferings and successes.

But these considerations, however powerfully they address themselves to your sensibility are greatly outweighed by those which apply more immediately to your Interest. Here every portion of our country finds the most commanding motives for carefully guarding and preserving the Union of the whole.

The *North*, in an unrestrained intercourse with the *South*, protected by the equal Laws of a common government, finds in the productions of the latter, great additional resources of Maritime and commercial enterprise and precious materials of manufacturing industry. The *South*, in the same Intercourse, benefiting by the same Agency of the *North*, sees its agriculture grow and its commerce expand. Turning partly into its own channels the seamen of the *North*, it finds its particular navigation invigorated; and while it contributes, in different ways, to nourish and increase the general mass of the National navigation, it looks forward to the protection of a Maritime strength, to which itself is unequally adapted. The *East*, in a like Intercourse with the *West*, already finds, and in the progressive improvement of interior communications, by land and water, will more and more find a valuable vent for the commodities which it brings from abroad, or manufactures at home. The *West* derives from the *East* supplies requisite to its growth and comfort, and what is perhaps of still greater consequence, it must of necessity owe the *secure* enjoyment of indispensable *outlets* for its own productions to the weight, influence, and the future Maritime strength of the Atlantic side of the Union, directed by an indissoluble community of Interest as *one Nation*. Any other tenure by which the *West* can hold this essential advantage, whether derived from its own separate strength, or from an apostate and unnatural connection with any foreign Power, must be intrinsically precarious.

While then every part of our country thus feels an immediate and particular Interest in Union, all the parts combined cannot fail to find in the united mass of means and efforts greater strength, greater resource, proportionally greater security from external danger, a less frequent interruption of their Peace by foreign Nations; and what is of inestimable value, they must derive from Union an exemption from those broils and Wars between themselves, which so frequently afflict neighboring countries, not tied together by the same government; which their own rivalships alone would be sufficient to produce, but which opposite foreign alliances, attachments, and intrigues would stimulate and embitter. Hence, likewise, they will avoid the necessity of those overgrown Military establishments, which under any form of Government are inauspicious to liberty, and which are to be regarded as particularly hostile to Republican Liberty: In this sense it is, that your Union ought to be considered as a main prop of your liberty, and that the love of the one ought to endear to you the preservation of the other.

These considerations speak a persuasive language to every reflecting and virtuous mind, and exhibit the continuance of the UNION as a primary object of Patriotic desire. Is there a doubt, whether a common government can embrace so large a sphere? Let experience solve it. To listen to mere speculation in such a case were criminal. We are authorized to hope that a proper organization of the whole, with the auxiliary agency of governments for the respective Subdivisions, will afford a happy issue to the experiment. 'Tis well worth a fair and full experiment. With such powerful and obvious motives to Union, affecting all parts of our country, while experience shall not have demonstrated its impracticability, there will always be reason, to distrust the patriotism of those, who in any quarter may endeavor to weaken its bands.

In contemplating the causes which may disturb our Union, it occurs as matter of serious concern, that any ground should have been furnished for characterizing parties by *Geographical* discriminations: *Northern* and *Southern*; *Atlantic* and *Western*; whence designing men may endeavor to excite a belief that there is a real difference of local interests and views. One of the expedients of Party to acquire influence, within particular districts, is to misrepresent the opinions and aims of other Districts. You cannot shield yourselves too much against the jealousies and heart burnings which spring from these misrepresentations. They tend to render Alien to each other those who ought to be bound together by fraternal affection. The Inhabitants of our Western country have lately had a useful lesson on this head. They have seen, in the Negotiation by the Executive, and in the unanimous ratification by the Senate, of the Treaty with Spain, and in the universal satisfaction at that event, throughout the United States, a decisive proof how unfounded were the suspicions propagated among them of a policy in the General Government and in the Atlantic States unfriendly to their Interests in regard to the Mississippi. They have been witnesses to the formation of two Treaties, that with Great Britain and that with Spain, which secure to them every thing they could desire, in respect to our

Foreign relations, towards confirming their prosperity. Will it not be their wisdom to rely for the preservation of these advantages on the Union by which they were procured? Will they not henceforth be deaf to those advisers, if such there are, who would sever them from their Brethren and connect them with Aliens?

To the efficacy and permanency of Your Union, a Government for the whole is indispensable. No Alliances however strict between the parts can be an adequate substitute. They must inevitably experience the infractions and interruptions which all Alliances in all times have experienced. Sensible of this momentous truth, you have improved upon your first essay, by the adoption of a Constitution of Government, better calculated than your former for an intimate Union, and for the efficacious management of your common concerns. This government, the offspring of our own choice uninfluenced and unawed, adopted upon full investigation and mature deliberation, completely free in its principles, in the distribution of its powers, uniting security with energy, and containing within itself a provision for its own amendment, has a just claim to your confidence and your support. Respect for its authority, compliance with its Laws, acquiescence in its measures, are duties enjoined by the fundamental maxims of true Liberty. The basis of our political systems is the right of the people to make and to alter their Constitutions of Government. But the constitution which at any time exists, 'till changed by an explicit and authentic act of the whole People, is sacredly obligatory upon all. The very idea of the power and the right of the People to establish Government presupposes the duty of every Individual to obey the established Government.

All obstructions to the execution of the Laws, all combinations and Associations, under whatever plausible character, with the real design to direct, control counteract, or awe the regular deliberation and action of the Constituted authorities, are destructive of this fundamental principle and of fatal tendency. They serve to organize faction, to give it an artificial and extraordinary force; to put in the place of the delegated will of the Nation, the will of a party; often a small but artful and enterprising minority of the Community; and, according to the alternate triumphs of different parties, to make the public administration the Mirror of the ill concerted and incongruous projects of faction, rather than the organ of consistent and wholesome plans digested by common councils and modified by mutual interests. However combinations or Associations of the above description may now and then answer popular ends, they are likely in the course of time and things, to become potent engines, by which cunning, ambitious and unprincipled men will be enabled to subvert the Power of the People, and to usurp for themselves the reins of Government; destroying afterwards the very engines which have lifted them to unjust dominion.

Towards the preservation of your Government and the permanency of your present happy state, it is requisite, not only that you steadily discountenance irregular oppositions to its acknowledged authority, but also that you resist with care the spirit of innovation upon its principles, however specious the pretexts. One method of assault may be to effect, in the forms of the Constitution, alterations which will impair the energy of the system, and thus to undermine what cannot be directly overthrown. In all the changes to which you may be invited, remember that time and habit are at least as necessary to fix the true character of Governments, as of other human institutions; that experience is the surest standard by which to test the real tendency of the existing Constitution of a country; that facility in changes upon the credit of mere hypotheses and opinion exposes to perpetual change, from the endless variety of hypotheses and opinion: and remember, especially, that for the efficient management of your common interests, in a country so extensive as ours, a Government of as much vigor as is consistent with the perfect security of Liberty is indispensable. Liberty itself will find in such a Government, with powers properly distributed and adjusted, its surest Guardian. It is indeed little else than a name, where the Government is too feeble to withstand the enterprises of faction, to confine each member of the Society within the limits prescribed by the laws and to maintain all in the secure and tranquil enjoyment of the rights of person and property.

I have already intimated to you the danger of Parties in the State, with particular reference to the founding of them on Geographical discriminations. Let me now take a more comprehensive view, and warn you in the most solemn manner against the baneful effects of the Spirit of Party, generally.

This spirit, unfortunately, is inseparable from our nature, having its root in the strongest passions of the human Mind. It exists under different shapes in all Governments, more or less stifled, controlled, or repressed; but, in those of the popular form it is seen in its greatest rankness and is truly their worst enemy.

The alternate domination of one faction over another, sharpened by the spirit of revenge natural to party dissention, which in different ages and countries has perpetrated the most horrid enormities, is itself a frightful despotism. But this leads at length to a more formal and permanent despotism. The disorders and miseries, which result, gradually incline the minds of men to seek security and repose in the absolute power of an Individual: and sooner or later the chief of some prevailing faction more able or more fortunate than his competitors, turns this disposition to the purposes of his own elevation, on the ruins of Public Liberty.

Without looking forward to an extremity of this kind (which nevertheless ought not to be entirely out of sight) the common and continual mischiefs of the spirit of Party are sufficient to make it the interest and duty of a wise People to discourage and restrain it.

It serves always to distract the Public Councils and enfeeble the Public administration. It agitates the Community with ill-founded jealousies and false alarms, kindles the animosity of one part against another; foments occasionally riot and insurrection. It opens the door to foreign influence and corruption, which find a facilitated access to the government itself through the channels of party passions. Thus the policy and the will of one country, are subjected to the policy and will of another.

There is an opinion that parties in free countries are useful checks upon the Administration of the Government and serve to keep alive the spirit of Liberty. This within certain limits is probably true, and in Governments of a Monarchical cast Patriotism may look with indulgence, if not with favor, upon the spirit of party. But in those of the popular character, in Governments purely elective, it is a spirit not to be encouraged.

From their natural tendency, it is certain there will always be enough of that spirit for every salutary purpose. And there being constant danger of excess, the effort ought to be, by force of public opinion, to mitigate and assuage it. A fire not to be quenched; it demands a uniform vigilance to prevent its bursting into a flame, lest instead of warming it should consume.

It is important, likewise, that the habits of thinking in a free Country should inspire caution in those entrusted with its administration, to confine themselves within their respective Constitutional spheres; avoiding in the exercise of the Powers of one department to encroach upon another. The spirit of encroachment tends to consolidate the powers of all the departments in one, and thus to create whatever the form of government, a real despotism. A just estimate of that love of power, and proneness to abuse it, which predominates in the human heart is sufficient to satisfy us of the truth of this position. The necessity of reciprocal checks in the exercise of political power; by dividing and distributing it into different depositories, and constituting each the Guardian of the Public Weal against invasions by the others, has been evinced by experiments ancient and modern; some of them in our country and under our own eyes. To preserve them must be as necessary as to institute them. If in the opinion of the People the distribution or modification of the Constitutional powers be in any particular wrong, let it be corrected by an amendment in the way which the Constitution designates. But let there be no change by usurpation; for though this, in one instance, may be the instrument of good, it is the customary weapon by which free governments are destroyed. The precedent must always greatly overbalance in permanent evil any partial or transient benefit which the use can at any time yield.

Of all the dispositions and habits which lead to political prosperity, Religion and morality are indispensable supports. In vain would that man claim the tribute of Patriotism who should labor to subvert these great Pillars of human happiness, these firmest props of the duties of Men and citizens. The mere Politician, equally with the pious man ought to respect and to cherish them. A volume could not trace all their connections with private and public felicity. Let it simply be asked where is the security for property, for reputation, for life, if the sense of religious obligation *desert* the oaths, which are the instruments of investigation in Courts of Justice? And let us with caution indulge the supposition that morality can be maintained without religion. Whatever may be conceded to the influence of refined education on minds of peculiar structure, reason and experience both forbid us to expect that National morality can prevail in exclusion of religious principle.

'Tis substantially true, that virtue or morality is a necessary spring of popular government. The rule indeed extends with more or less force to every species of free Government. Who that is a sincere friend to it, can look with indifference upon attempts to shake the foundation of the fabric.

Promote then as an object of primary importance, Institutions for the general diffusion of knowledge. In proportion as the structure of a government gives force to public opinion, it is essential that public opinion should be enlightened.

As a very important source of strength and security, cherish public credit. One method of preserving it is to use it as sparingly as possible: avoiding occasions of expense by cultivating peace, but remembering also that timely disbursements to prepare for danger frequently prevent much greater disbursements to repel it; avoiding likewise the accumulation of debt, not only by shunning occasions of expense, but by vigorous exertions in time of Peace to discharge the Debts which unavoidable wars may have occasioned, not ungenerously throwing upon posterity the burthen which we ourselves ought to bear. The execution of these maxims belongs to your Representatives; but it is necessary that public opinion should cooperate. To facilitate to them the performance of their duty it is essential that you should practically bear in mind, that towards the payment of debts there must be Revenue; that to have Revenue there must be taxes; that no taxes can be devised which are not more or less inconvenient and unpleasant; that the intrinsic embarrassment inseparable from the selection of the proper objects (which is always a choice of difficulties) ought to be a decisive motive for a candid construction of the Conduct of the Government in making it, and for a spirit of acquiescence in the measures for obtaining Revenue which the public exigencies may at any time dictate.

Observe good faith and justice towards all Nations. Cultivate peace and harmony with all. Religion and morality enjoin this conduct; and can it be that good policy does not equally enjoin it? It will be worthy of a free, enlightened, and, at no distant period, a great Nation, to give to mankind the magnanimous and too novel example of a People always guided by an exalted justice and benevolence. Who can doubt that in the course of time and things the fruits of such a plan would richly repay any temporary advantages which might be lost by a steady adherence to it? Can it be, that Providence has not connected the permanent felicity of a Nation with its virtue? The experiment, at least, is recommended by every sentiment which ennobles human Nature. Alas! is it rendered impossible by its vices?

In the execution of such a plan nothing is more essential than that permanent, inveterate antipathies against particular Nations and passionate attachments for others should be excluded; and that in place of them just and amicable feelings towards all should be cultivated. The Nation, which indulges towards another an habitual hatred, or an habitual fondness, is in some degree a slave. It is a slave to its animosity or to its affection, either of which is sufficient to lead it astray from its duty and its interest. Antipathy in one Nation against another, disposes each more readily to offer insult and injury, to lay hold of slight causes of umbrage, and to be haughty and intractable, when accidental or trifling occasions of dispute occur. Hence frequent collisions, obstinate envenomed, and bloody contests. The Nation, prompted by ill will and resentment sometimes impels to War the Government, contrary to the best calculations of policy. The government sometimes participates in the national propensity, and adopts through passion what reason would reject; at other times, it makes the animosity of the Nation subservient to projects of hostility instigated by pride, ambition and other sinister and pernicious motives. The peace often, sometimes perhaps the Liberty, of Nations has been the victim.

So, likewise, a passionate attachment of one Nation for another produces a variety of evils. Sympathy for the favorite nation, facilitating the illusion of an imaginary common interest, in cases where no real common interest exists, and infusing into one the enmities of the other, betrays the former into a participation in the quarrels and Wars of the latter without adequate inducement or justification: It leads also to concessions to the favorite Nation of privileges denied to others, which is apt doubly to injure the Nation making the concessions; by unnecessarily parting with what ought to have been retained; and by exciting jealousy, ill will, and a disposition to retaliate, in the parties from whom equal privileges are withheld: And it gives to ambitious, corrupted, or deluded citizens (who devote themselves to the favorite Nation) facility to betray, or sacrifice the interests of their own country, without odium, sometimes even with popularity; gilding with the appearances of a virtuous sense of obligation a commendable deference for public opinion, or a laudable zeal for public good, the base or foolish compliances of ambition corruption or infatuation.

As avenues to foreign influence in innumerable ways, such attachments are particularly alarming to the truly enlightened and independent Patriot. How many opportunities do they afford to tamper with domestic factions, to practice the arts of seduction, to mislead public opinion, to influence or awe the public Councils! Such an attachment of a small or weak, towards a great and powerful Nation, dooms the former to be the satellite of the latter.

Against the insidious wiles of foreign influence (I conjure you to believe me fellow citizens) the jealousy of a free people ought to be *constantly* awake; since history and experience prove that foreign influence is one of the most baneful foes of Republican Government. But that jealousy to be useful must be impartial; else it becomes the instrument of the very influence to be avoided, instead of a defense against it. Excessive partiality for one foreign nation and excessive dislike of another, cause those whom they actuate to see danger only on one side, and serve to veil and even second the arts of influence on the other. Real Patriots, who may resist the intrigues of the favorite, are liable to become suspected and odious; while its tools and dupes usurp the applause and confidence of the people, to surrender their interests.

The Great rule of conduct for us, in regard to foreign Nations is in extending our commercial relations to have with them as little *political* connection as possible. So far as we have already formed engagements let them be fulfilled, with perfect good faith. Here let us stop.

Europe has a set of primary interests, which to us have none, or a very remote relation. Hence she must be engaged in frequent controversies, the causes of which are essentially foreign to our concerns. Hence therefore it must be unwise in us to implicate ourselves, by artificial ties, in the ordinary vicissitudes of her politics, or the ordinary combinations and collisions of her friendships, or enmities:

Our detached and distant situation invites and enables us to pursue a different course. If we remain one People, under an efficient government, the period is not far off, when we may defy material injury from external annoyance; when we may take such an attitude as will cause the neutrality we may at any time resolve upon to be scrupulously respected; when belligerent nations, under the impossibility of making acquisitions upon us, will not lightly hazard the giving us provocation; when we may choose peace or war, as our interest guided by justice shall Counsel.

Why forego the advantages of so peculiar a situation? Why quit our own to stand upon foreign ground? Why, by interweaving our destiny with that of any part of Europe, entangle our peace and prosperity in the toils of European Ambition, Rivalship, Interest, Humor or Caprice?

'Tis our true policy to steer clear of permanent Alliances, with any portion of the foreign world. So far, I mean, as we are now at liberty to do it, for let me not be understood as capable of patronizing infidelity to existing engagements (I hold the maxim no less applicable to public than to private affairs, that honesty is always the best policy). I repeat it therefore, let those engagements be observed in their genuine sense. But in my opinion, it is unnecessary and would be unwise to extend them.

Taking care always to keep ourselves, by suitable establishments, on a respectably defensive posture, we may safely trust to temporary alliances for extraordinary emergencies.

Harmony, liberal intercourse with all Nations, are recommended by policy, humanity, and interest. But even our Commercial policy should hold an equal and impartial hand: neither seeking nor granting exclusive favors or preferences; consulting the natural course of things; diffusing and diversifying by gentle means the streams of Commerce, but forcing nothing; establishing with Powers so disposed; in order to give trade a stable course, to define the rights of our Merchants, and to enable the Government to support them; conventional rules of intercourse, the best that present circumstances and mutual opinion will permit, but temporary, and liable to be from time to time abandoned or varied, as experience and circumstances shall dictate; constantly keeping in view, that 'tis folly in one Nation to look for disinterested favors from another; that it must pay with a portion of its Independence for whatever it may accept under that character; that by such acceptance, it may place itself in the condition of having given equivalents for nominal favors and yet of being reproached with ingratitude for not giving more. There can be no greater error than to expect or calculate upon real favors from Nation to Nation. 'Tis an illusion which experience must cure, which a just pride ought to discard.

In offering to you, my Countrymen these counsels of an old and affectionate friend, I dare not hope they will make the strong and lasting impression, I could wish; that they will control the usual current of the passions, or prevent our Nation from running the course which has hitherto marked the Destiny of Nations: But if I may even flatter myself, that they may be productive of some partial benefit, some occasional good; that they may now and then recur to moderate the fury of party spirit, to warn against the mischiefs of foreign Intrigue, to guard against the Impostures of pretended patriotism; this hope will be a full recompense for the solicitude for your welfare, by which they have been dictated.

How far in the discharge of my Official duties, I have been guided by the principles which have been delineated, the public Records and other evidences of my conduct must Witness to You and to the world. To myself, the assurance of my own conscience is, that I have at least believed myself to be guided by them.

In relation to the still subsisting War in Europe, my Proclamation of the 22d. of April 1793 is the index to my Plan. Sanctioned by your approving voice and by that of Your Representatives in both Houses of Congress, the spirit of that measure has continually governed me; uninfluenced by any attempts to deter or divert me from it.

After deliberate examination with the aid of the best lights I could obtain I was well satisfied that our Country, under all the circumstances of the case, had a right to take, and was bound in duty and interest, to take a Neutral position. Having taken it, I determined, as far as should depend upon me, to maintain it, with moderation, perseverance and firmness.

The considerations, which respect the right to hold this conduct, it is not necessary on this occasion to detail. I will only observe, that according to my understanding of the matter, that right, so far from being denied by any of the Belligerent Powers has been virtually admitted by all.

The duty of holding a Neutral conduct may be inferred, without any thing more, from the obligation which justice and humanity impose on every nation, in cases in which it is free to act, to maintain inviolate the relations of Peace and amity toward other Nations.

The inducements of interest for observing that conduct will best be referred to your own reflections and experience. With me, a predominant motive has been to endeavor to gain time to our country to settle and mature its yet recent institutions, and to progress without interruption, to that degree of strength and consistency, which is necessary to give it, humanly speaking, the command of its own fortunes.

Though in reviewing the incidents of my Administration, I am unconscious of intentional error, I am nevertheless too sensible of my defects not to think it probable that I may have committed many errors. Whatever they may be I fervently beseech the Almighty to avert or mitigate the evils to which they may tend. I shall also carry with me the hope that my Country will never cease to view them with indulgence; and that after forty-five years of my life dedicated to its Service, with an upright zeal, the faults of incompetent abilities will be consigned to oblivion, as myself must soon be to the Mansions of rest.

Relying on its kindness in this as in other things, and actuated by that fervent love toward it, which is so natural to a Man, who views in it the native soil of himself and his progenitors for several Generations; I anticipate with pleasing expectation that retreat, in which I promise myself to realize, without alloy, the sweet enjoyment of partaking, in the midst of my fellow Citizens, the benign influence of good Laws under a free Government, the ever favorite object of my heart, and the happy reward, as I trust, of our mutual cares, labors, and dangers.

✤ ✤ ✤

James Madison, A Memorial and Remonstrance (1785)

We, the subscribers, citizens of the said Commonwealth, having taken into serious consideration, a Bill printed by order of the last Session of General Assembly, entitled "A Bill establishing a provision for Teachers of the Christian Religion," and conceiving that the same, if finally armed with the sanctions of a law, will be a dangerous abuse of power, are bound as faithful members of a free State, to remonstrate against it, and to declare the reasons by which we are determined. We remonstrate against the said Bill,

1. Because we hold it for a fundamental and undeniable truth, "that Religion or the duty which we owe to our Creator and the Manner of discharging it, can be directed only by reason and conviction, not by force or violence."* The Religion then of every man must be left to the conviction and conscience of every man; and it is the right of every man to exercise it as these may dictate. This right is in its nature an unalienable right. It is unalienable; because the opinions of men, depending only on the evidence contemplated by their own minds, cannot follow the dictates

---

*Virginia Declaration of Rights, Article 16 (citation in the original).

of other men: It is unalienable also, because what is here a right towards men, is a duty towards the Creator. It is the duty of every man to render to the Creator such homage, and such only, as he believes to be acceptable to him. This duty is precedent both in order of time and degree of obligation, to the claims of Civil Society. Before any man can be considered as a member of Civil Society, he must be considered as a subject of the Governor of the Universe: And if a member of Civil Society, who enters into any subordinate Association, must always do it with a reservation of his duty to the general authority; much more must every man who becomes a member of any particular Civil Society, do it with a saving of his allegiance to the Universal Sovereign. We maintain therefore that in matters of Religion, no man's right is abridged by the institution of Civil Society, and that Religion is wholly exempt from its cognizance. True it is, that no other rule exists, by which any question which may divide a Society, can be ultimately determine, but the will of the majority; but it is also true, that the majority may trespass on the rights of the minority.

2. Because if religion be exempt from the authority of the Society at large, still less can it be subject to that of the Legislative Body. The latter are but the creatures and vicegerents of the former. Their jurisdiction is both derivative and limited: it is limited with regard to the co-ordinate departments, more necessarily is it limited with regard to the constituents. The preservation of a free government requires not merely, that the metes and bounds which separate each department of power may be invariably maintained; but more especially, that neither of them be suffered to overleap the great Barrier which defends the rights of the people. The Rulers who are guilty of such an encroachment, exceed the commission from which they derive their authority, and are Tyrants. The People who submit to it are governed by laws made neither by themselves, nor by an authority derived from them, and are slaves.

3. Because, it is proper to take alarm at the first experiment on our liberties. We hold this prudent jealousy to be the first duty of citizens, and one of [the] noblest characteristics of the late Revolution. The freemen of America did not wait till usurped power had strengthened itself by exercise, and entangled the question in precedents. They saw all the

consequences in principle, and they avoided the consequences by denying the principle. We revere this lesson too much, soon to forget it. Who does not see that the same authority which can establish Christianity, in exclusion of all other Religions, may establish with the same ease any particular sect of Christians, in exclusion of all other Sects? That the same authority which can force a citizen to contribute three pence only of his property for the support of any one establishment, may force him to conform to any other establishment in all cases whatsoever?

4. Because, the bill violates that equality which ought to be the basis of every law, and which is more indispensable, in proportion as the validity or expediency of any law is more liable to be impeached. If "all men are by nature equally free and independent,"* all men are to be considered as entering into Society on equal conditions; as relinquishing no more, and therefore retaining no less, one than another, of their natural rights. Above all are they to be considered as retaining an *"equal* title to the free exercise of Religion according to the dictates of conscience."** Whilst we assert for ourselves a freedom to embrace, to profess and to observe the Religion which we believe to be of divine origin, we cannot deny an equal freedom to those whose minds have not yet yielded to the evidence which has convinced us. If this freedom be abused, it is an offence against God, not against man: To God, therefore, not to men, must an account of it be rendered. As the Bill violates equality by subjecting some to peculiar burdens; so it violates the same principle, by granting to others peculiar exemptions. Are the Quakers and Mennonites the only sects who think a compulsive support of their religions unnecessary and unwarrantable? Can their piety alone be entrusted with the care of public worship? Ought their Religions to be endowed above all others, with extraordinary privileges, by which proselytes may be enticed from all others? We think too favorably of the justice and good sense of these denominations, to believe that they either covet pre-eminencies over their fellow citizens, or that they will be seduced by them, from the common opposi-

---

* Virginia Declaration of Rights, Article 1 (citation in the original).
** Virginia Declaration of Rights, Article 16 (citation in the original).

tion to the measure. Because the bill implies either that the Civil Magistrate is a competent Judge of Religious truth; or that he may employ Religion as an engine of Civil policy. The first is an arrogant pretension falsified by the contradictory opinions of Rulers in all ages, and throughout the world: The second an unhallowed perversion of the means of salvation.

6. Because the establishment proposed by the Bill is not requisite for the support of the Christian Religion. To say that it is, is a contradiction to the Christian Religion itself; for every page of it disavows a dependence on the powers of this world: it is a contradiction to fact; for it is known that this Religion both existed and flourished, not only without the support of human laws, but in spite of every opposition from them; and not only during the period of miraculous aid, but long after it had been left to its own evidence, and the ordinary care of Providence: Nay, it is a contradiction in terms; for a Religion not invented by human policy, must have pre-existed and been supported, before it was established by human policy. It is moreover to weaken in those who profess this Religion a pious confidence in its innate excellence, and the patronage of its Author; and to foster in those who still reject it, a suspicion that its friends are too conscious of its fallacies, to trust it to its own merits.

7. Because experience witnesseth that ecclesiastical establishments, instead of maintaining the purity and efficacy of Religion, have had a contrary operation. During almost fifteen centuries, had the legal establishment of Christianity been on trial. What have been its fruits? More or less in all places, pride and indolence in the Clergy; ignorance and servility in the laity; in both, superstition, bigotry and persecution. Enquire of the Teachers of Christianity for the ages in which it appeared in its greatest luster; those of every sect, point to the ages prior to its incorporation with Civil policy. Propose a restoration of this primitive state in which its Teachers depended on the voluntary rewards of their flocks; many of them predict its downfall. On which side ought their testimony to have greatest weight, when for or when against their interest?

8. Because the establishment in question is not necessary for the support of Civil Government. If it be urged as necessary for the support of Civil Government only as it is a means of supporting Religion, and it be

not necessary for the latter purpose, it cannot be necessary for the former. If Religion be not within [the] cognizance of Civil Government, how can its legal establishment be said to be necessary to civil Government? What influence in fact have ecclesiastical establishments had on Civil Society? In some instances they have been seen to erect a spiritual tyranny on the ruins of Civil authority; in many instances they have been seen upholding the thrones of political tyranny; in no instance have they been seen the guardians of the liberties of the people. Rulers who wished to subvert the public liberty, may have found an established clergy convenient auxiliaries. A just government, instituted to secure & perpetuate it, needs them not. Such a government will be best supported by protecting every citizen in the enjoyment of his Religion with the same equal hand which protects his person and his property; by neither invading the equal rights of any Sect, nor suffering any Sect to invade those of another.

9. Because the proposed establishment is a departure from that generous policy, which, offering an asylum to the persecuted and oppressed of every Nation and Religion, promised a luster to our country, and an accession to the number of its citizens. What a melancholy mark is the Bill of sudden degeneracy? Instead of holding forth an asylum to the persecuted, it is itself a signal of persecution. It degrades from the equal rank of Citizens all those whose opinions in Religion do not bend to those of Legislative authority. Distant as it may be, in its present form, from the Inquisition it differs from it only in degree. The one is the first step, the other the last in the career of intolerance. The magnanimous sufferer under this cruel scourge in foreign Regions, must view the Bill as a Beacon on our Coast, warning him to seek some other haven, where liberty and philanthropy in their due extent may offer a more certain repose from his troubles.

10. Because, it will have a like tendency to banish our Citizens. The allurements presented by other situations are every day thinning their number. To superadd a fresh motive to emigration, by revoking the liberty which they now enjoy, would be the same species of folly which has dishonored and depopulated flourishing kingdoms.

11. Because, it will destroy that moderation and harmony which the forbearance of our laws to intermeddle with Religion, has produced

amongst its several sects. Torrents of blood have been split in the old world, by vain attempts of the secular arm to extinguish Religious discord, by proscribing all difference in Religious opinions. Time has at length revealed the true remedy. Every relaxation of narrow and rigorous policy, wherever it has been tried, has been found to assuage the disease. The American Theatre has exhibited proofs, that equal and complete liberty, if it does not wholly eradicate it, sufficiently destroys its malignant influence on the health and prosperity of the State. If with the salutary effects of this system under our own eyes, we begin to contract the bonds of Religious freedom, we know no name that will too severely reproach our folly. At least let warning be taken at the first fruits of the threatened innovation. The very appearance of the Bill has transformed that "Christian forbearance,"* love and charity," which of the late mutually prevailed, into animosities and jealousies, which may not soon be appeased. What mischiefs may not be dreaded should this enemy to the public quiet be armed with the force of the law?

12. Because, the policy of the bill is adverse to the diffusion of the light of Christianity. The first wish of those who enjoy this precious gift, ought to be that it may be imparted to the whole race of mankind. Compare the number of those who have as yet received it with the number still remaining under the dominion of false Religions; and how small is the former! Does the policy of the Bill tend to lessen the disproportion? No; it at once discourages those who are strangers to the light of [revelation] from coming into the Religion of it; and countenances, by example the nations who continue in darkness, in shutting out those who might convey it to them. Instead of leveling as far as possible, every obstacle to the victorious progress of truth, the Bill with an ignoble and unchristian timidity would circumscribe it, with a wall of defense, against the encroachments of error.

13. Because attempts to enforce by legal sanctions, acts obnoxious to so great a proportion of Citizens, tend to enervate the laws in general, and to slacken the bands of Society. If it be difficult to execute any law which

---

*Virginia Declaration of Rights, Article 16 (citation is in the original).

is not generally deemed necessary or salutary, what must be the case where it is deemed invalid and dangerous? and what may be the effect of so striking an example of impotency in the Government, on its general authority.

14. Because a measure of such singular magnitude and delicacy ought not to be imposed, without the clearest evidence that is called for by a majority of citizens: and no satisfactory method is yet proposed by which the voice of the majority in this case may be determined, or its influence secured. "The people of the respective countries are indeed requested to signify their opinion respecting the adoption of the Bill to the next Session of Assembly." But the representation must be made equal, before the voice either of the Representatives or of the Counties, will be that of the people. Our hope is that neither of the former will, after due consideration, espouse the dangerous principle of the Bill. Should the event disappoint us, it will still leave us in full confidence, that a fair appeal to the latter will reverse the sentence against our liberties.

15. Because, finally, "the equal right of every citizen to the free exercise of his Religion according to the dictates of conscience" is held by the same tenure with all our other rights. If we recur to its origin, it is equally the gift of nature; if we weigh its importance, it cannot be less dear to us; if we consult the Declaration of those rights which pertain to the good people of Virginia, as the "basis and foundation of Government,"* it is enumerated with equal solemnity, or rather studied emphasis. Either then, we must say, that the will of the Legislature is the only measure of their authority; and that in the plentitude of this authority, they may sweep away all our fundamental rights; or, that they are bound to leave this particular right untouched and sacred: Either we must say, that they may control the freedom of the press, may abolish the trial by jury, may swallow up the Executive and Judiciary Powers of the State; nay that they may despoil us of our very right of suffrage, and erect themselves into an independent and hereditary assembly: or we must say, that they have no authority to enact into law the Bill under consideration. We the subscribers

*Virginia Declaration of Rights (citation is in the original).

say, that the General Assembly of this Commonwealth have no such authority: And that no effort may be omitted on our part against so dangerous an usurpation, we oppose to it, this remonstrance; earnestly praying, as we are in duty bound, that the Supreme Lawgiver of the Universe, by illuminating those to whom it is addressed, may on the one hand, turn their councils from every act which would affront his holy prerogative, or violate the trust committed to them: and on the other, guide them into every measure which may be worthy of his [blessing, may re]dound to their own praise, and may establish more firmly the liberties, the prosperity, and the Happiness of the Commonwealth.

THOMAS JEFFERSON, VIRGINIA STATUTE FOR RELIGIOUS LIBERTY (1786)

Section I. Well aware that the opinions and belief of men depend not on their own will, but follow involuntarily the evidence proposed to their minds; that Almighty God hath created the mind free, and manifested his supreme will that free it shall remain by making it altogether insusceptible of restraint; that all attempts to influence it by temporal punishments, or burthen, or by civil incapacitations, tend only to beget habits of hypocrisy and meanness, and are a departure from the plan of the holy author of our religion, who being lord both of body and mind, yet chose not to propagate it by coercions on either, as was in his Almighty power to do, but to extend it by its influence on reason alone; that the impious presumption of legislators and rulers, civil as well as ecclesiastical, who, being themselves but fallible and uninspired men, have assumed dominion over the faith of others, setting up their own opinions and modes of thinking as the only true and infallible, and as such endeavoring to impose them on others, hath established and maintained false religions over the greatest part of the world and through all time: That to compel a man to furnish contributions of money for the propagation of opinions which he disbelieves and abhors, is sinful and tyrannical; that event he forcing him to support this or that teachers of his own religious persuasion, is depriving him of the comfortable liberty of giving his contributions to the particular pastor whose morals he would make his pattern, and whose powers he feels most persuasive to righteousness; and is withdrawing from the ministry those temporary rewards, which proceeding from an approbation of their personal conduct, are an additional incitement to earnest and unremitting labors for the instruction of mankind; that our civil rights have no dependence on our religious opinions, any more than our opinions in physics or geometry; that therefore the proscribing any citizen as unworthy the public confidence by laying upon him an incapacity of being called to offices of trust and emolument, unless he profess or renounce this or that religious opinion, is depriving him injuriously of those privileges and advantages to which, in common with his fellow citizens, he has a natural right; that it tends also to corrupt the principles of that very religion it is meant to encourage, by bribing, with a monopoly of worldly honors and emoluments, those who will externally profess and conform to it; that though indeed these are criminal who do not withstand such temptation, yet neither are those innocent who lay the bait in their way; that the opinions of men are not the object of civil government, nor under its jurisdiction; that to suffer the civil magistrate to intrude his powers into the field of opinion and to restrain the profession or propagation of principles on supposition of their ill tendency is a dangerous fallacy, which at once destroys all religious liberty, because he being of course judge of that tendency will make his opinions the rule of judgment, and approve or condemn the sentiments of others only as they shall square with or differ from his own; that it is time enough for the rightful purposes of civil government for its officers to interfere when principles break out into overt acts against peace and good order; and finally, that truth is great and will prevail if left to herself; that she is the proper and sufficient antagonist to error, and has nothing to fear from the conflict unless by human interposition disarmed of her natural weapons, free argument and debate; errors ceasing to be dangerous when it is permitted freely to contradict them.

Sect. II. We the General Assembly of Virginia do enact that no man shall be compelled to frequent or support any religious worship, place, or ministry whatsoever, nor shall be enforced, restrained, molested, or burthened in his body or goods, nor shall otherwise suffer, on account of his religious opinions or belief; but that all men shall be free to profess, and by argument to maintain, their opinions in matters of religion, and that the same shall in no wise diminish, enlarge, or affect their civil capacities.

Sect. III. and though we well know that this Assembly, elected by the people for the ordinary purposes of legislation only, have no power to restrain the acts of succeeding Assemblies, constituted with powers equal to our own, and that therefore to declare this act irrevocable would be of no effect in law; yet we are free to declare, and do declare, that the rights hereby asserted are of the natural rights of mankind, and that if any act shall be hereafter passed to repeal the present or to narrow its operation, such act will be an infringement of natural right.

Thomas Jefferson, Letter to the Danbury Baptists (1802)

Gentlemen:

The affectionate sentiments of esteem and approbation which you are so good as to express towards me, on behalf of the Danbury Baptist Association, give me the highest satisfaction. My duties dictate a faithful and zealous pursuit of the interests of my constituents, and in proportion as they are persuaded of my fidelity to those duties, the discharge of them becomes more and more pleasing.

Believing with you that religion is a matter which lies solely between man and his God, that he owes account to none other for his faith or his worship, that the legislative powers of government reach actions only, and not opinions, I contemplate with sovereign reverence that act of the whole American people which declared that their legislature should "make no law respecting an establishment of religion, or prohibiting the free exercise thereof," thus building a wall of separation between Church and State. Adhering to this expression of the supreme will of the nation in behalf of the rights of conscience, I shall see with sincere satisfaction the progress of those sentiments which tend to restore to man all his natural rights, convinced he has no natural right in opposition to his social duties.

I reciprocate your kind prayers for the protection and blessing of the common Father and Creator of man, and tender you for yourselves and your religious association, assurances of my high respect and esteem.

✠✠✠

Samuel West,
Sermon on the Right to Rebel
Against Governors* (1776)

One of the most influential citizens in Massachusetts during the Founding era, Congregationalist minister Samuel West delivered this sermon before the Massachusetts Council and House of Representatives in Boston, 1776.

Put them in mind to be subject to principalities and powers, to obey magistrates, to be ready to every good work.—Titus iii.

1. The great Creator, having designed the human race for society, has made us dependent on one another for happiness. He has so constituted us that it becomes both our duty and interest to seek the public good; and that we may be the more firmly engaged to promote each other's welfare, the Deity has endowed us with tender and social affections, with generous and benevolent principles: hence the pain that we feel in seeing an object of distress; hence the satisfaction that arises in relieving the afflictions, and the superior pleasure which we experience in communicating happiness to the miserable. The Deity has also invested us with moral powers and faculties, by which we are enabled to discern the difference

*This is an edited version of the sermon.

between right and wrong, truth and falsehood, good and evil; hence the approbation of mind that arises upon doing a good action, and the remorse of conscience which we experience when we counteract the moral sense and do that which is evil. This proves that, in what is commonly called a state of nature, we are the subjects of the divine law and government; that the Deity is our supreme magistrate, who has written his law in our hearts, and will reward or punish us according as we obey or disobey his commands. Had the human race uniformly persevered in a state of moral rectitude, there would have been little or no need of any other law besides that which is written in the heart—for every one in such a state would be a law unto himself. There could be no occasion for enacting or enforcing of penal laws; for such are "not made for the righteous man, but for the lawless and disobedient, for the ungodly, and for sinners, for the unholy and profane, for murderers of fathers and murderers of mothers, for manslayers, for whoremongers, for them that defile themselves with mankind, for men-stealers, for liars, for perjured persons, and if there be any other thing that is contrary to" moral rectitude and the happiness of mankind. The necessity of forming ourselves into politic bodies, and granting to our rulers a power to enact laws for the public safety, and to enforce them by proper penalties, arises from our being in a fallen and degenerate state. The slightest view of the present state and condition of the human race is abundantly sufficient to convince any person of common sense and common honesty that civil government is absolutely necessary for the peace and safety of mankind; and, consequently, that all good magistrates, while they faithfully discharge the trust reposed in them, ought to be religiously and conscientiously obeyed. An enemy to good government is an enemy not only to his country, but to all mankind; for he plainly shows himself to be divested of those tender and social sentiments which are characteristic of a human temper, even of that generous and benevolent disposition which is the peculiar glory of a rational creature. An enemy to good government has degraded himself below the rank and dignity of a man, and deserves to be classed with the lower creation. Hence we find that wise and good men, of all nations and religions, have ever inculcated subjection to good government, and have borne their testimony against the licentious disturbers of the public peace.

Nor has Christianity been deficient in this capital point. We find our blessed Savior directing the Jews to render to Caesar the things that were Caesar's; and the apostles and first preachers of the gospel not only exhibited a good example of subjection to the magistrate, in all things that were just and lawful, but they have also, in several places in the New Testament, strongly enjoined upon Christians the duty of submission to that government under which Providence had placed them. Hence we find that those who despise government, and are not afraid to speak evil of dignities, are, by the apostles Peter and Jude, classed among those presumptuous, self-willed sinners that are reserved to the judgment of the great day. And the apostle Paul judged submission to civil government to be a matter of such great importance, that he thought it worth his while to charge Titus to put his hearers in mind to be submissive to principalities and powers, to obey magistrates, to be ready to every good work; as much as to say, none can be ready to every good work, or be properly disposed to perform those actions that tend to promote the public good, who do not obey magistrates, and who do not become good subjects of civil government. If, then, obedience to the civil magistrates is so essential to the character of a Christian, that without it he cannot be disposed to perform those good works that are necessary for the welfare of mankind—if the despisers of governments are those presumptuous, self-willed sinners who are reserved to the judgment of the great day—it is certainly a matter of the utmost importance to us all to be thoroughly acquainted with the nature and extent of our duty, that we may yield the obedience required; for it is impossible that we should properly discharge a duty when we are strangers to the nature and extent of it.

In order, therefore, that we may form a right judgment of the duty enjoined in our text, I shall consider the nature and design of civil government, and shall show that the same principles which oblige us to submit to government do equally oblige us to resist tyranny; or that tyranny and magistracy are so opposed to each other that where the one begins the other ends. I shall then apply the present discourse to the grand controversy that at this day subsists between Great Britain and the American colonies.

That we may understand the nature and design of civil government, and discover the foundation of the magistrate's authority to command, and the duty of subjects to obey, it is necessary to derive civil government from its original, in order to which we must consider what "state all men are naturally in, and that is (as Mr. Locke observes) a state of perfect freedom to order all their actions, and dispose of their possessions and persons as they think fit, within the bounds of the law of nature, without asking leave or depending upon the will of any man." It is a state wherein all are equal—no one having a right to control another, or oppose him in what he does, unless it be in his own defense, or in the defense of those that, being injured, stand in need of his assistance.

Had men persevered in a state of moral rectitude, every one would have been disposed to follow the law of nature, and pursue the general good. In such a state, the wisest and most experienced would undoubtedly be chosen to guide and direct those of less wisdom and experience than themselves—there being nothing else that could afford the least show or appearance of any one's having the superiority or precedence over another; for the dictates of conscience and the precepts of natural law being uniformly and regularly obeyed, men would only need to be informed what things were most fit and prudent to be done in those cases where their inexperience or want of acquaintance left their minds in doubt what was the wisest and most regular method for them to pursue. In such cases it would be necessary for them to advise with those who were wiser and more experienced than themselves. But these advisers could claim no authority to compel or to use any forcible measures to oblige any one to comply with their direction or advice. There could be no occasion for the exertion of such a power; for every man, being under the government of right reason, would immediately feel himself constrained to comply with everything that appeared reasonable or fit to be done, or that would any way tend to promote the general good. This would have been the happy state of mankind had they closely adhered to the law of nature, and persevered in their primitive state.

Thus we see that a state of nature, though it be a state of perfect freedom, yet is very far from a state of licentiousness. The law of nature gives men no right to do anything that is immoral, or contrary to the will of God, and injurious to their fellow-creatures; for a state of nature is properly a state of law and government, even a government founded upon the unchangeable nature of the Deity, and a law resulting from the eternal fitness of things. Sooner shall heaven and earth pass away, and the whole frame of nature be dissolved, than any part even the smallest iota, of this law shall ever be abrogated; it is unchangeable as the Deity himself, being a transcript of his moral perfections. A revelation, pretending to be from God, that contradicts any part of natural law, ought immediately to be rejected as an imposture; for the Deity cannot make a law contrary to the law of nature without acting contrary to himself—a thing in the strictest sense impossible, for that which implies contradiction is not an object of the divine power. Had this subject been properly attended to and under-stood, the world had remained free from a multitude of absurd and pernicious principles, which have been industriously propagated by art-ful and designing men, both in politics and divinity. The doctrine of nonresistance and unlimited passive obedience to the worst of tyrants could never have found credit among mankind had the voice of reason been hearkened to for a guide, because such a doctrine would immedi-ately have been discerned to be contrary to natural law.

In a state of nature we have a right to make the persons that have injured us repair the damages that they have done us; and it is just in us to inflict such punishment upon them as is necessary to restrain them from doing the like for the future—the whole end and design of punishing being either to reclaim the individual punished, or to deter others from being guilty of similar crimes. Whenever punishment exceeds these bounds it becomes cruelty and revenge, and directly contrary to the law of nature. Our wants and necessities being such as to render it impossible in most cases to enjoy life in any tolerable degree without entering into society, and there being innumerable cases wherein we need the assistance of others, which if not afforded we should very soon perish; hence the law of nature requires that we should endeavor to help one another to the ut-most of our power in all cases where our assistance is necessary. It is our duty to endeavor always to promote the general good; to do to all as we would be willing to be done by were we in their circumstances; to do justly, to love mercy, and to walk humbly before God. These are some of the laws of nature which every man in the world is bound to observe, and which whoever violates exposes himself to the resentment of mankind, the lashes of his own conscience, and the judgment of Heaven. This plainly shows that the highest state of liberty subjects us to the law of nature and the government of God. The most perfect freedom consists in obeying the dictates of right reason, and submitting to natural law. When a man goes beyond or contrary to the law of nature and reason, he becomes the slave of base passions and vile lusts; he introduces confusion and disorder into society, and brings misery and destruction upon himself. This, therefore, cannot be called a state of freedom, but a state of the vilest slavery and the most dreadful bondage. The servants of sin and corruption are subjected to the worst kind of tyranny in the universe. Hence we conclude that where licentiousness begins, liberty ends.

The law of nature is a perfect standard and measure of action for beings that persevere in a state of moral rectitude; but the case is far different with us, who are in a fallen and degenerate estate. We have a law in our members which is continually warring against the law of the mind, by which we often become enslaved to the basest lusts, and are brought into bondage to the vilest passions. The strong propensities of our animal nature often overcome the sober dictates of reason and conscience, and betray us into actions injurious to the public and destructive of the safety and happiness of society. Men of unbridled lusts, were they not restrained by the power of the civil magistrate, would spread horror and desolation all around them. This makes it absolutely necessary that societies should form themselves into politic bodies, that they may enact laws for the public safety, and appoint particular penalties for the violation of their laws, and invest a suitable number of persons with authority to put in execution and enforce the laws of the state, in order that wicked men may be restrained from doing mischief to their fellow-creatures, that the injured may have their rights restored to them, that the virtuous may be encouraged in doing good, and that every member of society may be protected and secured in the peaceable, quiet possession and enjoyment of all those liberties and privileges which the Deity has bestowed upon him; i.e., that he may safely enjoy and pursue whatever he chooses, that is consistent with the public good. This shows that the end and design of civil government cannot be to deprive men of their liberty or take away their freedom; but, on the contrary, the true design of civil government is to protect men in the enjoyment of liberty.

From hence it follows that tyranny and arbitrary power are utterly inconsistent with and subversive of the very end and design of civil government, and directly contrary to natural law, which is the true foundation of civil government and all politic law. Consequently, the authority of a tyrant is of itself null and void; for as no man can have a right to act contrary to the law of nature, it is impossible that any individual, or even the greatest number of men, can confer a right upon another of which they themselves are not possessed; i.e., no body of men can justly and lawfully authorize any person to tyrannize over and enslave his fellow-creatures, or do anything contrary to equity and goodness. As magistrates have no authority but what they derive from the people, whenever they act contrary to the public good, and pursue measures destructive of the peace and safety of the community, they forfeit their right to govern the people. Civil rulers and magistrates are properly of human creation; they are set up by the people to be the guardians of their rights, and to secure their persons from being injured or oppressed—the safety of the public being the supreme law of the state, by which the magistrates are to be governed, and which they are to consult upon all occasions. The modes of administration may be very different, and the forms of government may vary from each other in different ages and nations; but, under every form, the end of civil government is the same, and cannot vary: It is like the laws of the Medes and Persians—it altereth not.

Though magistrates are to consider themselves as the servants of the people, seeing from them it is that they derive their power and authority, yet they may also be considered as the ministers of God ordained by him for the good of mankind; for, under him, as the Supreme Magistrate of the universe, they are to act: and it is God who has not only declared in his word what are the necessary qualifications of a ruler, but who also raises up and qualifies men for such an important station. The magistrate may also, in a more strict and proper sense, be said to be ordained of God, because reason, which is the voice of God, plainly requires such an order of men to be appointed for the public good. Now, whatever right reason requires as necessary to be done is as much the will and law of God as though it were enjoined us by an immediate revelation from heaven, or commanded in the sacred Scriptures.

From this account of the origin, nature, and design of civil government, we may be very easily led into a thorough knowledge of our duty; we may see the reason why we are bound to obey magistrates, viz., because they are the ministers of God for good unto the people. While, therefore, they rule in the fear of God, and while they promote the welfare of the state— i.e., while they act in the character of magistrates—it is the indispensable duty of all to submit to them, and to oppose a turbulent, factious, and libertine spirit, whenever and wherever it discovers itself. When a people have by their free consent conferred upon a number of men a power to rule and govern them, they are bound to obey them. Hence disobedience becomes a breach of faith; it is violating a constitution of their own appointing, and breaking a compact for which they ought to have the most sacred regard. Such a conduct discovers so base and disingenuous a temper of mind, that it must expose them to contempt in the judgment of all the sober, thinking part of mankind. Subjects are bound to obey lawful magistrates by every tender tie of human nature, which disposes us to consult the public good, and to seek the good of our brethren, our wives, our children, our friends and acquaintance; for he that opposes lawful authority does really oppose the safety and happiness of his fellow-creatures. A factious, seditious person, that opposes good government, is a monster in nature; for he is an enemy to his own species, and destitute of the sentiments of humanity.

Subjects are also bound to obey magistrates, for conscience' sake, out of regard to the divine authority, and out of obedience to the will of God; for if magistrates are the ministers of God, we cannot disobey them without being disobedient to the law of God; and this extends to all men in authority, from the highest ruler to the lowest officer in the state. To oppose them when in the exercise of lawful authority is an act of disobedience to the Deity, and, as such, will be punished by him. It will, doubtless, be readily granted by every honest man that we ought cheerfully to obey the magistrate, and submit to all such regulations of government as tend to promote the public good; but as this general definition may be liable to be misconstrued, and every man may think himself at liberty to disregard any laws that do not suit his interest, humor, or fancy, I would observe that, in a multitude of cases, many of us, for want of being properly acquainted with affairs of state, may be very improper judges of particular laws, whether they are just or not. In such cases it becomes us, as good members of society, peaceably and conscientiously to submit, though we cannot see the reasonableness of every law to which we submit, and that for this plain reason: if any number of men should take it upon themselves to oppose authority for acts, which may be really necessary for the public safety, only because they do not see the reasonableness of them, the direct consequence will be introducing confusion and anarchy into the state.

It is also necessary that the minor part should submit to the major; e.g., when legislators have enacted a set of laws which are highly approved by a large majority of the community as tending to promote the public good, in this case, if a small number of persons are so unhappy as to view the matter in a very different point of light from the public, though they have an undoubted right to show the reasons of their dissent from the judgment of the public, and may lawfully use all proper arguments to convince the public of what they judge to be an error, yet, if they fail in their attempt, and the majority still continue to approve of the laws that are enacted, it is the duty of those few that dissent peaceably and for conscience' sake to submit to the public judgment, unless something is required of them which they judge would be sinful for them to comply with; for in that case they ought to obey the dictates of their own consciences rather than any human authority whatever. Perhaps, also, some cases of intolerable oppression, where compliance would bring on inevitable ruin and destruction, may justly warrant the few to refuse submission to what they judge inconsistent with their peace and safety; for the law of self-preservation will always justify opposing a cruel and tyrannical imposition, except where opposition is attended with greater evils than submission, which is frequently the case where a few are oppressed by a large and powerful majority.* Except the above-named cases, the minor ought always to submit to the major; otherwise, there can be no peace nor harmony in society. And, besides, it is the major part of a community that have the sole right of establishing a constitution and authorizing magistrates; and consequently it is only the major part of the community that can claim the right of altering the constitution, and displacing the magistrates; for certainly common sense will tell us that it requires as great an authority to set aside a constitution as there was at first to establish it. The collective body, not a few individuals, ought to constitute the supreme authority of the state.

The only difficulty remaining is to determine when a people may claim a right of forming themselves into a body politic, and assume the powers of legislation. In order to determine this point, we are to remember that all men being by nature equal, all the members of a community have a natural right to assemble themselves together, and act and vote for such regulations as they judge are necessary for the good of the whole. But when a community is become very numerous, it is very difficult, and in many cases impossible, for all to meet together to regulate the affairs of the state; hence comes the necessity of appointing delegates to represent the people in a general assembly. And this ought to be looked upon as a sacred and inalienable right, of which a people cannot justly divest themselves, and which no human authority can in equity ever take from them,

---

* This shows the reason why the primitive Christians did not oppose the cruel persecutions that were inflicted upon them by the heathen magistrates. They were few compared with the heathen world, and for them to have attempted to resist their enemies by force would have been like a small parcel of sheep endeavoring to oppose a large number of ravening wolves and savage beasts of prey. It would, without a miracle, have brought upon them inevitable ruin and destruction. Hence the wise and prudent advice of our Savior to them is, "When they persecute you in this city, flee you to another."

viz., that no one be obliged to submit to any law except such as are made either by himself or by his representative.

If representation and legislation are inseparably connected, it follows, that when great numbers have emigrated into a foreign land, and are so far removed from the parent state that they neither are or can be properly represented by the government from which they have emigrated, that then nature itself points out the necessity of their assuming to themselves the powers of legislation; and they have a right to consider themselves as a separate state from the other, and, as such, to form themselves into a body politic.

In the next place, when a people find themselves cruelly oppressed by the parent state, they have an undoubted right to throw off the yoke, and to assert their liberty, if they find good reason to judge that they have sufficient power and strength to maintain their ground in defending their just rights against their oppressors; for, in this case, by the law of self-preservation, which is the first law of nature, they have not only an undoubted right, but it is their indispensable duty, if they cannot be re-dressed any other way, to renounce all submission to the government that has oppressed them, and set up an independent state of their own, even though they may be vastly inferior in numbers to the state that has op-pressed them. When either of the aforesaid cases takes place, and more especially when both concur, no rational man, I imagine, can have any doubt in his own mind whether such a people have a right to form them-selves into a body politic, and assume to themselves all the powers of a free state. For, can it be rational to suppose that a people should be sub-jected to the tyranny of a set of men who are perfect strangers to them, and cannot be supposed to have that fellow-feeling for them that we gen-erally have for those with whom we are connected and acquainted; and, besides, through their unacquaintedness with the circumstances of the people over whom they claim the right of jurisdiction, are utterly unable to judge, in a multitude of cases, which is best for them?

It becomes me not to say what particular form of government is best for a community—whether a pure democracy, aristocracy, monarchy, or a mixture of all the three simple forms. They have all their advantages and disadvantages, and when they are properly administered may, any of them, answer the design of civil government tolerably. Permit me, however, to say, that an unlimited, absolute monarchy, and an aristocracy not subject to the control of the people, are two of the most exceptionable forms of government: firstly, because in neither of them is there a proper representation of the people; and, secondly, because each of them being entirely independent of the people, they are very apt to degenerate into tyranny. However, in this imperfect state, we cannot expect to have government formed upon such a basis but that it may be perverted by bad men to evil purposes. A wise and good man would be very loath to undermine a constitution that was once fixed and established, although he might discover many imperfections in it; and nothing short of the most urgent necessity would ever induce him to consent to it; because the unhinging a people from a form of government to which they had been long accustomed might throw them into such a state of anarchy and confusion as might terminate in their destruction, or perhaps, in the end, subject them to the worst kind of tyranny.

Having thus shown the nature, end, and design of civil government, and pointed out the reasons why subjects are bound to obey magistrates— viz., because in so doing they both consult their own happiness as individuals, and also promote the public good and the safety of the state— I proceed, in the next place, to show that the same principles that oblige us to submit to civil government do also equally oblige us, where we have power and ability, to resist and oppose tyranny; and that where tyranny begins government ends. For, if magistrates have no authority but what they derive from the people; if they are properly of human creation; if the whole end and design of their institution is to promote the general good, and to secure to men their just rights—it will follow, that when they act contrary to the end and design of their creation they cease being magistrates, and the people which gave them their authority have the right to take it from them again. This is a very plain dictate of common sense, which universally obtains in all similar cases; for who is there that, having employed a number of men to do a particular piece of work for him, but what would judge that he had a right to dismiss them from his service when he found that they went directly contrary to his orders, and that, instead of accomplishing the business he had set them about, they would infallibly ruin and destroy it? If, then, men, in the common affairs of life, always judge that they have a right to dismiss from their service such persons as counteract their plans and designs, though the damage will affect only a few individuals, much more must the body politic have a right to depose any persons, though appointed to the highest place of power and authority, when they find that they are unfaithful to the trust reposed in them, and that, instead of consulting the general good, they are disturbing the peace of society by making laws cruel and oppressive, and by depriving the subjects of their just rights and privileges. Whoever pretends to deny this proposition must give up all pretence of being master of that common sense and reason by which the Deity has distinguished us from the brutal herd.

As our duty of obedience to the magistrate is founded upon our obligation to promote the general good, our readiness to obey lawful authority will always arise in proportion to the love and regard that we have for the welfare of the public; and the same love and regard for the public will inspire us with as strong a zeal to oppose tyranny as we have to obey magistracy. Our obligation to promote the public good extends as much to the opposing every exertion of arbitrary power that is injurious to the state as it does to the submitting to good and whole—some laws. No man, therefore, can be a good member of the community that is not as zealous to oppose tyranny as he is ready to obey magistracy. A slavish submission to tyranny is a proof of a very sordid and base mind. Such a person cannot be under the influence of any generous human sentiments, nor have a tender regard for mankind.

Further: if magistrates are no farther ministers of God than they promote the good of the community, then obedience to them neither is nor can be unlimited; for it would imply a gross absurdity to assert that, when magistrates are ordained by the people solely for the purpose of being beneficial to the state, they must be obeyed when they are seeking to ruin and destroy it. This would imply that men were bound to act against the great law of self-preservation, and to contribute their assistance to their own ruin and destruction, in order that they may please and gratify the greatest monsters in nature, who are violating the laws of God and destroying the rights of mankind. Unlimited submission and obedience is due to none but God alone. He has an absolute right to command; he alone has an uncontrollable sovereignty over us, because he alone is unchangeably good; he never will nor can require of us, consistent with his nature and attributes, anything that is not fit and reasonable; his commands are all just and good; and to suppose that he has given to any particular set of men a power to require obedience to that which is unreasonable, cruel, and unjust, is robbing the Deity of his justice and goodness, in which consists the peculiar glory of the divine character, and it is representing him under the horrid character of a tyrant.

If magistrates are ministers of God only because the law of God and reason points out the necessity of such an institution for the good of mankind, it follows, that whenever they pursue measures directly destructive of the public good they cease being God's ministers, they forfeit their right to obedience from the subject, they become the pests of society, and the community is under the strongest obligation of duty, both to God and to its own members, to resist and oppose them, which will be so far from resisting the ordinance of God that it will be strictly obeying his commands. To suppose otherwise will imply that the Deity requires of us an obedience that is self-contradictory and absurd, and that one part of his law is directly contrary to the other; i.e., while he commands us to pursue virtue and the general good, he does at the same time require us to persecute virtue, and betray the general good, by enjoining us obedience to the wicked commands of tyrannical oppressors. Can any one not lost to the principles of humanity undertake to defend such absurd sentiments as these? As the public safety is the first and grand law of society, so no community can have a right to invest the magistrate with any power or authority that will enable him to act against the welfare of the state and the good of the whole. If men have at any time wickedly and foolishly given up their just rights into the hands of the magistrate, such acts are null and void, of course; to suppose otherwise will imply that we have a right to invest the magistrate with a power to act contrary to the law of

God—which is as much as to say that we are not the subjects of divine law and government. What has been said is, I apprehend, abundantly sufficient to show that tyrants are no magistrates, or that whenever magistrates abuse their power and authority to the subverting the public happiness, their authority immediately ceases, and that it not only becomes lawful, but an indispensable duty to oppose them; that the principle of self-preservation, the affection and duty that we owe to our country, and the obedience we owe the Deity, do all require us to oppose tyranny.

If it be asked, Who are the proper judges to determine when rulers are guilty of tyranny and oppression? I answer, the public. Not a few disaffected individuals, but the collective body of the state, must decide this question; for, as it is the collective body that invests rulers with their power and authority, so it is the collective body that has the sole right of judging whether rulers act up to the end of their institution or not. Great regard ought always to be paid to the judgment of the public. It is true the public may be imposed upon by a misrepresentation of facts; but this may be said of the public, which cannot always be said of individuals, viz., that the public is always willing to be rightly informed, and when it has proper matter of conviction laid before it its judgment is always right.

This account of the nature and design of civil government, which is so clearly suggested to us by the plain principles of common sense and reason, is abundantly confirmed by the sacred Scriptures, even by those very texts which have been brought by men of slavish principles to establish the absurd doctrine of unlimited passive obedience and nonresistance, as will abundantly appear by examining the two most noted texts that are commonly brought to support the strange doctrine of passive obedience. The first that I shall cite is in 1 Peter ii. 13, 14: "submit yourselves to every ordinance of man,"—or, rather, as the words ought to be rendered from the Greek, submit yourselves to every human creation, or human constitution—"for the Lord's sake, whether it be to the king as supreme, or unto governors, as unto them that are sent by him for the punishment of evildoers, and for the praise of them that do well." Here we see that the apostle asserts that magistracy is of human creation or appointment; that is, that magistrates have no power or authority but what they derive from the people; that this power they are to exert for the punishment of evil-doers, and for the praise of them that do well; i.e., the end and design of the appointment of magistrates is to restrain wicked men, by proper penalties, from injuring society, and to encourage and honor the virtuous and obedient. Upon this account Christians are to submit to them for the Lord's sake; which is as if he had said, Though magistrates are of mere human appointment, and can claim no power or authority but what they derive from the people, yet, as they are ordained by men to promote the general good by punishing evil-doers and by rewarding and encouraging the virtuous and obedient, you ought to submit to them out of a sacred regard to the divine authority; for as they, in the faithful discharge of their office, do fulfill the will of God, so ye, by submitting to them, do fulfill the divine command. If the only reason assigned by the apostle why magistrates should be obeyed out of a regard to the divine authority is because they punish the wicked and encourage the good, it follows, that when they punish the virtuous and encourage the vicious we have a right to refuse yielding any submission or obedience to them; i.e., whenever they act contrary to the end and design of their institution, they forfeit their authority to govern the people, and the reason for submitting to them, out of regard to the divine authority, immediately ceases; and they being only of human appointment, the authority which the people gave them the public have a right to take from them, and to confer it upon those who are more worthy. So far is this text from favoring arbitrary principles, that there is nothing in it but what is consistent with and favorable to the highest liberty that any man can wish to enjoy; for this text requires us to submit to the magistrate no further than he is the encourager and protector of virtue and the punisher of vice; and this is consistent with all that liberty which the Deity has bestowed upon us.

The other text which I shall mention, and which has been made use of by the favorers of arbitrary government as their great sheet anchor and main support, is in Rom. xiii., the first six verses: "Let every soul be subject to the higher powers; for there is no power but of God. The powers that be are ordained of God. Whosoever therefore resisteth the power, resisteth the ordinance of God; and they that resist shall receive to themselves damnation; for rulers are not a terror to good works, but to the evil. Wilt thou then not be afraid of the power? Do that which is good, and thou shalt have praise of the same: for he is the minister of God to thee for good. But if thou do that which is evil, be afraid; for he beareth not the sword in vain: for he is the minister of God, a revenger to execute wrath upon him that doth evil. Wherefore ye must needs be subject not only for wrath, but also for conscience' sake. For, for this cause pay you tribute also; for they are God's ministers, attending continually upon this very thing." A very little attention, I apprehend, will be sufficient to show that this text is so far from favoring arbitrary government, that, on the contrary, it strongly holds forth the principles of true liberty. Subjection to the higher powers is enjoined by the apostle because there is no power but of God; the powers that be are ordained of God; consequently, to resist the power is to resist the ordinance of God: and he repeatedly declares that the ruler is the minister of God. Now, before we can say whether this text makes for or against the doctrine of unlimited passive obedience, we must find out in what sense the apostle affirms that magistracy is the ordinance of God, and what he intends when he calls the ruler the minister of God.

I can think but of three possible senses in which magistracy can with any propriety be called God's ordinance, or in which rulers can be said to be ordained of God as his ministers. The first is a plain declaration from the word of God that such a one and his descendants are, and shall be, the only true and lawful magistrates: thus we find in Scripture the kingdom of Judah to be settled by divine appointment in the family of David. Or,

Secondly, By an immediate commission from God, ordering and appointing such a one by name to be the ruler over the people: thus Saul and David were immediately appointed by God to be kings over Israel. Or,

Thirdly, Magistracy may be called the ordinance of God, and rulers may be called the ministers of God, because the nature and reason of things, which is the law of God, requires such an institution for the preservation and safety of civil society. In the two first senses the apostle cannot be supposed to affirm that magistracy is God's ordinance, for neither he nor any of the sacred writers have entailed the magistracy to any one particular family under the gospel dispensation. Neither does he nor any of the inspired writers give us the least hint that any person should ever be immediately commissioned from God to bear rule over the people. The third sense, then, is the only sense in which the apostle can be supposed to affirm that the magistrate is the minister of God, and that magistracy is the ordinance of God; viz., that the nature and reason of things require such an institution for the preservation and safety of mankind. Now, if this be the only sense in which the apostle affirms that magistrates are ordained of God as his ministers, resistance must be criminal only so far forth as they are the ministers of God, i.e., while they act up to the end of their institution, and ceases being criminal when they cease being the ministers of God, i.e., when they act contrary to the general good, and seek to destroy the liberties of the people...

Thus we see that both reason and revelation perfectly agree in pointing out the nature, end, and design of government, viz., that it is to promote the welfare and happiness of the community; and that subjects have a right to do everything that is good, praiseworthy, and consistent with the good of the community, and are only to be restrained when they do evil and are injurious either to individuals or the whole community; and that they ought to submit to every law that is beneficial to the community for conscience' sake, although it may in some measure interfere with their private interest; for every good man will be ready to forgo his private interest for the sake of being beneficial to the public. Reason and revelation, we see, do both teach us that our obedience to rulers is not unlimited, but that resistance is not only allowable, but an indispensable duty in the case of intolerable tyranny and oppression. From both reason and revelation we learn that, as the public safety is the supreme law of the state—being the true standard and measure by which we are to judge whether any law or body of laws are just or not—so legislatures have a right to make, and require subjection to, any set of laws that have a tendency to promote the good of the community.

Our governors have a right to take every proper method to form the minds of their subjects so that they may become good members of society. The great difference that we may observe among the several classes of mankind arises chiefly from their education and their laws: hence men become virtuous or vicious, good commonwealthsmen or the contrary, generous, noble, and courageous, or base, mean-spirited, and cowardly, according to the impression that they have received from the government that they are under, together with their education and the methods that have been practiced by their leaders to form their minds in early life. Hence the necessity of good laws to encourage every noble and virtuous sentiment, to suppress vice and immorality, to promote industry, and to punish idleness, that parent of innumerable evils; to promote arts and sciences, and to banish ignorance from among mankind.

And as nothing tends like religion and the fear of God to make men good members of the commonwealth, it is the duty of magistrates to become the patrons and promoters of religion and piety, and to make suitable laws for the maintaining public worship, and decently supporting the teachers of religion. Such laws, I apprehend, are absolutely necessary for the well-being of civil society. Such laws may be made, consistent with all that liberty of conscience which every good member of society ought to be possessed of; for, as there are few, if any, religious societies among us but what profess to believe and practice all the great duties of religion and morality that are necessary for the well-being of society and the safety of the state, let every one be allowed to attend worship in his own society, or in that way that he judges most agreeable to the will of God, and let him be obliged to contribute his assistance to the supporting and defraying the necessary charges of his own meeting. In this case no one can have any right to complain that he is deprived of liberty of conscience, seeing that he has a right to choose and freely attend that worship that appears to him to be most agreeable to the will of God; and it must be very unreasonable for him to object against being obliged to contribute his part towards the support of that worship which he has chosen. Whether some such method as this might not tend, in a very eminent manner, to promote the peace and welfare of society, I must leave to the wisdom of our legislators to determine; be sure it would take off some of the most popular objections against being obliged by law to support public worship while the law restricts that support only to one denomination.

But for the civil authority to pretend to establish particular modes of faith and forms of worship, and to punish all that deviate from the standard which our superiors have set up, is attended with the most pernicious consequences to society. It cramps all free and rational inquiry, fills the world with hypocrites and superstition bigots—nay, with infidels and skeptics; it exposes men of religion and conscience to the rage and malice of fiery, blind zealots, and dissolves every tender tie of human nature; in short, it introduces confusion and every evil work. And I cannot but look upon it as a peculiar blessing of Heaven that we live in a land where every one can freely deliver his sentiments upon religious subjects, and have the privilege of worshipping God according to the dictates of his own conscience without any molestation or disturbance—a privilege which I hope we shall ever keep up and strenuously maintain. No principles ought ever to be discountenanced by civil authority but such as tend to the subversion of the state. So long as a man is a good member of society, he is accountable to God alone for his religious sentiments; but when men are found disturbers of the public peace, stirring up sedition, or practicing against the state, no pretence of religion or conscience ought to screen them from being brought to condign punishment. But then, as the end and design of punishment is either to make restitution to the injured or to restrain men from committing the like crimes for the future, so, when these important ends are answered, the punishment ought to cease; for whatever is inflicted upon a man under the notion of punishment after these important ends are answered, is not a just and lawful punishment, but is properly cruelty and base revenge.

From this account of civil government we learn that the business of magistrates is weighty and important. It requires both wisdom and integrity. When either are wanting, government will be poorly administered; more especially if our governors are men of loose morals and abandoned principles; for if a man is not faithful to God and his own soul, how can we expect that he will be faithful to the public? There was a great deal of propriety in the advice that Jethro gave to Moses to provide able men—men of truth, that feared God, and that hated covetousness—and to appoint them for rulers over the people. For it certainly implies a very gross absurdity to suppose that those who are ordained of God for the public good should have no regard to the laws of God, or that the ministers of God should be despisers of the divine commands. David, the man after God's own heart, makes piety a necessary qualification in a ruler: "He that ruleth over men (says he) must be just, ruling in the fear of God." It is necessary it should be so, for the welfare and happiness of the state; for, to say nothing of the venality and corruption, of the tyranny and oppression, that will take place under unjust rulers, barely their vicious and irregular lives will have a most pernicious effect upon the lives and manners of their subjects: their authority becomes despicable in the opinion of discerning men. And, besides, with what face can they make or execute laws against vices which they practice with greediness? A people that have a right of choosing their magistrates are criminally guilty in the sight of Heaven when they are governed by caprice and humor, or are influenced by bribery to choose magistrates that are irreligious men, who are devoid of sentiment, and of bad morals and base lives. Men cannot be sufficiently sensible what a curse they may bring upon themselves and their posterity by foolishly and wickedly choosing men of abandoned characters and profligate lives for their magistrates and rulers.

We have already seen that magistrates who rule in the fear of God ought not only to be obeyed as the ministers of God, but that they ought also to be handsomely supported, that they may cheerfully and freely attend upon the duties of their station; for it is a great shame and disgrace to society to see men that serve the public laboring under indigent and needy circumstances; and, besides, it is a maxim of eternal truth that the laborer is worthy of his reward.

It is also a great duty incumbent on people to treat those in authority with all becoming honor and respect—to be very careful of casting any aspersion upon their characters. To despise government, and to speak evil of dignities, is represented in Scripture as one of the worst of characters; and it was an injunction of Moses, "Thou shalt not speak evil of the ruler of thy people." Great mischief may ensue upon reviling the character of good rulers; for the unthinking herd of mankind are very apt to give ear to scandal, and when it falls upon men in power, it brings their authority into contempt, lessens their influence, and disheartens them from doing that service to the community of which they are capable; whereas, when they are properly honored, and treated with that respect which is due to their station, it inspires them with courage and a noble ardor to serve the public: their influence among the people is strengthened, and their authority becomes firmly established. We ought to remember that they are men like to ourselves, liable to the same imperfections and infirmities with the rest of us, and therefore, so long as they aim at the public good, their mistakes, misapprehensions, and infirmities, ought to be treated with the utmost humanity and tenderness.

But though I would recommend to all Christians, as a part of the duty that they owe to magistrates, to treat them with proper honor and respect, none can reasonably suppose that I mean that they ought to be flattered in their vices, or honored and caressed while they are seeking to undermine and ruin the state; for this would be wickedly betraying our just rights, and we should be guilty of our own destruction. We ought ever to persevere with firmness and fortitude in maintaining and contending for all that liberty that the Deity has granted us. It is our duty to be ever watchful over our just rights, and not suffer them to be wrested out of our hands by any of the artifices of tyrannical oppressors. But there is a wide difference between being jealous of our rights, when we have the strongest reason to conclude that they are invaded by our rulers, and being unreasonably suspicious of men that are zealously endeavoring to support the constitution, only because we do not thoroughly comprehend all their designs. The first argues a noble and generous mind; the other, a low and base spirit.

✦✦✦

SAMUEL COOPER,
SERMON ON THE COMMENCEMENT OF THE MASSACHUSSETTS CONSTITUTION*
(1780)

Their Congregation shall be established before me: and their Nobles shall be of themselves, and their Governor shall proceed from the mist of them.
Jeremiah 30:20, 21

Nothing can be more applicable to the solemnity in which we are engaged, than this passage of sacred writ. The prophecy seems to have been made for ourselves, it is so exactly descriptive of that important, that comprehensive, that essential civil blessing, which kindles the luster, and diffuses the joy of the present day. Nor is this the only passage of holy scripture that holds up to our view a striking resemblance between our own circumstances and those of the ancient Israelites; a nation chosen by God a theatre for the display of some of the most astonishing dispensations of his providence. Like that nation we rose from oppression, and emerged "from the House of Bondage." Like that nation we were led into a wilderness, as a refuge from tyranny, and a preparation for the enjoyment of our civil and religious rights. Like that nation we have been pursued

*This is an edited version of the sermon.

through the sea, by the armed hand of power, which, but for the signal interpositions of heaven, must before now have totally defeated the noble purpose of our emigration. And, to omit many other instances of similarity, like that nation we have been ungrateful to the Supreme Ruler of the world, and too "lightly esteemed the Rock of our Salvation"; accordingly, we have been corrected by his justice, and at the same time remarkably supported and defended by his mercy. So that we may discern our own picture in the figure of the ancient church divinely exhibited to Moses in vision, "a bush burning and not consumed." This day, this memorable day, is a witness, that the Lord, he whose "hand maketh great, and giveth strength unto all, hath not forsaken us, nor our God forgotten us." This day, which forms a new era in our annals, exhibits a testimony to all the world, that contrary to our deserts, and amidst all our troubles, the blessing promised in our text to the afflicted seed of Abraham is come upon us; "Their Nobles shall be of themselves, and their Governor shall proceed from the midst of them...."

To mention all the passages in sacred writ which prove that the Hebrew government, tho' a theocracy, was yet as to the outward part of it, a free republic, and that the sovereignty resided in the people, would be to recite a large part of it's history....

Such was the civil constitution of the Hebrew nation, till growing weary of the gift of heaven, they demanded a king. After being admonished by the prophet Samuel of the ingratitude and folly of their request, they were punished in the grant of it. Impiety, corruption and disorder of every kind afterwards increasing among them, they grew ripe for the judgments of heaven in their desolation and captivity. Taught by these judgments the value of those blessings they had before despised, and groaning under the hand of tyranny more heavy than that of death, they felt the worth of their former civil and religious privileges, and were prepared to receive with gratitude and joy a restoration not barely to the land flowing with milk and honey, but to the most precious advantage, they ever enjoyed in that land, their original constitution of government. They were prepared to welcome with the voice of mirth and thanksgiving the re-establishment of their congregations; nobles chosen from among themselves, and a governor proceeding from the midst of them.

Such a constitution, twice established by the hand of heaven in that nation, so far as it respects civil and religious liberty in general, ought to be regarded as a solemn recognition from the Supreme Ruler himself of the rights of human nature. Abstracted from those appendages and formalities which were peculiar to the Jews, and designed to answer some particular purposes of divine Providence, it points out in general what kind of government infinite wisdom and goodness would establish among mankind.

We want not, indeed, a special revelation from heaven to teach us that men are born equal and free; that no man has a natural claim of dominion over his neighbors, nor one nation any such claim upon another; and that as government is only the administration of the affairs of a number of men combined for their own security and happiness, such a society have a right freely to determine by whom and in what manner their own affairs shall be administered. These are the plain dictates of that reason and common sense with which the common parent of men has informed the human bosom. It is, however, a satisfaction to observe such everlasting maxims of equity confirmed, and impressed upon the consciences of men, by the instructions, precepts, and examples given us in the sacred oracles; one internal mark of their divine original, and that they come from him "who hath made of one blood all nations to dwell upon the face of the earth," whose authority sanctifies only those governments that instead of oppressing any part of his family, vindicate the oppressed, and restrain and punish the oppressor.

Unhappy the people who are destitute of the blessing promised in our text; who have not the ulterior powers of government within themselves; who depend upon the will of another state, with which they are not incorporated as a vital part, the interest of which must in many respects be opposite to their own; and who at the same time have no fixed constitutional barrier to restrain this reigning power. There is no meanness or misery to which such a people is not liable. There is not a single blessing, tho' perhaps indulged to them for a while, that they can call their own; there is nothing they have not to dread. Whether the governing power be itself free or despotic, it matters not to the poor dependent. Nations who are jealous of their own liberties often sport with those of others; nay, it has been remarked, that the dependent provinces of free states have enjoyed less freedom than those belonging to despotic powers. Such was our late dismal situation, from which heaven hath redeemed us by a signal and glorious revolution. We thought, indeed, we had a charter to support our rights: but we found a written charter, a thin barrier against all-prevailing power, that could construe it to its own purpose, or rescind it by the sword at its own pleasure.

Upon our present independence, sweet and valuable as the blessing is, we may read the inscription, "I am found of them that sought me not." Be it to our praise or blame, we cannot deny, that when we were not searching for it, it happily found us. It certainly must have been not only innocent but laudable and manly, to have desired it even before we felt the absolute necessity of it. It was our birth right; we ought to have valued it highly, and never to have received a mess of pottage, a small temporary supply, as an equivalent for it. Going upon the trite metaphor of a mother country, which has so often been weakly urged against us, like a child grown to maturity, we had a right to a distinct settlement in the world, and to the fruits of our own industry; and it would have been but justice, and no great generosity, in her who so much boasted her maternal tenderness to us, had she not only readily acquiesced, but even aided us in this settlement. It is certain, however, that we did not seek an independence; and it is equally certain that Britain, though she meant to oppose it with all her power, has by a strange infatuation, taken the most direct, and perhaps the only methods that could have established it. Her oppressions, her unrelenting cruelty, have driven us out from the family of which we were once a part. This has opened our eyes to discern the inestimable blessing of a separation from her; while, like children that have been inhumanly treated and cast out by their parents, and at the same time are capable of taking care of themselves, we have found friendship and respect from the world, and have formed new, advantageous, and honorable connections.

Independence gives us a rank among the nations of the earth, which no precept of our religion forbids us to understand and feel, and which we should be ambitious to support in the most reputable manner. It opens to us a free communication with all the world, not only for the improvement of commerce, and the acquisition of wealth, but also for the cultivation of the most useful knowledge. It naturally unfetters and expands the human mind, and prepares it for the impression of the most exalted virtues, as well as the reception of the most, important science. If we look into the history and character of nations, we shall find those that have been for a long time, and to any considerable degree dependent upon others, limited and cramped in their improvements; corrupted by the court, and stained with the vices of the ruling state; and debased by an air of servility and depression marking their productions and manners. Servility is not only dishonorable to human nature, but commonly accompanied with the meanest vices, such as adulation, deceit, falsehood, treachery, cruelty, and the basest methods of supporting and procuring the favor of the power upon which it depends.

Neither does the time allow, nor circumstances require, that I should enter into a detail of all the principles and arguments upon which the right of our present establishment is grounded. They are known to all the world; they are to be found in the immortal writings of Sidney and Locke, and other glorious defenders of the liberties of human nature; they are also to be found, not dishonored, in the acts and publications of America on this great occasion, which have the approbation and applause of the wise and impartial among mankind, and even in Britain itself. They are the principles upon which her own government and her own revolution under William the third were founded; principles which brutal force may oppose, but which reason and scripture will forever sanctify. The citizens of these states have had sense enough to comprehend the full force of these principles, and virtue enough, in the face of uncommon dangers, to act upon so just, so broad, and stable a foundation.

It has been said, that every nation is free that deserves to be so. This may not be always true. But had a people so illuminated as the inhabitants of these states, so nurtured by their ancestors in the love of freedom; a people to whom divine Providence was pleased to present so fair an opportunity of asserting their natural right as an independent nation, and who were even compelled by the arms of their enemies to take sanctuary in the temple of liberty; had such a people been disobedient to the heavenly call, and refused to enter, who could have asserted their title to the glorious wreaths and peculiar blessings that are nowhere bestowed but in that hallowed place?

It is to the dishonor of human nature, that liberty, wherever it has been planted and flourished, has commonly required to be watered with blood. Britain, in her conduct towards these states, hath given a fresh proof of the truth of this observation. She has attempted to destroy by her arms in America, what she professes to defend by these very arms on her own soil. Such is the nature of man, such the tendency of power in a nation as well as a single person. It makes a perpetual effort to enlarge itself, and presses against the bounds that confine it. It loses by degrees all idea of right but its own; and therefore that people must be unhappy indeed, who have nothing but humble petitions and remonstrances, and the feeble voice of a charter to oppose to the arms of another nation, that claims *a right to bind them in all cases whatsoever.* . . .

To the disappointment of our enemies, and the joy of our friends, we have now attained a settled government with a degree of peace and unanimity, all circumstances considered, truly surprising. The sagacity, the political knowledge, the patient deliberation, the constant attention to the grand principles of liberty, and the mutual condescension and candor under a diversity of apprehension respecting the modes of administration, exhibited by those who were appointed to form this constitution, and by the people who ratified it, must do immortal honor to our country. It is, we believe, "an happy foundation for many generations"; and the framers of it are indeed the fathers of their country; since nothing is so essential to the increase, and universal prosperity of a community, as a constitution of government founded in justice, and friendly to liberty. Such men have a monument of glory more durable than brass or marble. . . .

When a people have the rare felicity of choosing their own government, every part of it should first be weighed in the balance of reason, and nicely adjusted to the claims of liberty, equity and order; but when this is done, a warm and passionate patriotism should be added to the result of cool deliberation, to put in motion and animate the whole machine. The citizens of a free republic should reverence their constitution. They should not only calmly approve, and readily submit to it, but regard it also with veneration and affection rising even to an enthusiasm, like that which prevailed at Sparta and at Rome. Nothing can render a commonwealth more illustrious, nothing more powerful, than such a manly, such a sacred fire. Every thing will then be subordinated to the public welfare; every labor necessary to this will be cheerfully endured, every expense readily submitted to, every danger boldly confronted.

May this heavenly flame animate all orders of men in the state! May it catch from bosom to bosom, and the glow be universal! May a double portion of it inhabit the breasts of our civil rulers, and impart a luster to them like that which sat upon the face of Moses, when he came down from the holy mountain with the tables of the Hebrew constitution in his hand! Thus will they sustain with true dignity the first honors, the first marks of esteem and confidence, the first public employments bestowed by this new commonwealth, and in which they this day appear. Such men must naturally care for our state; men whose abilities and virtues have obtained a sanction from the free suffrages of their enlightened and virtuous fellow citizens. Are not these suffrages, a public and solemn testimony that in the opinion of their constituents, they are men who have steadily acted upon the noble principles on which the frame of our government now rests? Men who have generously neglected their private interest in an ardent pursuit of that of the public—men who have intrepidly opposed one of the greatest powers on earth, and put their fortunes and their lives to no small hazard in fixing the basis of our freedom and honor. Who can forbear congratulating our rising state, and casting up a thankful eye to heaven, upon this great and singular occasion, the establishment of our congregation; our nobles freely chosen by ourselves; and our governor coming forth, at the call of his country, from the midst of us? . . .

The people of a free state have a right to expect from those whom they have honored with the direction of their public concerns, a faithful and unremitting attention to these concerns. He who accepts a public trust, pledges himself, his sacred honor, and by his official oath appeals to his God, that with all good fidelity, and to the utmost of his capacity he will discharge this trust. And that commonwealth which doth not keep an eye of care upon those who govern, and observe how they behave in their several departments, in order to regulate its suffrages upon this standard, will soon find itself in perplexity, and cannot expect long to preserve either its dignity or happiness.

Dignity of conduct is ever connected with the happiness of a state; particularly at its rise, and the first appearance it makes in the world. Then all eyes are turned upon it; they view it with attention; and the first impressions it makes are commonly lasting. This circumstance must render the conduct of our present rulers peculiarly important, and fall with particular weight upon their minds. We hope from their wisdom and abilities, their untainted integrity and unshaken firmness, this new-formed commonwealth will rise with honor and applause, and attract that respect, which the number and quality of its inhabitants, the extent of its territory and commerce, and the natural advantages with which it is blest, cannot fail, under a good government, to command.

From our present happy establishment we may reasonably hope for a new energy in government; an energy that shall be felt in all parts of the state. We hope that the sinews of civil authority through its whole frame will be well braced, and the public interest in all its extended branches be well attended to; that no officer will be permitted to neglect the duties, or transgress the bounds of his department; that peculations, frauds, and even the smaller oppressions in any office, will be watchfully prevented, or exemplarily punished; and that no corruption will be allowed to rest in any part of the political body, no not in the extremest, which may spread by degrees, and finally reach the very vitals of the community.

Righteousness, says one of the greatest politicians and wisest princes that ever lived, "Righteousness exalteth a nation." This maxim doth not barely rest upon his own but also on a divine authority; and the truth of it hath been verified by the experience of all ages.

Our civil rulers will remember, that as piety and virtue support the honor and happiness of every community, they are peculiarly requisite in a free government. Virtue is the spirit of a republic; for where all power is derived from the people, all depends on their good disposition. If they are impious, factious and selfish; if they are abandoned to idleness, dissipation, luxury, and extravagance; if they are lost to the fear of God, and the love of their country, all is lost. Having got beyond the restraints of a divine authority, they will not brook the control of laws enacted by rulers of their own creating. We may therefore rely that the present government will do all it fairly can, by authority and example, to answer the end of its institution, that the members of this commonwealth may *lead a quiet and peaceable life in all godliness as well as honesty*, and our liberty never be justly reproached as licentiousness.

I know there is a diversity of sentiment respecting the extent of civil power in religious matters. Instead of entering into the dispute, may I be allowed from the warmth of my heart, to recommend, where conscience is pleaded on both sides, mutual candor and love, and an happy union of all denominations in support of a government, which though human, and therefore not absolutely perfect, is yet certainly founded on the broadest basis of liberty, and affords equal protection to all. Warm [sic] parties upon civil or religious matters, or from personal considerations, are greatly injurious to a free state, and particularly so to one newly formed. We have indeed less of this than might be expected. We shall be happy to have none at all; happy indeed, when every man shall love and serve his country, and have that share of public influence and respect, without distinction of parties, which his virtues and services may justly demand. This is the true spirit of a commonwealth, centering all hearts, and all hands in the common interest.

Neither piety, virtue, or liberty can long flourish in a community, where the education of youth is neglected. How much do we owe to the care of our venerable ancestors upon this important object? Had not they laid such foundations for training up their children in knowledge and religion, in science, and arts, should we have been so respectable a community as we this day appear? Should we have understood our rights so clearly? or valued them so highly? or defended them with such advantage? Or should we have been prepared to lay that basis of liberty, that happy constitution, on which we raise such large hopes, and from which we derive such uncommon joy? We may therefore be confident that the schools, and particularly the university, founded and cherished by our wise and pious fathers, will be patronized and nursed by a government which is so much indebted to them for its honor and efficacy, and the very principles of its existence. The present circumstances of those institutions call for the kindest attention of our rulers; and their close connection with every public interest, civil and religious, strongly enforces the call.

The sciences and arts, for the encouragement of which a new foundation (The American Academy of Arts and Sciences [citation in the original]) hath lately been laid in this commonwealth, deserve the countenance and particular favor of every government. They are not only ornamental but useful. They not only polish, but support, enrich, and defend a community. As they delight in liberty, they are particularly friendly to free states. Barbarians are fierce and ungovernable, and having the grossest ideas of order, and the benefits resulting from it, they require the hand of a stern master; but a people enlightened and civilized by the sciences and liberal arts, have sentiments that support liberty and good laws. They may be guided by a silken thread; and the mild punishments proper to a free state are sufficient to guard the public peace.

An established honor and fidelity in all public engagements and promises, form a branch of righteousness that is wealth, is power, and security to a state. It prevents innumerable perplexities. It creates confidence in the government from subjects and from strangers. It facilitates the most advantageous connections. It extends credit; and easily obtains supplies in the most pressing public emergencies, and when nothing else can obtain them. While the want of it, whatever benefits some shortsighted politicians may have promised from delusive expedients, and deceitful arts, renders a state weak and contemptible; strips it of its defense; grieves and provoke[s] its friends, and delivers it up to the will of its enemies. Upon what does the power of the British nation chiefly rest at this moment? That power that has been so unrighteously employed against America? Upon the long and nice preservation of her faith in all monied matters. With all her injustice in other instances, mere policy hath obliged her to maintain a fair character with her creditors. The support this hath given her in frequent and expensive wars, by the supplies it has enabled her to raise upon loan, is astonishing. By this her government hath availed itself of the whole immense capital of the national debt, which hath been expended in the public service, while the creditors content themselves with the bare payment of the interest. It may be demonstrated that the growing resources of these states, under the conduct of prudence and justice, are sufficient to form a fund of credit for prosecuting the present war, so ruinous to Britain, much longer than that nation, loaded as she now is, can possibly support it.

But need I urge, in a Christian audience, and before Christian rulers, the importance of preserving inviolate the public faith? If this is allowed to be important at all times, and to all states, it must be peculiarly so to those whose foundations are newly laid, and who are but just numbered among the nations of the earth. They have a national character to establish, upon which their very existence may depend. Shall we not then rely that the present government will employ every measure in their power, to maintain in this commonwealth a clear justice, an untainted honor in all public engagements; in all laws respecting property; in all regulations of taxes; in all our conduct towards our sister states, and towards our allies abroad....

While we receive in the settlement of our commonwealth a reward of our achievements and sufferings, we have the further consolation to reflect, that they have tended to the general welfare, and the support of the rights of mankind. The struggle of America hath afforded to oppressed Ireland a favorable opportunity of insisting upon her own privileges. Nor do any of the powers in Europe oppose our cause, or seem to wish it may be unsuccessful. Britain has maintained her naval superiority with such marks of haughtiness and oppression as have justly given umbrage to the nations around her. They cannot therefore but wish to see her power confined within reasonable bounds, and such as may be consistent with the safety of their own commercial rights. This, they know would at least be exceeding difficult, should the rapidly increasing force of these states be reunited with Britain, and wielded by her, as it hath been in time past, against every nation upon whom she is pleased to make war. So favorable, through the divine superintendence, is the present situation of the powers in Europe, to the liberties and independence for which we are contending. But as individuals must part with some natural liberties for the sake of the security and advantages of society; the same kind of commutation must take place in the great republic of nations. The rights of kingdoms and states have their bounds; and as in our own establishment we are not likely to find reason, I trust we shall never have an inclination to exceed these bounds, and justly to excite the jealousy and opposition of other nations. It is thus wisdom, moderation and sound policy would connect kingdoms and states for their mutual advantage, and preserve the order and harmony of the world. In all this these free states will find their own security, and rise by natural and unenvied degrees to that eminence, for which, I would fain persuade myself, we are designed.

It is laudable to lay the foundations of our republics with extended views. Rome rose to empire because she early thought herself destined for it. The great object was continually before the eyes of her sons. It enlarged and invigorated their minds; it excited their vigilance; it elated their courage, and prepared them to embrace toils and dangers, and submit to every regulation friendly to the freedom and prosperity of Rome. They did great things because they believed themselves capable, and born to do them. They reverenced themselves and their country; and animated with unbounded respect for it, they every day added to its strength and glory. Conquest is not indeed the aim of these rising states; sound policy must ever forbid it. We have before us an object more truly great and honorable. We seem called by heaven to make a large portion of this globe a seat of knowledge and liberty, of agriculture, commerce, and arts, and what is more important than all, of Christian piety and virtue. A celebrated British historian observes, if I well remember, that the natural features of America are peculiarly striking. Our mountains, our rivers and lakes have a singular air of dignity and grandeur. May our conduct correspond to the face of our country! At present an immense part of it lies as nature hath left it, and human labor and art have done but little, and brightened only some small specks of a continent that can afford ample means of subsistence to many, many millions of the human race. It remains with us and our posterity, to "make the wilderness become a fruitful field, and the desert blossom as the rose"; to establish the honor and happiness of this new world, as far as it may be justly our own, and to invite the injured and oppressed, the worthy and the good to these shores, by the most liberal governments, by wise political institutions, by cultivating the confidence and friendship of other nations, and by a sacred attention to that gospel that breaths "peace on earth, and good will towards men." Thus will our country resemble the new city which St. John saw "coming down from God out of heaven, adorned as a bride for her husband." Is there a benevolent spirit on earth, or on high, whom such a prospect would not delight?

But what are those illustrious forms that seem to hover over us on the present great occasion, and to look down with pleasure on the memorable transactions of this day? Are they not the founders and lawgivers, the skilful pilots and brave defenders of free states, whose fame "flows down through all ages, enlarging as it flows"? They, who thought no toils or vigilance too great to establish and protect the rights of human nature; no riches too large to be exchanged for them; no blood too precious to be shed for their redemption? But who are they who seem to approach nearer to us, and in whose countenances we discern a peculiar mixture of gravity and joy upon this solemnity? Are they not the venerable fathers of the Massachusetts; who though not perfect while they dwelt in flesh, were yet greatly distinguished by an ardent piety, by all the manly virtues, and by an unquenchable love of liberty—they, who to form a retreat for it, crossed the ocean, through innumerable difficulties, to a savage land. They, who brought with them a broad charter of liberty, over which they wept when it was wrested from them by the hand of power, and an insidious one placed in its room. With what pleasure do they seem to behold their children, like the ancient seed of Abraham, this day restored to their original foundations of freedom! their Governor "as at the first, and their Counselors as at the beginning"? Do they not call upon us to defend these foundations at every hazard, and to perpetuate their honor in the liberty and virtue of the state they planted?

O thou supreme Governor of the world, whose arm hath done great things for us, establish the foundations of this commonwealth! and evermore defend it with the saving strength of thy right hand! Grant that here the divine constitutions of Jesus thy Son may ever be honored and maintained! Grant that it may be the residence of all private and patriotic virtues, of all that enlightens and supports, all that sweetens and adorns human society, till the states and kingdoms of this world shall be swallowed up in thine own kingdom. In that, which alone is immortal, may we obtain a perfect citizenship, and enjoy in its completion, "the glorious Liberty of the Sons of God!" And let all the people say, *Amen!*

✢ ✢ ✢

ABOUT THE AUTHORS

Thomas L. Krannawitter is a Claremont Institute Senior Fellow, and Assistant Professor of Political Science at Hillsdale College in Hillsdale, Michigan. He holds an M.A. and Ph.D. in political science from Claremont Graduate University. He is a contributing author to *Challenges to the American Founding: Slavery, Historicism, and Progressivism in the Nineteenth Century* (Lexington Books, 2005) and he has been published in *Interpretation: A Journal of Political Philosophy* and the *Claremont Review of Books*, as well as the *Los Angeles Times, Chicago Tribune, Houston Chronicle, Atlanta Journal-Constitution*, and *Orange County Register*. Dr. Krannawitter has made multiple appearances on nationally syndicated radio and he is editor of a PBS website on George Washington (www.pbs.org/georgewashington).

Daniel C. Palm is a Claremont Institute Senior Fellow, and Associate Professor of Political Science at Azusa Pacific University in Azusa, California, where he teaches American Government and International Relations. He holds a Ph.D. in Government from Claremont Graduate University, and an M.A. in Religious Studies from the University of Chicago Divinity School. His articles and reviews have appeared in *Political Communication and Persuasion, Perspectives in Political Science, National Review, The Claremont Review of Books, The Indianapolis Star*, and *The San Gabriel Valley Tribune*, and he is contributing editor of a book titled, *On Faith and Free Government* (Rowman and Littlefield, 1997).

243

INDEX